The Fall of France
DISASTER IN THE WEST · 1939-1940

George Forty

&

John Duncan

THE NUTSHELL PUBLISHING CO LTD
Tunbridge Wells · Kent

Contents

	Page
Acknowledgements	v
Selected Bibliography	vi
Brief Chronology	vii

Part I: Preparations for War

CHAPTER 1 **The Fruits of Versailles**	1
CHAPTER 2 **Strategic Considerations**	18
CHAPTER 3 **Opposing Tactical Doctrines**	25
CHAPTER 4 **German Organisation and Equipment**	40
CHAPTER 5 **Allied Organisation and Equipment**	64
CHAPTER 6 **Morale in Peace and War**	96

Part II: The Clash

CHAPTER 7 **Blitzkrieg in Poland**	111
CHAPTER 8 **The Phoney War**	126
CHAPTER 9 **The Hammer Blow Falls**	141
CHAPTER 10 **Advance to the Sea**	160
CHAPTER 11 **The Battle of France**	172

Index ... 182

Acknowledgements

First my thanks are due to Roland Groom, the Tank Museum resident photographer, for his invaluable assistance. Some of the battle photographs he has supplied come from German wartime propaganda material, while others were 'liberated' by members of the Royal Armoured Corps and later presented to the Tank Museum Library. Mrs Ingrid Randle has once again given me invaluable help translating letters from German maps and diagrams, which help so much to make clear what actually happened in the major battles.

Space and the disciplines of modern book design have made it impossible for me to use all the material, photographs and stories which so many kind people have helped to collect. But I must mention the work of my good friends, Max Flemming and Hans Teske. The former has helped to translate some of the graphic battle accounts, while the latter has provided me with invaluable information, photographs and contacts with men of the *Fallschirmjaeger*. I should also like to express my sincere thanks to Mr Mike Willis of the Imperial War Museum photographic department; Mr James Lucas, writer of so many excellent books on the Second World War; Mr Georges Mazy of the Brussels Tank Museum; Miss Anne-Marie Lammers of the Royal Netherlands Army and Arms Museum; Colonel Jan Smit, Military Attaché at the Royal Netherlands Embassy in London; Mr P. H. Kampuis, Deputy Chief Army Historical Section, Royal Netherlands Army; Oberstleutnant Jan Kraft, German Liaison Officer at the RAC Centre; Colonel Gerard Berthelot, French Liaison Officer, also at the RAC Centre, Oberst aD Fabian von Bonin von Ostau for his personal accounts of actions; Miss Nicola Scadding of the Royal Naval Museum; Mr Peter Elliott of the RAF Museum; Major John Carroll, Regimental Secretary, Devon and Dorsets; Lt-Col Walter Robins, Regimental Secreatry, RHQ, the Duke of Wellington's Regiment; the Rev Canon David Strangeways; Herr Arnold von Roon; Colonel Hubert Puga, President of the Association of Friends of the *Musée des Blindes*, Saumur. I must also thank all those authors who have kindly allowed to quote from their books, in particular the various British and German Home HQs and Old Comrades Association, whose histories are not normally on sale to the public.

I must thank my wife Anne, for her help and encouragement with yet another book: to be asked to comment constructively at 0700hrs on subjects such as the morale of the French Army is certainly well above and beyond the call! And lastly my thanks must also go to my son, Adam, who has patiently helped me to unravel at least some of the mysteries of a word processor.

GEORGE FORTY
Bryantspuddle   July 1989

In the preparation for the press of this manuscript and the material acknowledged above, I should like to pay tribute to the invaluable advice I have received at every stage from my friend and colleague, John Walton. My sincere thanks are also due to George Forty for the patience and understanding he has shown in the treatment of his original draft without which, of course, publication of this volume would simply not have been possible. Any errors, omissions or lapses of style which may persist, despite our mutual scrutiny, are down to me rather than to him.

JOHN DUNCAN
Royal Tunbridge Wells   January 1990

Every effort has been made to trace the owners of copyright material quoted in this book, but this has not proved possible in every case. We should therefore be glad to hear from any copyright owner whose material has not been fully acknowledged and credited.

The Nutshell Publishing Co Ltd

Select Bibliography

ADAMTHWAITE, Anthony P. *The Making of the Second World War*, Allen & Unwin, 1977

BARBER, Noel *The Week France Fell*, Macmillan, 1976

BARCLAY, Brigadier C. N. ed. *History of the Duke of Wellington's Regiment 1919-1952*, William Clowes & Sons Ltd, 1963

BEAUFRE, Gen André *1940: The Fall of France*, Cassell, 1968

BENOIST-MECHIN, J. *Sixty Days That Shook the West*, Jonathan Cape, 1963

BRERETON, J. M. *History of the 4th/7th Royal Dragoon Guards*, published by the Regiment, 1982

BULLOCK, Alan *Hitler: A Study in Tyranny*, Odhams, 1952

BUTLER, J. R. M. *History of the Second World War: Grand Strategy, Vol 2*, HMSO, 1967

COOPER, Matthew *The German Army 1939-1945*, Macdonald and Janes, 1978

COURAGE, Major G. *History of the 15/19 The King's Royal Hussars, 1939-1945*, Gale & Polden Ltd, 1949

DETWILER, Donald S. ed. *World War II German Military Studies, Vols 6, 7, 12 & 15*, Garland Publishing Inc, 1979

ELLIS, Major L. F. *The War in France and Flanders 1939-1940*, HMSO, 1963

EVANS, Maj-Gen Roger *The Story of the Fifth Royal Inniskilling Dragoon Guards*, Gale & Polden Ltd, 1951

FARRAR-HOCKLEY, Anthony *Infantry Tactics 1939-1945*, Almark Publishing Co Ltd, 1976

FORTY, George *German Tanks of World War Two 'In Action'*, Blandford Press, 1988

FOSTER, Major R. C. G. *History of the Queen's Royal Regiment, Vol VIII 1924-1948*, Gale & Polden Ltd, 1953

GIBBS, N. H. *History of the Second World War, Grand Strategy Vol 1*, HMSO, 1976

GRIESS, Thomas E, series ed. *The Second World War: Europe & The Mediterranean*, Department of History, United States Military Academy, West Point

GUDERIAN, Gen Heinz *Panzer Leader*, Michael Joseph, 1952

HITLER, Adolf *Mein Kampf*, trans Ralph Manheim, Hutchinson & Co and Radius Books, 1972

HORNE, Alistair *To Lose a Battle*, Macmillan, 1969

HOYT, Edwin P. *Hitler's War*, McGraw-Hill, 1988

KEMP, Anthony *The Maginot Line: Myth & Reality* Frederick Warne, 1981

KENNEDY, Robert M. *The German Campaign in Poland (1939)*, Department of the Army, USA, 1956

LIDDELL HART, Basil *The Other Side of the Hill*, Cassell, 1948

—— *The Tanks*, Cassell, 1959

—— *The Rommel Papers*, Collins, 1953

LONGMATE, Norman *How We Lived Then*, Hutchinson & Co. 1971

MACKSEY, Kenneth *Guderian Panzer General* Macdonald & Co Ltd, 1975

MANSTEIN, Field Marshal Erich von *Lost Victories*, Methuen & Co Ltd, 1958

MILLER, Harry *Service to the Services, The story of NAAFI*, Newman Neame, 1971

MILLER, Maj-Gen Charles H. *History of the 13th/18th Royal Hussars (Queen Mary's Own) 1922-1947*, Chisman, Bradshaw Ltd

MITCHAM, Samuel W. *Hitler's Legions*, Leo Cooper, 1985

MONTGOMERY, Field Marshal *The Memoirs of Field Marshal The Viscount Montgomery of Alamein, KG*, Collins, 1958

MURPHY Raymond *National Socialism*, Washington, 1943

MURRAY, Williamson *Luftwaffe*, Allen & Unwin, 1985

NOFI, Albert A. ed. *The War Against Hitler, Military Strategy in the West*, Hippocrene Books Inc, 1982

OSGOOD, Samuel M. *The Fall of France 1940, Causes and Responsibilities*, D. C. Heath & Co, 1965

PIEKALKIEWICZ, Janusz *Tank War 1939-1945*, Press, 1986

PORTEN, Edward P. von der *The German Navy in World War II*, Thomas Y Crowell Co, 1936

PRICE, Alfred *Luftwaffe Handbook*, Ian Allan Ltd, 1977

RICHARDS, Denis *Royal Air Force 1939-1945 Vol I The fight at Odds*, HMSO, 1953

ROON, Arnold von and Werner Ewald *Die Geschichte des Fallschirmjaeger-Regiment 2*, Druckhaus Goldammer, 1987

ROSKILL, Captain S. W. *The War at Sea 1939-1945, Vol I*, HMSO, 1954

SCHAUFLER, Heinrich *So Lebten Und So Starben Sie, Das Buch Von Panzer Regiment 35*, Kameradschaft ehem Pz Regt 35eV, 1983

SCHROEDER, Gerd *Die 1(H) 14 Pz im Westen 1940*, privately published

SHEFFIELD, Major O. F. *The York and Lancaster Regiment 1919-1953*, Gale & Polden Ltd, 1956

SHEPHERD, Christopher *German Aircraft of World War II*, Sidgwick & Jackson Ltd, 1975

SHERMER, David *World War I*, Octopus Books Ltd, 1973

SHIRER, William L. *The Rise and Fall of the Third Reich*, Secker & Warburg Ltd, 1960

SPEARS, Gen Sir Edward *Assignment to Catastrophe*, The Reprint Society Ltd, 1956

STEWART, Capt P. F. *History of the XII Royal Lancers (Prince of Wales)*, Oxford University Press, 1950

TOLAND, John *Adolf Hitler*, Doubleday and Co Inc, New York, 1976

TREVOR-ROPER, H. R. *Hitler's War Directives 1939-1945*, Sidgwick and Jackson, 1964

WEIDMANN, Gert-Axel *Unser Regiment*, Ernst J. Dohany, 1984

WHALEY, Barton *Covert German Re-Armament 1919-1939*, University Publications of America, 1934

WHITE, Lt-Col D. G. W. *Straight on for Tokyo, The War History of the 2nd Battalion, the Dorsetshire Regiment 1939-1948*, Gale & Polden, 1948

YOUNG, Desmond *Rommel*, Collins, London, 1950

Pamphlets Etc

Infantry Training, Training & War, 1937. 26 Manuals 1447, dated 21 August 1937.

Supplement to the *London Gazette* of Friday, 10 October 1941. The Despatches received by the Secretary of State for War from General the Viscount Gort, VC, KCB, CBE, DSO, MVO, MC, Commander-in-Chief, British Expeditionary Force (France and Belgium 1039-1940).

Brief Chronology

10 May 1940 0535hrs, Germany launches its *Fall Gelb* operation in the West, invading Holland, Belgium and Luxembourg. Allies move to Dyle Line. Churchill becomes Prime Minister.
11 May Eban Emael falls. Rapid German advance in Holland.
12 May French dig in on west bank of Meuse. Leading panzer troops reach Meuse. Luftwaffe bombs Allied lines of communication.
13 May Germans cross the Meuse at Sedan and Dinant. British and French divisions now manning Dyle Line. Dutch withdraw to 'Fortress Holland', while Queen Wilhelmina and her family take refuge in UK.
14 May 1330hrs, Rotterdam bombed. German bridgehead over Meuse increased, despite Allied bombing raids to knock out German floating bridges.
15 May 1100hrs, Dutch sign capitulation. Rommel's 7th Panzer Division breaks through at Philippeville, while Army Group B brings pressure against Allied forces on Dyle Line.
16 May Belgian Government withdraws to Ostend. Gamelin orders general retreat, including BEF, from Belgium. Rommel now 50 miles within France in direction of Cambrai, while Guderian is some 60 miles west of Sedan.
17 May Germans enter Brussels which has been declared an open city. Reynaud recalls Marshal Pétain and Gen Weygand. Guderian ordered to halt.
18 May Germans take Antwerp. Guderian allowed to start moving again on a 'reconaissance in force'. Panzers sweep through northern France to reach Amiens.
19 May Weygand appointed C-in-C.
20 May Rommel reaches Arras, Guderian at Abbeville and, by 2000hrs, reaches the coast at Noyelles.
21 May British counter-attack at Arras.
22 May Rommel restores situation and the panzers move on towards Boulogne and Calais.
24 May Hitler gives 'Halt' order; panzers not to cross the Aa canal.
25 May Boulogne taken, Allies fall back on Dunkirk.
26 May Calais surrenders. Hitler's order rescinded, panzer divisions unleashed, British and French driven back to a beach-head perimeter around Dunkirk. Operation 'Dynamo' commences.
27 May King Leopold asks for an end to hostilities.
28 May Belgian unconditional surrender becomes effective.
29 May Germans take Ostend and Ypres.
31 May French defence of Lille ends. Lord Gort hands over to Gen Alexander and leaves for UK. Churchill visits Paris.
3 June End of Dunkirk evacuation. Germans bomb Paris.
4 June Allies abandon Dunkirk.
5 June Battle of France begins. Army Group B attacks in west, opposite the French 10th Army.
9 June Army Group A launch main assault in centre.
10 June Italy declares war.
11 June German advance into central France continues, Rheims falls. Paris declared an open city.
12 June Guderian launches his XXXIX Corps against Chalons-sur-Marne.
13 June Churchill meets Reynaud for last time.
14 June Germans enter Paris. Maginot Line breached south of Saarbrucken by troops of Army Group C. French Government moves from Tours to Bordeaux. Gen Spears leaves Paris with de Gaulle in his aeroplane.
15 June Germans take Verdun. Reynaud decides to sue for peace.
16 June Guderian's panzers are now on the Saone. Dijon falls. Army Group C crosses Rhine at Colmar. Reynaud resigns, Pétain forms new government and asks Germans for peace terms.
17 June Guderian's leading panzers reach Swiss border near Pontarlier.
18 June De Gaulle's first broadcast from London. Rommel takes Cherbourg.
19 June Loire reached, Saumur cadets brave defence ends. Brest and Nantes taken.
20 June Germans enter Lyons. France asks Italy for an armistice.
21 June Italians attack in Alps and towards Menton on the Côte d'Azur. Hitler meets French delegation at Compiègne for surrender.
22 June France accepts German terms, Gen Huntziger and Gen Keitel sign armistice. French forces trapped between Epinal and Belfort surrender.
24 June French sign armistice with Italians.
25 June Fighting ends in France as armistice takes effect.

Chapter 1

Phase One
DAYS OF PEACE, PREPARATIONS FOR WAR

The Fruits of Versailles

Victory in the West
On the afternoon of 21 June 1940, one of the loveliest days of that momentous summer, a Nazi motorcade arrived at an old wooden railway dining-car standing in a small circular clearing in the middle of the forest near Compiègne, some 50 miles north-east of Paris. Adolf Hitler got out of his gleaming Mercedes and, accompanied by Goering, Brauchitsch, Keitel, Raeder, Ribbentrop and Hess, walked over to a large granite block which bore the following inscription: 'Here on the Eleventh of November 1918 succumbed the criminal pride of the German Empire – vanquished by the free people which it tried to enslave.' One observer (William Shirer, the CBS correspondent in Berlin) reported that Hitler's expression was '. . . afire with scorn, anger, hate, revenge, triumph', while Hitler's valet, Heinz Linge, later recalled that the Führer was muttering something that sounded like: 'We will

THE SITUATION IN 1919

Territory lost by Germany in Europe under the Treaty of Versailles

A triumphant Hitler with his entourage at Compiègne in July 1940, when the French signed the instrument of surrender after Allied forces were routed by Germany's fast-moving panzer divisions.

TM

destroy everything that can remind the world of that shameful day in 1918.'[1]

The railway dining car was of course the place where the Kaiser's representatives had surrendered at the end of the First World War to Marshal Foch. German engineers had taken it out of its museum building and moved it to the exact spot on which it had stood twenty-two years earlier. Hitler was clearly determined to humiliate the French as much as possible, to repay them for the way in which they had humbled the Germans in 1919. At that time, the Hall of Mirrors at Versailles was deliberately chosen as the place in which to sign the Armistice, because that was where, in 1871, King Wilhelm of Prussia had proclaimed himself Kaiser. The Führer's cup of happiness was full – at least for the time being!

True to his word, after the surrender was signed and the *wagon-lit* taken back to its museum, Hitler had the granite block with its damning inscription razed to the ground.

The Treaty of Versailles imposed very strict conditions on Germany, including having to accept sole responsibility for starting the war, the payment of reparations,[2] the loss of territory such as Alsace-Lorraine to France, most of Posen and West Prussia to Poland and the Malmédy area to Belgium. Danzig was to become a free state, plebiscites were to be held in the Saar, Schleswig and East Prussia, while an Allied Army of Occupation was to occupy the Rhineland. In all, there was a loss of some 10% of population and territory. Germany would also lose her colonies and, most humiliating of all, the army would be limited to 100,000 men. Submarines and military aircraft were totally banned.

These conditions, imposed to prevent Germany from starting a war again, unfortunately had the opposite effect. They sowed the seeds of resentment in the hearts of the German people, especially the military, who were more determined than ever that the Fatherland would rise again. Abetted by indus-

A mere two decades earlier Germany was herself suffering the humiliation of total defeat. This photograph, taken in June 1919, shows British occupation forces in Cologne. Tanks of the 12th Battalion, Tank Corps, make their way towards the Cathedral precinct for an inspection by the commander of VII Corps. IWM

trialists, like Krupp, they began to rearm in secret.

Allied Control Commission

To ensure that Germany kept to the letter of the Treaty, Inter-Allied Commissions of Control were established. The inspectors were faced with a well-nigh impossible task as they tried to keep track of all the covert double-dealing that took place. Germany was assisted in its endeavours by other European countries such as Sweden, which had remained neutral during the war and would do so again in 1939. Joseph Vollmer, the only German tank designer of any merit, was able to dismantle his latest model of the *Leichte Kampfwagen* – the LK II – and slip abroad to Sweden, taking with him all ten of the LK II tank kits which had been produced so far in Germany. Safe in a neutral country, he reassembled his tanks and sold them to the obliging Swedes who used them to form their very first tank company. By 1921 the giant Ruhr armaments firm of Krupp had exchanged enough patents and licences with the Bofors steel and cannon works in Sweden to enable them to gain control of its production. They then sent one of their chief production engineers to Bofors where he oversaw the development and production of a whole series of Krupp-designed field artillery pieces, AA guns and light tanks. Next, a member of Krupp's board of directors arrived and took over the management. Similarly a number of Dutch companies readily provided Krupp and others with cover for their illegal dealings.

How Germany's military power was crushed by the Treaty of Versailles in 1919

MILITARY CLAUSES
Article 159
The German military forces shall be demobilized and reduced as prescribed hereinafter.

Article 160
By a date which must not be later than March 31, 1920, the German Army must not comprise more than seven divisions of infantry and three divisions of cavalry *(see below)*. After that date the total number of effectives in the Army of the States constituting Germany must not exceed 100,000 men, including officers and establishments of depots. The Army shall be devoted exclusively to the maintenance of order within the territory and to the control of the frontiers. The total effective strength of officers, including the personnel of staffs, whatever their composition, must not exceed 4,000.

Article 173
Universal compulsory military service shall be abolished in Germany. The German army may only be constituted and recruited by means of voluntary enlistment.

Article 180
All fortified works, fortresses and fieldworks situated in German territory to the west of a line drawn 50 kilometres to the east of the Rhine shall be disarmed and dismantled.

NAVAL CLAUSES
Article 181
After the expiration of a period of two months from the coming into force of the present Treaty the German naval forces in commission must not exceed: 6 battleships of the *Deutschland* or *Lothringen* type, 6 light cruisers, 12 destroyers and 12 torpedo boats... No submarines are to be included.

Article 183
After the expiration of a period of two months from the coming into force of the present Treaty the total personnel of the German Navy, including the manning of the fleet, coast defences, signal stations, administration and other land services, must not exceed 15,000 including officers and men of all grades and corps. The total strength of officers and warrant officers must not exceed 1,500.

Article 194
The personnel of the Germany Navy shall be recruited entirely by voluntary engagements...

AIR CLAUSES
Article 198
The armed forces of Germany must not include any military or naval air forces...

Establishment of an Infantry Division

Unit	Max no of units in div	Max strength Offrs	NCOs & men
HQ	1	25	70
HQ div inf	1	4	30
HQ div arty	1	4	30
inf regt	3	70	2300
trench mortar coy	3	6	150
div sqn	1	6	150
fd arty regt	1	85	1300
pnr bn	1	12	400
sig det	1	12	300
div med svc	1	20	400
parks and convoys	–	14	800
Total Infantry Division		410	10,830

Establishment of a Cavalry Division

Unit	Max no of units in div	Max strength Offrs	NCOs & men
HQ	1	15	50
cav regt	6	40	800
horse arty gp	1	20	400
Total Cavalry Division		275	5,250

A great deal of ingenuity was shown by the Germans first in circumventing the provisions of the Versailles Treaty, and then ignoring them altogether as their war production machine got under way. For example, these dummy tanks made from canvas and wood and mounted on small cars, were used with considerable success during the early 1930s in panzer training.
TM

A British soldier lowers the Union Jack as men of the occupation forces leave the city of Cologne in January 1926. IWM

Hitler reviews his growing number of supporters during a street rally held in 1927. A year later the Nazis had 12 seats in the Reichstag. By 1930, this number had grown to 107, and by 1932 there were 230 Nazi members. IWM

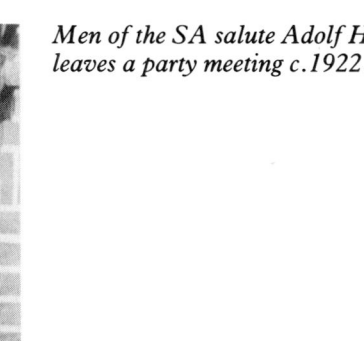

Men of the SA salute Adolf Hitler as he leaves a party meeting c.1922. IWM

It was no different in the aircraft industry. Germany was only allowed to keep 140 aircraft, strictly for commercial use. Tony Fokker of the great Fokker Aircraft works in Schwerin, had the prototype of his latest aeroplane (the F-2) flown secretly to Holland. Back in Germany, realising that the control commission inspectors would dismantle his factory, he personally master-minded the removal and concealment of over half the inventory moving it secretly to Holland, where he calmly started to manufacture planes once more, even selling them to the Dutch government.

Enter Adolf Hitler

In 1919 an obscure but highly decorated corporal, who was awarded both the Iron Cross 2nd & 1st Class during the First World War, began his rise in politics when, as a low grade army political officer, he was sent to investigate the right-wing German Workers' Party. Less than two years later, in July 1921, Adolf Hitler had become its leader and changed the title to the National Socialist German Workers' Party (*Nationalsozialistische Deutsche Arbeiterpartei* – NSDAP – or Nazis for short). The party programme was now radical, violently anti-communist and strongly in opposition to the Versailles Treaty. Hitler and his compatriot, Ernst Röhm, were not afraid to use violence in order to achieve their aims.

In 1923 France and Belgium occupied the Ruhr in an effort to get Germany to keep up with their reparation payments. One of the reasons why payments had fallen behind was inflation which, by November 1923, had reached such ludicrous limits that the rate of exchange for a single US dollar was 130,000,000,000 marks. Taking full advantage of the political unrest caused by these financial problems in Germany, the NSDAP attempted a *putsch*, but failed mainly because the army was not included. Hitler was put into prison for nine months and used the time to write his book *Mein Kampf* which set out his political ideas, such as his anti-communist and anti-semitic feelings, together with his ideals of seeking 'living room' (*lebensraum*) for the German people.

In 1929 after the party congress in Nuremberg, Hitler, who had by then learnt a great deal about politics, publicly joined with the Stabhelm – a party of rabidly nationalistic veterans and the right-wing German National Peoples Party, led by an industrialist named Hugenberg. This link gave the Nazis financial clout. In the elections of 1930 the Nazis became the second largest party, but it took another two years before they became the dominant force in German politics when, in January 1933, Adolf Hitler was appointed Chancellor, under President Paul von Hindenburg.

The New Order and the Old Guard. Hitler and the aged President Paul von Hindenburg at a memorial service in Berlin. On 30 January 1933 Hitler became Chancellor, and after Hindenburg's death in 1934 he declared himself 'Führer and Chancellor'. IWM

The Führer inspects a guard of honour mounted by men of the SS Leibstandarte *'Adolf Hitler'.*   IWM

The burning of the Reichstag on 27 February 1933 was used as an excuse to get rid of as many Communists as possible. They were made convenient scapegoats, but it is still not clear if any political party actually encouraged the mentally-retarded Dutch anarchist who was arrested for starting the fire, or whether it was his own idea. The Nazis took full advantage of the situation and Hitler seized the opportunity to outlaw all other political parties. When Hindenburg died a year later, Hitler had himself declared Reichsführer as well as Chancellor. 'One People, One Nation, One Leader!' (*Ein Volk, Ein Reich, Ein Führer!*), became the rallying cry of the emerging 'New Order'.

On the other side of the hill

While the Germans were plotting and dreaming of battles yet to come, the rest of Europe had other priorities. The 'War to end all Wars' had touched nearly every home in Great Britain and France. The French alone had suffered over 1.3 million casualties: 27% of all their young men between the ages of eighteen and twenty-seven had been killed, while the British had lost over three-quarters of a million men. The total military loss of life worldwide had been in excess of eight million. So it was hardly surprising that there was a determination, especially among those who had fought in the bloody battles on the Western Front, never to go to war again. Military budgets were pared to the bone. There was precious little money to spare for new equipment or new weapons, so it was a question of making do with what remained from the First World War. Other ways had to be found, such as the construction of permanent defence lines, to meet the threat of possible future aggression.

Of course, there were dissenting voices. One of the loudest and strongest was that of Winston Churchill, but no one wanted to listen. Later, Paul Reynaud, France's Premier in 1940, would write with feeling but not, perhaps, entirely with complete accuracy; 'France was no better organized for the preparation and waging of war than she was allied, fortified or armed. We did not think in terms of war. It was because we did not think in terms of it that we had neither allied ourselves, nor fortified ourselves, nor armed ourselves.'[3] This emotive statement does conveniently ignore France's main ally Great Britain with its magnificent Navy, also that vastly expensive 'White Elephant', the Maginot Line and, for that matter, France's own large standing army. However, had he been talking about the mood of the people, then undoubtedly he spoke not just for France, but for all those who had endured the horrors of the First World War. They were heartily sick of war, would ignore all the warning signs, and gladly take every step along the slippery road of appeasement if only another conflict could be avoided.

Covert rearmament

The Inter-Allied Control Commission inspectors left Germany early in 1927, thus removing the only outside 'eyes' capable of watching events closely. From then on the Council of the League of Nations was the only body authorised to look into German disarmament violations. This did not mean that Germany could immediately start overt rearming. As Barton Whaley explains in his book on German re-armament between the

One of the many ways in which the Nazis expressed their intolerance and racial hatred was by organizing the burning of thousands of books, especially those by Jewish authors. IWM

After the Inter-Allied Control Commissioners left Germany early in 1927, arms production was resumed in earnest, 'Guns before Butter' was one of the slogans used to rally the German people behind the rearmament programme, and huge factories like this Rheinmetal-Borsig plant in Düsseldorf were soon working to full capacity. TM

Build-up of German Forces 1933-40

(*NB* Strengths in 1918 were: Army – 2 million plus; Air Force – 306 sqns. By 1930 these figures had dropped to 100,000 men in the Army and just three sqns in the Air Force.)

Dates	Strengths in 000s	Active divs	No of tanks	Air sqns	first line aircraft
1933	102,500	10	?	?	
1934	240,000	10	?	16	
1935	c350,000	10	353	48	c502
1937	550,000	39	?	213	
1938	550,000	42	?	243	1,230
Sep '39	1,400,000	117	2,240+	266	
May '40	2,400,000	157	2,574		2,500

(Source: extracted from a table in *Covert German Re-armament* by Barton Whaley.)

wars: '... It only meant that design, testing and training could proceed under thinner, less hampering cover.' It was now safe for the Krupp's representatives to go home and for their factories to launch into a period of 'black production' (*schwarze produktion*), as it was called. One of the many milestones achieved was the designing of the now world-famous 88mm AA/anti-tank gun which was to cause such havoc among Allied tank forces. It is true to say that the majority of the guns that were to prove so successful in 1939-40 were already fully developed by 1933. When Adolf Hitler became Chancellor all was well in hand to fulfil his dreams of building an all-powerful Third Reich.

This period also saw the birth of the panzer forces, the building of the new German tanks and the evolution of the *Blitzkrieg* tactics, as will be explained in a later chapter.

Overt rearmament

In the spring of 1935 Hitler decided to break the Versailles Treaty and to start openly building up his forces. On 16 March 1935 he decreed that universal military conscription should begin, with the aim of enlarging the existing 10 divisions (100,000 men) to 36 divisions (550,000). Part of his policy was also to endeavour to make the Allies believe that the German forces were larger, better equipped and better trained than in fact they were. An example of this double bluff took place on 14 March 1934 over Berlin, when Goering put on a flying demonstration with over 400 aircraft. The mass of bombers and fighters looked awesome enough to those watching, but a closer inspection would have revealed that many of the 'bombers' were actually cleverly-painted Ju 52 transport planes, and that none of the 'fighters' had any weapons fitted.

But it was not all double bluff. As the adjacent table shows, there was a rapid expansion in the German forces, consistent with Hitler's dreams, and the new weapons to arm these forces had begun to roll off the assembly lines. For example, in early 1935 the first Heinkel He 111 medium bomber was tested and the hull of the first *Scharnhorst*-class battleship was laid down; in June 1935 the first U 1 submarine was commissioned after its

The civil war that broke out in Spain in 1936, seen by many as the first armed clash in an inevitable confrontation between Fascism and Communism, fired the imagination of young idealists from many different countries. These men of Major Clement Attlee's Company, part of the British Battalion of the 15th International Brigade, were typical of those who went out to fight the Nationalists led by General Franco. But after nearly three years of intense, bitter fighting – which in many ways foreshadowed the much larger struggle to come – Franco, strengthened by 'volunteers' from Germany and Italy, won the final battle and established a dictatorship more enduring that that of Hitler or of Mussolini. IWM

As war-clouds gathered over Europe, Japan pressed on with her military adventure in the Far East by launching a full-scale assault on China in July 1937.
IWM

secret construction and by the end of the year a further eleven had joined it. Also Germany now had both the Italians and the Japanese as their allies. Thus, Hitler felt secure enough to reoccupy the demilitarised Rhineland in March 1936. Not one of the other countries raised more than a brief verbal protest.

War in Spain

It was also time for Germany to test its new forces in battle and the Spanish Civil War provided the ideal opportunity. In July 1936 the Luftwaffe began secretly to lift Franco's troops from Morocco to Spain. In November the German Condor Legion, disguised as volunteers, entered Spain in force. They included four tank battalions plus thirty anti-tank companies. As Gen von Thoma recalled later to Liddell Hart: 'It could be seen that Spain would serve as the "European Aldershot". I was in command of all the German ground troops in Spain during the war ... They were used to train Franco's tank force.'[4] They were also able to perfect new tactics, including air to ground support. In addition to the Germans, the Italians had sent a large number of 'volunteers' to fight for Franco even before the Germans arrived; while the Russians joined in on the other side, supplying the Republicans with arms, despite the fact that Stalin had said he would not become involved. The Spanish Civil War was thus used as the arena for all three nations to 'blood' some of their soldiers, try out new weapons and to gain battle experience. The League of Nations condemned the foreign powers for stepping in, but nothing was done to stop them.

Spain was not the only place where Germany's new allies were flexing their newly acquired muscle. In October 1935 Italy had invaded Abyssinia and for nearly a year Mussolini's forces, numbering some 100,000 and supported by modern bombers, fought Emperor Haile Selassie's ill-armed, but heroic, tribesmen. The League of Nations made some half-hearted attempts to impose sanctions against Italy, but nothing positive was done to stop the Italians from creating the 'Empire' which 'Il Duce' had promised them. The attack on Abyssinia helped to reduce political discontent by diverting attention from economic deterioration in Italy. Conscription reduced the level of unemployment, while the production of armaments helped Italy's industry to prosper.

In the Far East, the Japanese had declared the independence of their puppet state of Manchukuo (formerly Manchuria) in February 1932, and in November 1936 signed the 'Anti-Comintern Pact' with Germany, ostensibly as a bastion against communism. A few months later, in July 1937, the Japanese launched a full-scale assault on China. The League of Nations declared Japan to be an aggressor but, as usual, did nothing else. America decided to keep away, while the European powers were all far too busy with their own problems. The Japanese had the full support of Germany in all their acts of aggression because it was clearly in Hitler's best interests to keep both Britain and America on tenterhooks in the Far East.

Versailles Treaty abrogated

1937 opened with Hitler formally abrogating the provisions of the Versailles Treaty, when he claimed in a speech in the Reichstag that it was impossible for a great power like Germany to accept such restrictions any longer. Just over a year later, in March 1938, he annexed Austria and on 13 March it was proclaimed a province of the German Reich. President Beneš of Czechoslovakia resigned seven months later when Germany moved into the Sudetenland and his country was split into three autonomous provinces. The following March German troops were once again on the move. Hitler raised the Nazi banner on Hradzin Castle, late residence of the president of the now vanished republic of Czechoslovakia. The reception given to the German army when it entered Prague was very different to the tumultuous welcome they had received in both Austria and the Sudentenland. The crowds were openly hostile, as well they might be, for this was the very first time that Adolf

Hitler had occupied a country not inhabited by people of the Germanic race. It is interesting to note that the annexation of Czechoslovakia also gained for the Germans a fleet of excellent Czech-built tanks designed by the indefatigable Joseph Vollmer, who had moved there from Sweden some years earlier. These tanks were to prove invaluable in the coming battle for France.

In direct contravention of the Versailles Treaty, German cavalry re-entered the demilitarized Rhineland on 7 March 1936. IWM

Every German soldier had to swear an oath of personal allegiance to the Führer, seen here at a presentation of standards parade. IWM

Hitler's greatest single triumph in peacetime was the 'Anschluss' (Connection), by which Austria became an integral part of Germany. When he formally announced its successful completion to the Reichstag on 13 March 1938, the Führer received a standing ovation. IWM

In the Sudetenland plebiscite held on 4 December 1938 the German-speaking population voted overwhelmingly in favour of Hitler's annexation. As a result, a further 11,000 square miles of territory was added to the Third Reich without a shot being fired. IWM

Peace at any price

Mr Neville Chamberlain was the British Prime Minister from 1937 to 1940 and during that time devoted himself to preserving peace at any price. He tried to establish links with both Hitler and Mussolini in order to talk to them about preventing war. With the benefit of hindsight, many people now accuse him of being naive and much too trusting, but his purposes were honourable and he saw nothing wrong in appeasement if it would prevent war. In fact, the vast majority of British and French people felt exactly as he did, so strong was the desire for peace. After Germany marched into Austria in March 1938 he secured a promise from Hitler that there would be no further aggression and, in particular, that Germany had no intention of invading Czechoslovakia. Chamberlain then made a speech in the House of Commons, in which he implied that both Britain and France would not stand idly by if Czechoslovakia were attacked. However, events were to prove otherwise. When Hitler demanded self-government for the Sudentenland, which housed over three million Germans, France let it be known that they would not go to war over the issue. Chamberlain decided to fly to Berchtesgaden himself on 15 September 1938 in an attempt to persuade the Führer not to invade if the Sudentenland were to be given self-government. Hitler quickly agreed, and Chamberlain flew home to obtain the approval of the Cabinet.

This secured, Chamberlain met Hitler once more, this time at Godesberg on 22 September, only to discover that the Führer had changed his mind. He renewed his threat to attack Czechoslovakia earlier, at the same time announcing that this was to be his 'last territorial demand in Europe'. War seemed inevitable. The Czechs mobilised and the British Fleet was sent to its war stations. However, Hitler had decided to continue his cat-and-mouse game a little longer, and invited both Chamberlain and the French Premier, Daladier, to meet him in Munich on 29 September to discuss peace plans. The agreement concluded between them was supposed to guarantee 'Peace In Our Time': Chamberlain returned home to press and public acclaim as the saviour of Europe. But the heady atmosphere rapidly faded when the Germans invaded Czechoslovakia not long afterwards.

Even someone as hopeful of maintaining peace as Chamberlain was forced to realise that he could not trust the word either of Hitler or Mussolini. Unfortunately, by this time the dictators were both firmly of the opinion that they could do anything they liked. Whatever Britain and France might say, it was believed that they would never go to war to defend any country other than their own. So Hitler's excesses continued. On 15 March the Germans proclaimed the establishment of the Protectorate of Bohemia and Moravia. They followed this announcement a week later with an ultimatum to

After the Munich Agreement in September 1938, Neville Chamberlain waves the piece of paper 'bearing my name and that of Adolf Hitler' to an enthusiastic crowd gathered at the airport to greet him on his return. IWM

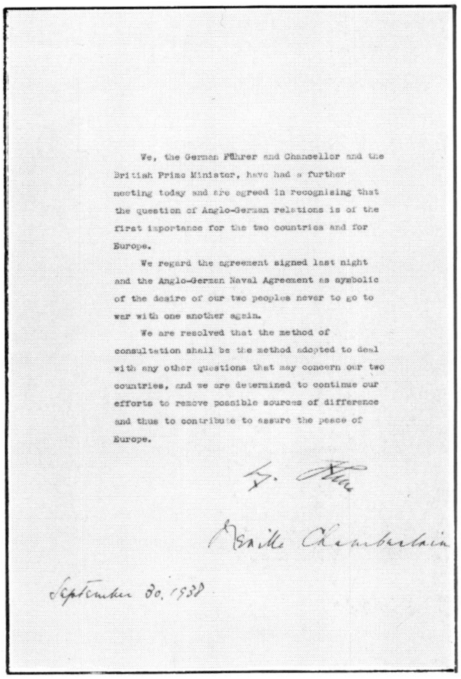

We, the German Führer and Chancellor and the British Prime Minister, have had a further meeting today and are agreed in recognising that the question of Anglo-German relations is of the first importance for the two countries and for Europe.

We regard the agreement signed last night and the Anglo-German Naval Agreement as symbolic of the desire of our two peoples never to go to war with one another again.

We are resolved that the method of consultation shall be the method adopted to deal with any other questions that may concern our two countries, and we are determined to continue our efforts to remove possible sources of difference and thus to contribute to assure the peace of Europe.

A. Hitler

Neville Chamberlain

September 30, 1938

On 20 March 1939 the German army mounted a huge parade in Wenceslas Square, Prague, at which the salute was taken by General von Schweppenburg, commander of the 3rd Panzer Division. IWM

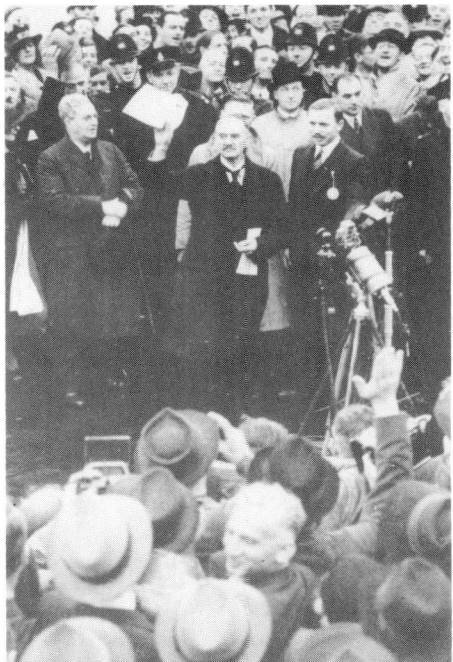

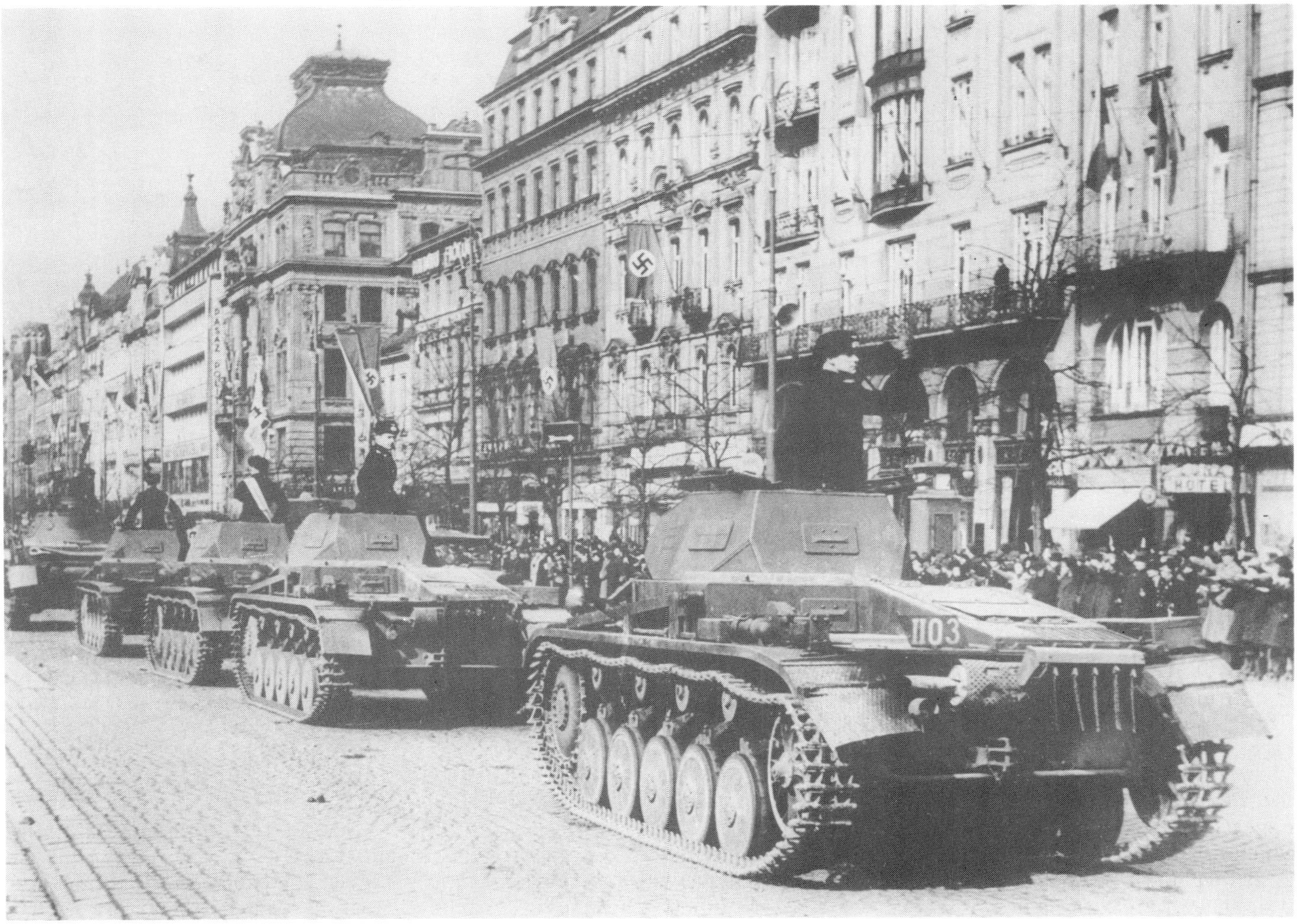

Adolf Hitler and Benito Mussolini in expansive mood after signing their 'Pact of Steel' on 22 May 1939. IWM

Lithuania to cede the area around Memel. This was done on 22 March. The next day Germany signed an economic agreement with Rumania to obtain oil on privileged terms.

The fuel for his panzers now secure, Hitler began to put pressure on the Poles, demanding that they give Germany sufficient land to build a road through the Polish Corridor linking Danzig to the German province of East Prussia and that Danzig itself should be returned to Germany. Not to be outdone, Mussolini invaded Albania in April 1939, and in Berlin on 22 May the Italians and Germans signed a formal alliance which they called 'The Pact of Steel'.

From appeasement to rearmament

As we have seen, after Hitler came to power the League of Nations followed a policy of appeasement led by Britain and France. This policy probably reached its zenith during the Munich crisis of September 1938 over the situation in Czechoslovakia, with Neville Chamberlain returning from Munich clutching his 'Peace in our Time' friendship agreement. However, the warning signs were all too plain and could no longer be ignored. After Germany marched into the Sudentenland on 1 October despite all Hitler's promises, it became clear that Poland would be the next target. Both Britain and France let it be known that they would declare war on Germany if the Nazis did invade their ally, but Hitler clearly did not believe them. His miscalculation of the Anglo-French will to fight led to the Second World War and to the eventual downfall of the Thousand Year Reich.

Despite the policy of appeasement Britain and France embarked upon a gradual programme of rearmament from the mid-Thirties, which became more and more frenetic as they realised just how far behind Germany they had allowed themselves to drift. Britain, for example, started a crash programme of aircraft construction, hoping that the quality of new fighters such as the Supermarine Spitfire and the Hawker Hurricane would compensate for lack of numbers.

The British Army also began to modernise, albeit very slowly, as was evidenced from the 1935-36 Army Estimates, which allowed for a paltry £4 million increase, of which a mere £270,000 was for the provision of tracked vehicles, including tanks. This state of affairs was hardly surprising when one considers the attitude of mind towards mechanisation which still pervaded the British Army at that time. The Secretary of State for War, for example, when introducing the Army Estimates for 1936-37, apologised to the cavalry for having made the unpalatable decision to mechanise eight of their regiments. 'It is like asking a great musical performer to throw away his violin,' he said, 'and to devote himself in future to the gramophone.'[5] Is there any wonder that by 1939 Britain only had two incomplete armoured divisions compared with the Germans' six?

To be fair to Neville Chamberlain, as Chancellor of the Exchequer in 1937 he actively promoted a rearmament plan which called for a five-year expansion on a scale far larger than anything attempted since the end of the First World War. It was proposed to spend £1,500 million over five years: three times as much as was spent when Hitler came to power, and a 50% increase on expenditure during the previous year.

On the Home Front

As early as 1924, a sub-committee of the Committee of Imperial Defence had been set up under John Anderson[6] (who would later give his name to the never-to-be-forgotten garden air-raid shelters) to consider Air Raid Precautions (ARP). However, the abbreviation did not become familiar to local authorities until July 1935, when a circular was issued urging them to prepare plans. Two years later the Air Raid Precautions Act was passed, and it became legally binding on

German might on display. Adolf Hitler inspects his panzer troops on parade in Berlin. In the foreground are Sd Kfz 232 six-wheeled armoured cars and troop-carrying Man *standard 3-ton trucks.* IWM

the Committee to submit their plans for approval with all possible speed. Unfortunately the ARP remained as rather a joke and, even when national recruiting began in 1938, there was little interest aroused or assistance given. However, during the twelve months following the Munich crisis, a new impetus was apparent as people realised all too clearly from the newsreels of the bombing in Spain and China the probable dangers they might soon have to face from enemy air-raids. An immense amount was done thereafter to prepare for war, which completely transformed the ARP. Civil Defence was no longer a laughing matter and now there were far more volunteers than there were instructors to train them.

Civilian resources were mobilized no less thoroughly than the armed forces in Hitler's pre-war Germany. Men of the Reich Labour Corps carry their spades like rifles as they march past their leader during a massive party rally. The Nazi propaganda machine took full advantage of carefully-staged events such as these to boost home morale and demoralize potential enemies. IWM

By comparison, British preparations for war at times seemed half-hearted and amateur. But this photograph shows Anderson shelters being delivered in Muswell Hill, a suburb of London, in February 1938 – well before the Munich Agreement was signed. When at last it became clear that Hitler's ambitions could not be satisfied by appeasement, a mood of quiet determination gripped the country. IWM

In France
'Thank God for the French Army!' exclaimed Winston Churchill in the House of Commons on 23 March 1933. Undoubtedly he was thinking and speaking about the great French Army of 1918, but was it still as good as it had been at the end of the First World War? Sadly the answer was definitely no.

Although France still had a large, well-equipped army, it was woefully behind the times as far as tactical thinking was concerned. This is clearly evidenced from remarks made by two famous French generals on the role of tanks. Marshal Pétain, while he was Supreme Commander in the early Twenties, had said that he considered the role of tanks was 'to assist the advance of the infantry, by breaking static obstacles and active resistance put up by the enemy'. Over a decade later, in 1936, Gamelin had this to say: 'You cannot hope to achieve real breakthroughs with tanks. The tank is not independent enough. It has to go ahead, but then must return for fuel and supplies.'[7]

Clearly France was alarmed by the rise of Germany during the mid-Thirties and took steps to modernise its force, but French hearts were really not in it and, like their Allies, they hoped for 'Peace at any Price'. The revoking of the Franco-Belgian Treaty by King Leopold III on 14 October 1936, with the Belgians opting for neutrality, undoubtedly caused the French many problems. No longer would they be able to occupy a defensive line in Belgium in peacetime, but would have to take up unprepared positions once the Germans had invaded. A very worrying situation, especially as it put at risk their Maginot Line strategy.

So as Europe enjoyed its last summer of peace the Germans confidently prepared for their 'lightning war' in Poland, firmly convinced that Britain and France would once again turn the other cheek.

ARP wardens, with their helmets painted white to make them more visible in the blackout, on patrol in Lambeth.   IWM

NOTES

1. J. Toland *Adolf Hitler* New York: Doubleday & Co. Inc., 1976.
2. At the Peace Conference the whole question of reparations to be paid by Germany became the source of considerable friction among the victors. Of a total of 400,000 million gold francs claimed by the Allies as a whole, the French demanded 209,000 million. British Treasury officials, on the other hand, calculated that Germany would not be able to pay more than 75,000 million altogether. As Alistair Horne put it in *To Lose A Battle*, this discord did not go unnoticed by the Germans and '. . . *fatally the sum to be paid by Germany was left open for future negotiations. It was an open sore that the issue of reparations remained open, gaining little from France but ill-will.*'
3. J. Benoist-Mechin *Sixty Days That Shook The West* London: Jonathan Cape, 1963.
4. B. Liddell Hart *The Other Side of the Hill* London: Cassell, 1964.
5. *The Tanks* Vol. 1.
6. Later Lord Waverley. He was put in charge of Air Raid Precautions in July 1939 and later as wartime Home Secretary, was described by Winston Churchill, as 'a man of singular capacity and firmness of character, imperturbable amid gathering peril and confusion.' Others were not so generous: he was known in the Civil Service, for example, as 'Pompous John' or 'Jehovah'! As explained in the text, he gave his name to the cheap, simple domestic air-raid shelter of which more than 2,300,000 had been erected by September 1940 to protect the civilian population of Great Britain.
7. A Horne *To Lose A Battle* London: Macmillan, 1969.

Chapter 2

Strategic Considerations

The Effects of the First World War

The First World War and the provisions of the Treaty of Versailles had a profound influence on the future strategies of the major nations of the world. It could scarcely have been otherwise, for the cost in human life and in the destruction of property was on a hitherto unimaginable scale. Civilian casualties amounted to nine million (although some historians put the figure as high as twelve million), and at least eight million military personnel lost their lives. If the wounded,

Death in action. No other image conveys the horror of trench warfare more powerfully than this photograph, taken in 1916, of a soldier lying outside his dug-out on the Western Front. IWM

prisoners-of-war and those reported missing are taken into account, that last figure increases fourfold, to at least 37 million. The economic cost to Europe was equally staggering. In those four disastrous years she lost her lead over the rest of the world in trade and industry, and in the political influence such commercial dominance brings.

However, the statistics alone do not tell the full story. As the 1920s dawned, ordinary people everywhere began to realize that the appalling sacrifices of the First World War were made largely in vain, and that all the talk about upholding Christian values, of making the world a safer place to live in, and of turning Britain 'into a land fit for heroes', was little more than the empty rhetoric of self-seeking politicians. The euphoria of victory soon gave way to a feeling of disillusionment. For the wealthy few, this found its expression in the pursuit of pleasure at any cost. But for the vast majority of people in Europe and elsewhere the bitter legacy of war was hopelessness and despair, fuelled by unemployment and recession.

German strategy

Adolf Hitler realized instinctively that one way of seizing power was to turn the frustration and despair of the German people to his political advantage. He did this by enlisting support in achieving a number of objectives, set out clearly in the pages of *Mein Kampf*. In the process, he fanned the smouldering flame of German nationalism and restored to ordinary people in all walks of life their natural pride, and sense of purpose. Top of the list was his desire for *lebensraum* for the German people. '... we National Socialists,' he wrote 'must hold unflinchingly to our aim in foreign policy, namely, to secure for the German people the land and soil to which they are entitled on this earth. And this action is the only one which, before God and our German posterity, would make any sacrifice of blood seem justified ... The right to possess soil can become a duty if without extension of its soil a great nation seems doomed to destruction. ... Germany will either be a world power or there will be no Germany.'[1]

This idea of a divine right to *lebensraum* was not Hitler's original brainchild, because expansionism had long been a German dream. As John Toland explains in his book on Adolf Hitler: '... In 1906 Klaus Wagner wrote that "every great people needs new territory.

Hitler was a man quite insignificant in stature, but what held the German nation in his thrall were his genius as an orator and the force of his magnetic personality. Long after it became obvious that he was leading Germany to total annihilation, he was still able to command the loyalty and devotion of those around him. IWM

It must expand over foreign soil. It must expel foreigners by the power of the sword." Combining it with anti-Semitism was Hitler's contribution.'

Hitler's other major strategic contribution, which eventually caused his downfall and the defeat of Germany, was his choice of the area for this *lebensraum*. 'And so we National Socialists consciously draw a line beneath the foreign policy tendency of our pre-war period. We take up where we broke off six hundred years ago. We stop the endless German movement to the south and west, and turn our gaze towards the land in the east. At long last we break off the colonial and commercial policy of the pre-war period and shift to the soil policy of the future. If we speak of soil in Europe today, we can primarily have in mind only Russia and her vassal border states.'[2] The invasion of Russia and the taking by force of Russian territory, was perhaps the most important strategic aim of Hitler and of the German people. Such conquest also, he hoped, would rid Europe for ever of Communism, the arch-enemy of Facism and of the Nazis.

Before starting his crusade in the east to subjugate the despised Russians and to capture by force of arms the necessary 'living room', he had first to gather back into the fold all those areas in which German-speaking people lived, which had been taken away at Versailles. This he achieved without a shot being fired – is it any wonder that the Germans thought their Führer was invincible?

Germany's second major strategic aim was the destruction of her erstwhile enemies Britain and France, especially the latter who had so humiliated the Fatherland in 1919. But these two strategic aims carried with them the risk

Villagers gather for a religious festival in the vast, open steppes of Russia. Hitler's plan was to seize country like this to satisfy the German demand for more living space (lebensraum). IWM

Another of Hitler's aims was to preserve the 'purity' of the Aryan race by driving out the Jews. What started as harrassment, such as the daubing of Jewish-owned shops, ended as genocide on an unimaginable scale. IWM

of having to fight on two fronts simultaneously, in the east and in the west. Hitler and his generals realised this was impossible: despite the rapid expansion and re-equipping of the German armed forces, they could not hope to take on all their enemies at the same time. Hitler therefore decided on a complicated game of bluff which the rest of the world obligingly took at face value. In 1934, for instance, he signed a ten-year non-aggression pact with Poland. He had no intention of honouring this treaty, but used it simply as a means of separating Poland from an existing alliance with France. Five years later, in March 1939, Hitler scrapped the pact, using the extending of the Anglo/Polish guarantee as his excuse. On 23 August 1939 Germany signed a non-aggression pact with Russia much to the amazement and chagrin of Britain and France, who never imagined for a moment that two such obvious enemies could sign such an agreement. Stalin and Hitler actually detested one another, but both saw advantages in the pact. For example, one secret clause agreed that Germany and Russia would divide Poland between them once the Poles had been crushed. After the pact had served its purpose Hitler would have no qualms about breaking it and invading Russia.

The order in which he dealt with his three main enemies was dictated by the way in which events unfolded after the invasion of Poland. Hitler and his cronies were undoubtedly both surprised and scared by Britain's firm reaction and the declaration of war which followed. It is a pity that this firm resolve was not backed up by more positive action.

Hitler's first wartime directive

In Hitler's first directive to his Service chiefs for the prosecution of the war, planned to begin on 1 September with the invasion of Poland, he set out his major strategy, indicating that he required the Army to hold the West Wall and prevent England and France from interfering with operations against Poland. The Navy would start warfare against British shipping, while the primary task of the Luftwaffe was to defend the Fatherland against France and England. (See Chapter 7 for details.)

Allied Strategy
Of the major powers beside whom Britain fought in the Second World War, only France was seriously considered as a potential ally during the inter-war years. America was reckoned to be more isolationist than ever while it was felt that Russia would only take an active part if they were under a direct threat themselves. On the other hand, the security of Britain and France was considered to be indivisible and that both would fight if the other came under attack. During the Chamberlain administration there was a school of thought which argued that Britain would only participate in a continental war in a limited way using only her sea and air power. However, neither the British nor the French agreed to an alliance on such a basis. Shortly before the war the British and French staff delegations had summed up their conclusions on the 'broad strategic policy for the conduct of the war' as follows: 'We should be faced by enemies who would be more fully prepared than ourselves for war on a national scale, would have superiority in air and land forces, but would be inferior at sea and in general economic strength. In these circumstances, we must be prepared to face a major offensive directed at either France or Great Britain or against both. To defeat such an offensive we should have to concentrate all our initial efforts, and during this time our major strategy would be defensive.'[3]

They went on to say that it might be possible to carry out counter-offensive operations against the Italians, both in North and East Africa, thus reducing Italy's will to fight without, as they put it, 'undue cost'. Subsequent policy would be directed against holding Germany and dealing decisively with Italy, whilst building up military strength to a point when it would be possible to take the offensive against Germany. Meanwhile, everything should be done by diplomatic means to secure the '. . . benevolent neutrality or active assistance of other powers, particularly the United States of America.'

No mention was made of Japan, but in the last few weeks before war was declared in Europe relations between Britain and Japan were certainly under strain. On the other hand the Japanese had quite enough on their plate dealing with China, while the Russo-German agreement made them suspicious about Hitler's long-term motives.

Major Allied strategic considerations
Just before the outbreak of war the British and French staff delegations listed a number of strategic considerations which they believed were of major importance. These included naval matters such as the protection of trade; the military assistance which Britain could offer if France were attacked; the timetable for the despatch of an expeditionary force; and finally, the employment of the British and French air forces. To summarise the main points:

Naval tasks The essential task was to protect the merchant ships carrying the supplies on which the Allies depended. The Germans had no 'High Seas Fleet' but rather a small number of potential 'raiders' which, nevertheless, could be highly dangerous. Admiralty policy was to place the main fleet where it could give covering protection to shipping, namely at Scapa Flow in the Orkneys. There were agreed operational zones between the surface vessel of both navies in the Channel, the Atlantic and the Mediterranean. The French proposed to maintain a powerful *force de raid* in the Atlantic. Both navies would have free use of each other's bases and the secrets of the British anti-submarine device ASDIC were given to the French.

Military tasks Anglo-French strategy would aim at maintaining the integrity of French territory. If the Low Countries were involved then the Allies would attempt to stop the enemy as far forward as possible. Allied troops would be unable to enter Belgium unless invited by the Belgian government, but: '. . . chances of successful intervention would be enhanced if previous arrangements

Smirking Nazi thugs look on as elderly Jews are forced to scrub the streets of Vienna. But outrages such as these were only minor affairs compared with those to follow, as Hitler's, 'final solution' gathered momentum. IWM

Newsreel film of the bombing of towns and cities in Spain and China brought home, for the first time, the horror of air attacks on civilian populations. In France, as in Britain, national appeals went out for civil defence workers. TM

had been made with Belgium.' The British Army would fight in France, but the size of the Expeditionary Force would be much smaller than in the First World War. Many politicians and soldiers did not approve of a 'Continental military commitment'. However there was no disagreement over the need to maintain an adequate army in the Middle East. Egypt was considered to be of prime strategic importance in view of the Suez Canal, while Palestine was needed as a buffer against an invasion of Egypt from the north. India and the Far East were not thought to be in any immediate danger.

Air tasks Despite a major expansion, the RAF was a long way behind the Luftwaffe in bombers and, so long as the Low Countries remained neutral, British bombers would find it difficult to reach potential enemy targets. This could be countered by basing bombers in France and it was agreed in April 1938 that an advanced air striking force would move to French airfields on the outbreak of war. Initial bombing objectives would '. . . not involve loss of civil life' and there would be co-operation between the Allies to strike at the invading German armies and their supply services.

French strategy

In 1933 Gen Weygand, then inspector general of the army, reviewed French defence policy. His report gives a good summary of the basic tenets of France's inter-war years defence strategy. 'France is profoundly pacifist,' he wrote. 'This is true, this is simple, but it is just too simple to be sufficient to define her policy. The policy of a great country like ours, which through her possessions has spread over the whole surface of the globe, has to reckon with various complex elements which are the results of her geographic and demographic situation, the nature of her frontiers and the inclinations of her neighbours, the treaties in force and the agreements made with other powers.'[4]

Gen Weygand then explains how France had over 1,000km of land frontiers, of which she shared about one-third with Italy which was reinforced by the barrier of the Alps; one-third with Germany which had no natural protection to the west of the Rhine. Also, France was the only European country with maritime frontiers opening on the north, west and south, all of which were ice-free all year round. Her eastern and south-eastern neighbours had aggressive intentions and might attack without warning. The result was that the first duty of the military, air and naval forces was: '. . . to defend the territory while defending themselves against these attacks.' Despite the fact that theirs was a 'defensive army', Weygand maintained that the defence system must include large manoeuvring units as well as fortress units.

As to the 120km of frontier which neighbouring Belgium shared with Germany, from the south of Luxembourg to Dutch Limbourg, France had a duty to: '. . . go to her rescue without delay in order to stop the enemy on this line.' This was sensible because not only would the French enjoy the support of the Belgian army, but the frontier was also much shorter than the 350km border between France and Belgium, where they would be on their own. There was a need, he argued, for '. . . new large manoeuvring units, certain of which must be capable of special speed.'

Weygand then went on to discuss the treaties with Poland and Great Britain, and France's requirements to defend its overseas territories. He concluded by saying that it was essential to begin a methodical and exhaustive study without delay, which would result in a major reorganisation of the national defence forces. As a result, French forces were on the whole both large and well-equipped by the time war came. What had not changed since the end of the First World War was the tactical thinking of the French generals.

Defence of Britain

Since 1934, when Germany started to rearm her air force, the minds of people in Britain were increasingly prepared for a 'knock-out' blow by German bombers aimed at the commercial and industrial centres of Great Britain and, in particular, at the sprawling mass of London. The Air Staff estimated in May 1939 that for a fortnight the Germans could maintain an attack on London by 1,000 bombers daily.'[5] The air defence of Britain, controlled by RAF Fighter Command and agreed as early as November 1938, was based upon co-operation between fighters, AA artillery, searchlight companies and balloons. Information on approaching aircraft would be greatly enhanced by the new radar direction-finding posts set up along the south and south-east coasts. All three Services would play their part in the defence of the coasts and coastal waters, including Territorial Army troops manning the defences of twenty-eight defended ports.

Certain other matters affected both Allied and Axis strategic policy, so we must look briefly at them.

Naval policy

Naval strategy on both sides was affected by the various treaties which laid down total tonnages. In Germany's case the limits were initially imposed by the Versailles Treaty. The rest of the world was governed by international agreements, such as the Washington Treaty of 1922 and the two London treaties which followed in 1930 and 1936. In 1922 the total tonnages were limited to approximately 500,000 tons for Britain and the United States; 300,000 for Japan; 220,000 for France; and 180,000 for Italy. The treaty also endeavoured to impose a size limit of 35,000 tons, with guns no larger than 16in. However, the Japanese refused to ratify the 1936 London Treaty, so that they could build bigger, more powerfully armed ships in secret. America followed

Despite drastic cuts after the First World War, the Royal Navy was still seen as the guardian of vital links with Empire rather than as the first line of defence in a European conflict. IWM

Dunkirk town centre, May 1940. TM

suit, raising the limit to 45,000 tons. The German Navy used subterfuge to get around the Versailles provisions, and when Hitler abrogated the treaty they began building pocket-battleships to counter those of the Allies. Details of the respective navies at the start of the war are given later.

An Anglo-French declaration on the conduct of warfare, made on 2 September 1939, included an assurance that they would strictly abide by the rules laid down in the Submarine Protocol of 1936 which had been accepted by nearly all civilised nations. They would also only employ their aircraft against merchant shipping at sea in conformity with the recognised rules applicable to the exercise of belligerent rights by warships.[6]

Military policy
The same declaration covered the promise that there would be no artillery bombardment of objectives which had no strictly defined military importance, particularly large urban areas outside the battle zone. They would also make every effort to avoid the destruction of localities or buildings which were, as they put it 'of value to civilisation'.

The two Allied Governments also affirmed their intention to abide by the terms of the German Protocol of 1925, prohibiting the use in war of asphyxiating, poisonous or other gases, or of bacteriological methods of warfare.

Air bombing policy
On 1 September 1939 President Roosevelt made an appeal to each of the co-belligerents to '. . . publicly affirm its determination that its armed forces shall in no event and under no circumstances undertake bombardment from the air of civilian populations or unfortified cities, upon the understanding that the same rules of warfare will be scrupulously observed by all their opponents.'

These principles, which had been unanimously approved by the League of Nations Assembly, were quoted in Air Ministry Instructions on 22 August 1939. Hitler also replied to President Roosevelt, stating that the German Air Force had received a similar command to confine itself to military objectives. Sadly this did not prove to be the case once the invasion of Poland began when it rapidly became clear that the Luftwaffe was bombing open towns, including Warsaw. In mid-October the Chief of the Air Staff informed the Head of No 1 Air Mission in France: 'Owing to German action in Poland we are no longer bound under the instructions . . . nor by our acceptance of Roosevelt's appeal.'[7]

A cartload of bewildered old men, driven from their homes by the rapid German advance, flee westwards out of Belgium, 13 May 1940. IWM

NOTES

1. A. Hitler *Mein Kampf* trs. R. Manheim. London: Hutchinson & Co. 1973.
2. Ibid.
3. N. H. Gibbs, *History of the Second World War* London: HMSO, 1976.
4. Weygand *The Makings of the Second World War*.
5. As note 3.
6. The Submarine Protocol of 1936 dealt with the sinking of merchant ships by submarines and surface vessels and laid down that, except in the case of ships which refuse to stop or offer active resistance, a warship may not sink or render incapable of navigation a merchant vessel without first placing the passengers, crew and ship's papers in a place of safety (not the ship's boats, unless they could be assured of reaching land or another vessel). After the unrestricted engagement of merchant ships by her submarines and aircraft, Germany was regarded as having violated all such agreements.
7. J. R. M. Butler *History of the Second World War, Vol II 'Grand Strategy'* London: HMSO, 1957.

Chapter 3

Opposing Tactical Doctrines

GERMANY

Blitzkrieg

Perhaps the most emotive word to emerge from the battles of 1939-40 is *Blitzkrieg* which means literally 'lightning war'. It conjures up visions of vast mobile, armoured forces, moving swiftly across country and sweeping all before them, while from the air comes a rain of bombs onto the enemy positions. To those who were on the receiving end of the first *Blitzkrieg* attacks this is exactly what it must have appeared to be, and it is entirely consistent with the image of the invincibility of the *Panzerwaffe* which the Germans had been actively promoting since before the war. It is also true to say that the effect which the new tactics had on their opponents' morale was out of all proportion to the number of troops involved.

In order to put things into perspective it is as well to appreciate that in 1939-40 the mechanised portion of the German Army which was responsible for carrying out these new tactics represented only a tiny fraction of the whole. In general terms, as we shall see in the next chapter, the Wehrmacht was still predominantly comprised of foot soldiers who marched into battle, supported by artillery that was still horsedrawn. As General Heinz Guderian, the 'Father of the Panzers' and chief architect of the build-up of the panzer arm later wrote: 'The development of tracked vehicles for the tank supporting arms never went as fast as we wished. It was clear that the effectiveness of the tanks would gain in proportion to the ability of the infantry, artillery and other divisional arms to follow them across country'.[1]

The origins of *Blitzkrieg*

As Matthew Cooper explains in his history of *The German Army (1933-1945)*, the basic tactics of 'lightning war' go back to much earlier times. He quotes an example of a 14th-century Sultan who was known as 'The Thunderbolt' because of his method of rapid attack. The need for 'war in a hurry' had been an essential part of Prussian military thinking since well before Bismarck; however, it is now indissolubly linked to the German *panzertruppe* of the Second World War.

It is not entirely clear how the word *Blitzkrieg* originated. Some historians say that it was invented by Hitler, yet Len Deighton in his book entitled *Blitzkrieg* states that General Walther Nehring was sure that it was not of German origin. This would add credence to the claim that it was used for the first time by an

One of the young tank commanders who helped to create a myth of invincibility as the Panzerwaffe *raced across Belgium and France sweeping all opposition aside.* IWM

25

The spectacular success of the panzer division hides the fact that in 1939-40 Hitler's army was less mechanised than the British. The majority of infantrymen still had to march, while most German artillery was still drawn by horses. TM

General Heinz Guderian, the 'Father of the Panzers', was the architect of Hitler's most powerful weapon. TM

American *Time* magazine correspondent who, when describing the events which had taken place in Poland in 1939, wrote of them as being '. . . no war of occupation but a war of quick penetration and obliteration – *Blitzkrieg* – lightning war'.[2] Cooper goes on to explain how even Guderian agreed that 'our enemies coined the word *Blitzkrieg*'.

Blitzkrieg tactics as we know them today did not come about until the invention of that revolutionary new weapon the tank, which came into being as the result of a pressing need to break the stalemate which existed on the Somme battlefields of 1914-15. War had ground to a halt, thanks to the deadly effectiveness of the machine gun and the artillery shell. The opposing armies were bogged down in trench warfare and all that it entailed; the morass of muddy, shell-torn ground that separated them needed a very special vehicle to cross it.

The tank itself could not have been produced without the earlier invention of the internal combustion engine or of the means of fabricating armour plate which, between them, provided two of its three basic characteristics, namely mobility and protection. The third, and most important – firepower – was already available and merely needed to be adapted to suit. In simple terms a tank is a means of carrying a weapon system and the crew needed to serve it, safely and speedily, on the battlefield.

The British, the inventors of the tank, used them with increasing success in the First World War, yet chose to ignore their potential in the period of peace that followed. There were plenty of voices telling those in authority what to do, but the 'Back to 1914' brigade did not want to listen.[3] On the other hand Generaloberst Hans von Seeckt, first commander of the *Reichswehr* in the days of the Weimar Republic, wrote: 'In brief, the whole future of warfare appears to me to lie in the employment of mobile armies, relatively small but of high quality and rendered more effective by the addition of aircraft.' Seeckt was convinced that any future war would be a much more fluid affair than previously and that the successful forces would be those composed of integrated, mobile units, with close air support.

Seeckt ensured that every member of his 100,000-strong army was trained as both a leader and an instructor so that they would be fully able to cope with expansion when the time came. He also supported the covert rearmament programme and took every opportunity to send his officers abroad to visit other armies and learn new ideas. The theories of mechanised warfare expounded in Britain by men like Fuller, Broad and Liddell Hart found a much more receptive audience in the *Reichswehr* than in their own army. Among these German officers was one Heinz Guderian who, more than anyone else, clearly appreciated the decisive role which tanks could play in the battles to come.

The all-arms team

Guderian and his mentors saw the tank not as a unit operating in isolation, but as an important – perhaps the most important – element of a team in which tanks, infantry, artillery, engineers and other arms all worked closely together with close air support. Tanks could play a vital role acting as 'mobile artillery', constantly on call to support the leading troops. In German parlance this was known as *einheit* (unity). We take this for granted on the modern battlefield, but in those days such ideas were considered heresy. For example, while British tankmen had to work within the constraints of a severe lack of funding plus the need to help police a vast worldwide Empire. In sharp contrast to the general dislike and distrust of mechanisation by many senior British officers, the Germans were more willing to accept the new philosophy. It should not be assumed that Guderian had everything his own way: he did encounter some opposition from the 'Old Order' in the Wehrmacht and had to fight hard to overcome it.

Einheit did not signify only that the various arms would operate in a coordinated manner, but that they were integrated down to the lowest level possible. Each tank battalion in the attack would have one or more motorised infantry companies assigned to it. The lucky infantrymen travelled in half-tracked armoured personnel carriers; others were lorry-borne, with one or more troops of assault engineers. A battalion or more of field artillery would also be on call plus a flight or two of Stuka dive-bombers. There might well be other weapons involved, such as anti-tank guns used offensively, or even anti-aircraft artillery – particularly effective

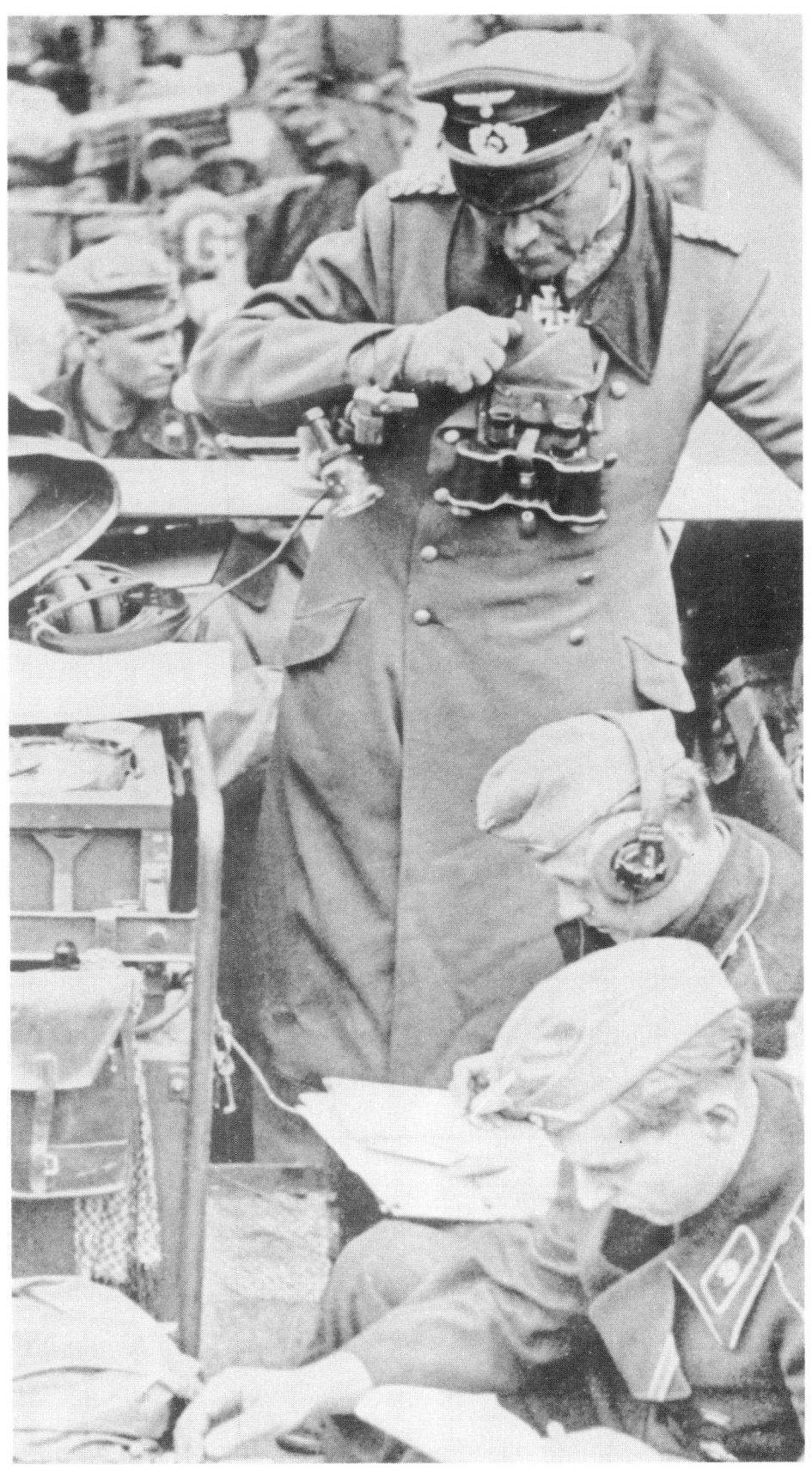

Effective communications played a crucial part in the successful panzer campaigns. Standing in the back of a half-track, Guderian looks on as his men use an Enigma encoding machine to transmit his orders during field operations. The Germans believed that their system was unbreakable – an error of judgement that was to cost them dear once Enigma's secrets were unravelled by British cryptologists. The intelligence so gathered, code-named 'Ultra', was used to great effect by the Allies to the end of the war. TM

against enemy armour when used in the ground role. Armoured cars might be used to protect vulnerable flanks, while overhead a screen of fighter aircraft would ensure that the dive-bombers could get on with their job unhindered by enemy aircraft. Each of these arms would bring their own special skills and weapons to enhance the fighting ability of the whole group.

Communications
To enable a group to operate effectively, there was a major requirement for command and control on an immediate person-to-person basis. This was impossible if commanders had to rely on runners, land-laid telephone lines, despatch riders, liaison officers or the humble carrier-pigeon. The essential new ingredient was radio which was used for communications down to the level of tank and infantry platoon commanders. Individual tanks did not get radios until later in the war. The new communications tool was, without doubt, the key to the success of *Blitzkrieg* tactics. Company commanders had two-way radios so that they could talk with the battlegroup commander and pass on his orders to their platoons. Tank platoon commanders had only radio receivers, so they were able to receive orders but not reply; they still relied upon flag or hand signals to control their individual tanks. Even this scale of use of radio sets was a major step forward. Similarly, all infantry, artillery, engineer and other commanders were able to talk to one another and to the overall commander, while there were additional ground-to-air communications to the dive-bombers. We now take all this for granted but Kenneth Macksey graphically reveals how revolutionary this was in his book on Guderian, when he quotes from a pre-war conversation between Guderian and the then Chief of the General Staff, Generaloberst Ludwig Beck: '. . . Beck: How many divisions do you want? Guderian: Two to begin with, later twenty. Beck: And how will you lead these divisions? Guderian: From the front – by wireless. Beck: Nonsense! A divisional commander sits back with maps and a telephone. Anything else is Utopian!'[4]

For the *Blitzkrieg* tactics to work there was a need for the commander to be forward, on the spot, right where the action was taking place, where he could stamp his authority on the battle, and for every commander in his group to be able to talk to one other and to him. After the experience panzer leaders gained in the early battles in Poland, HQs were trimmed to a small number of armoured vehicles so that commanders would be able to get forward uncluttered, leaving the rest of their HQ further back. In modern parlance this small HQ is known as the commander's Tactical HQ, or just TAC for short.

Principles of *Blitzkrieg*
Stated simply, *Blitzkrieg* was a tactical system employed to pierce the enemy's front, and then encircle and destroy all or part of his forces. Its major elements were surprise, speed of manoeuvre, shock action from ground and air, and retention of the initiative by the attacking force. This called for a high standard of training by all the troops involved and for everyone, at all levels, to use their initiative to the full.

Let us imagine that the panzer division, a force of all arms, is advancing with recce elements out in front to locate the main enemy positions. These recce

Reconnaissance on the ground was also vitally important. Fast-moving armoured cars and scout cars, often working with motor-cycle patrols, operated ahead of the main body of the division to reconnoitre the routes forward and so maintain the momentum of the attack. TM

A TYPICAL BLITZKRIEG ATTACK

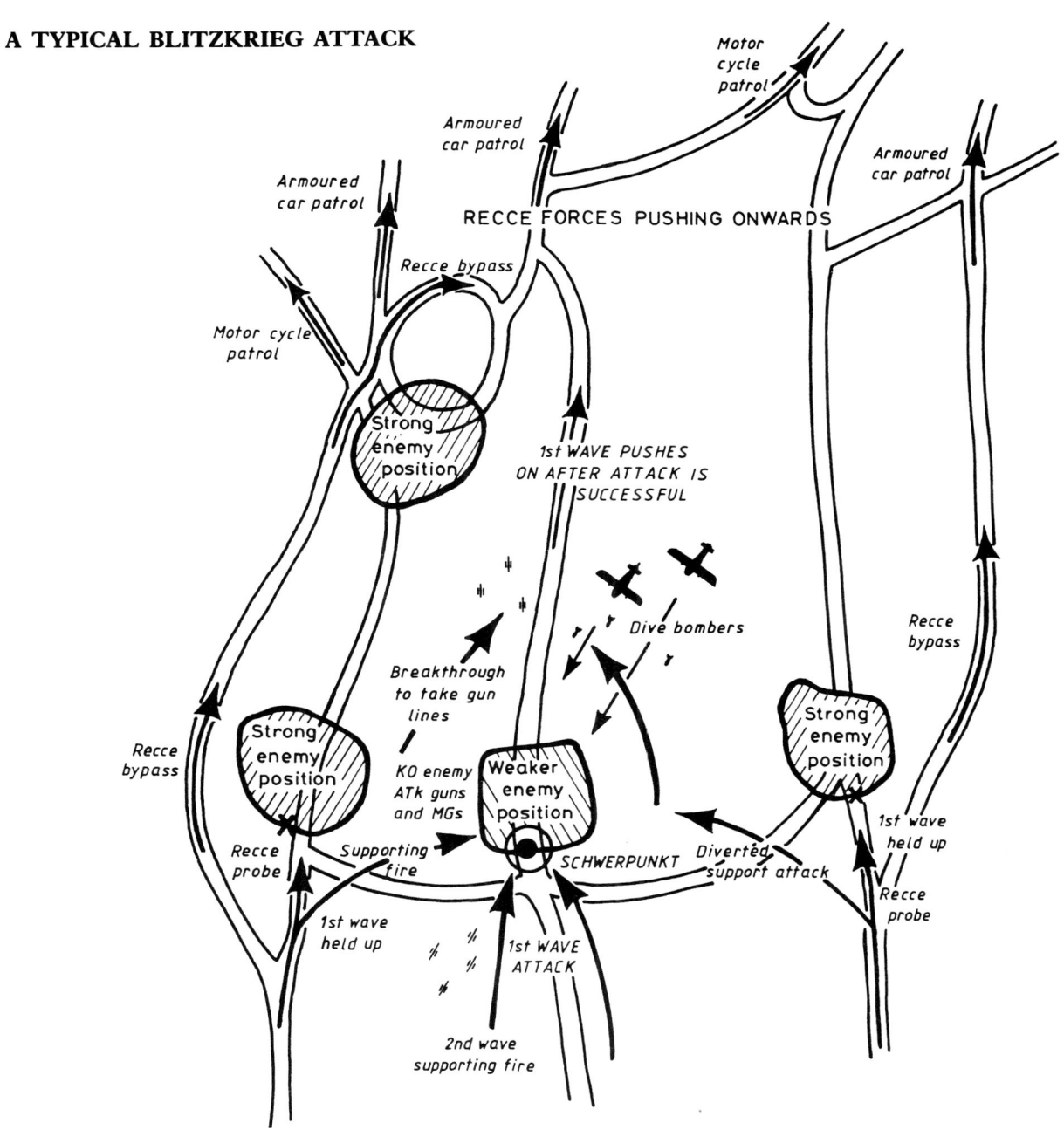

elements will probably consist of armoured cars on the main routes, with motor-cycle patrols on the side roads. They will almost certainly have an artillery forward observation officer with them, who can call quickly over the radio for fire support if it is needed. Having located the enemy and reported back, they will try to bypass the main enemy positions and keep going, so as to maintain the momentum of the advance. They will of course be in constant radio communication with the force commander, who will regulate their speed of movement, and decide whether the whole force should bypass or engage the enemy positions discovered. The commander will be well forward, travelling just behind the vanguard. If and when he decides that an attack is necessary, he will probably give out his orders over the radio and the requisite striking force will then concentrate as quickly as possible – *aufmarsch* – (immediately off the line of march) to concentrate on a narrow sector of the enemy front.

The centre of gravity of the attack, the *Schwerpunkt*, will be where the commander considers is the best place to assault, and not where the enemy is strongest. The attack will be put in with overwhelming force, making use of all the firepower at the commander's disposal, including air – in the words of Guderian: '*Klotzen nicht kleckern!*' (Thump them hard – don't pat them!) The main aim of the attack is to achieve a penetration of the enemy's line and, once this is successful, a follow-up force will pass through and press on with the advance avoiding the main enemy positions. These tactics were known as *flachen und luckentakit* (space and gap tactics), their aim being to get armoured forces behind the main enemy positions

Infantry-tank co-operation in a French cornfield in May 1940. The secret of success then, as now, is for tanks and infantry to work closely together in a fully planned and co-ordinated manner. TM

Blitzkrieg! By driving deep into enemy lines the panzers created panic. Here, a Czech-built Pz Kpfw 38t rounds up French prisoners. TM

so as to be able to take control of his lines of communication.

Meanwhile, behind the leading armoured groups would be additional forces, probably based upon motorised infantry, whose task it was to mop up any pockets of enemy left, and generally tidy up and make safe the tattered ends of the enemy line – *aufrollen* as it was called – so that the breakthrough would remain open. The spearhead would continue to exploit, pressing forwards with the aim of encircling as many of the enemy forces as possible. The faster and deeper they could penetrate into the enemy rear areas, the larger would be these envelopments. The dictum was to reinforce success and abandon failure, switching forces from any dead ends to other parts of the battlefield where they could be of more use.

Such manoeuvres required excellent teamwork, good command and control, careful timing and, above all, continuous voice communications. In addition to the speed and strength of the attack, the element of surprise was also essential to the success of the *Blitzkrieg*, so there could be no massive build-up and long drawn out manoeuvring, giving the enemy time to prepare. Instead, an overwhelmingly powerful attack force would hit the enemy without prior warning, smashing through them on a relatively narrow front.

The other essential ingredient of a successful *Blitzkrieg* attack was a continual supply of fuel, ammunition, rations and other necessaries. Petrol was of prime importance if the momentum of the attack was to be maintained.

A panzer division used about 2,000 gallons a mile on cross-country movement, less of course if they stuck to the roads. Each division had its own main supply route (*Rollbahn*) and the supply columns needed very careful handling so that they got to the right place at the right time. Panzer troops would also to some extent 'live off the land', filling up their tanks at the civilian garages they happened to pass. In the campaign in France each panzer division carried about 125 miles' worth of fuel and was resupplied by airdrop. They also had nine days of rations within divisional resources so the bulk of the resupply vehicles could be used to bring up ammunition.

Summary

To summarise the main points of *Blitzkrieg*: its success lay partly in the tactical combination of a force of all arms (of which tanks were the most important ingredient) with aircraft attacking without warning from an unexpected direction and partly from the exploitation of the breakthrough thus achieved. This exploitation had to be carried out as quickly as possible by armoured forces racing ahead of the main army, acting independently and driving as deeply as possible into the enemy's rear areas.

A combat example

The following short extract is taken from the regimental history of Panzer Regiment 35, which fought in France as part of 5th Panzer Division, during fighting on the Somme, and shows some of the tactics of the *Blitzkrieg* in action: 'The belated arrival of the 88 Flak Battery enables us to knock out four enemy tanks. The captured anti-tank gun of the Pioneer Section knocks out two more tanks in the village. In the meantime, our riflemen have arrived. They are under orders, together with strong artillery, to attack Liancourt. Not until this township is in our hands will the Brigade renew its main attack. It takes until 1800 hours for our riflemen to clear the village, with the help of IV Panzer Company. The Regiment renews its attack at 1830 hours, and makes good progress by moving quickly as far as Roiglise. It is from there that we meet enemy anti-tank and artillery fire. The village is full of obstacles, which are covered by fire from the houses. Protected by I Battalion, our panzer pioneers go forward to clear the obstacles. The infantry then clear the village house by house, while the withdrawing enemy columns are being blasted by our artillery. V Panzer Company goes around the village from the left to silence an enemy artillery gun. However, it is not until 2030 hours that we reach Verpiliers.' In this example we have tanks, infantry, artillery and engineers, working together in an all arms team to achieve their objective.

Massed tanks and lorry-borne infantry prepare to advance from their concentration area during the 1940 campaign in France.
TM

'Thanks for your help!' An infantryman shakes hands with the commander of a supporting tank after a successful action.
TM

Achtung Stuka!. *A Junkers 87 dive-bomber releases its bombs at 3,000 feet. With sirens fitted to produce a morale-shattering noise, this aircraft proved to be a highly successful and important ingredient in Blitzkrieg tactics.*   IWM

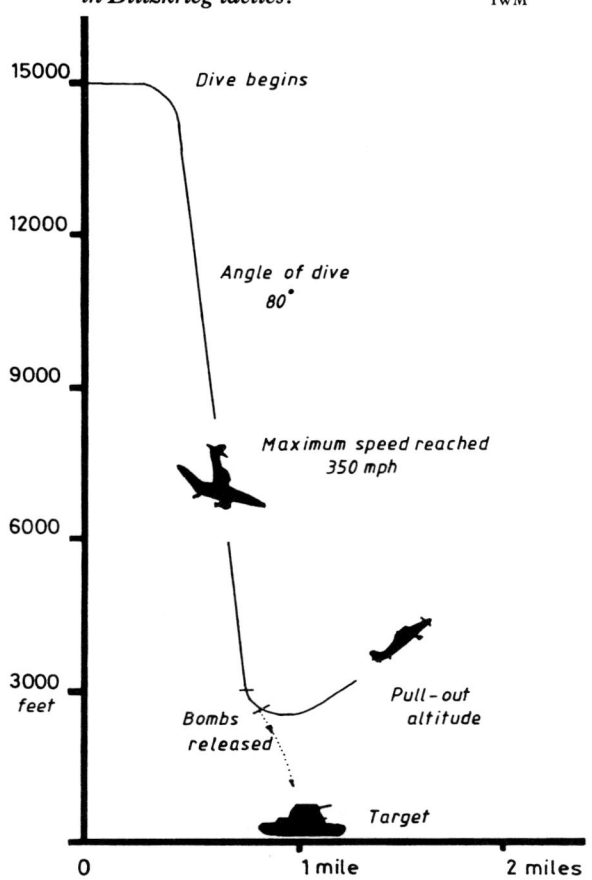

The dive bomber

Another essential ingredient of the *Blitzkrieg* tactics was the dive-bomber, the familiar, clumsy-looking Junkers 87. The Ju 88 was also used in a similar manner but its dive angle was a little shallower (60 degrees instead of the Ju 87's 80 degrees). The Stuka, as the Ju 87 was normally called, got its name from the shortening of the German dive-bomber – *Sturzkampfflugzeug* and its thick angled wings and fixed undercarriage made it instantly recognisable in the skies above the French countryside.

This method of delivering bombs was extremely accurate and once the crews (a Stuka carried two men) had completed their course at the special Dive-Bomber School, they were expected to be able to get at least 50% of their bombs within a 25 metre radius of the target. Various bomb loads were available (see table) dependent upon the nature of the target to be engaged.

As Alfred Price explains in his book on the Luftwaffe, when approaching their target the Ju 87s usually flew in threes in a Vee formation at a cruising altitude of about 15,000ft, speed around 150mph. Larger formations were made up of a number of Vees in line astern. To support a major attack an entire *Gruppe* of 30 aircraft might be employed, with protective fighters flying slightly behind and above the dive-bombers. As the target got closer the fighters split, some going down to about 3,000ft to be ready to protect the dive-bombers as they pulled out of their dives. Before commencing his dive, the Stuka pilot would switch on his reflector sight, trim his aircraft, set the pullout altitude on the contact altimeter (an automatic device, almost an autopilot, which ensured a proper pullout from the dive even if the pilot blacked out), close the radiator flaps, throttle back the engine and open the ventilation air supply to the windscreen. This was necessary to prevent misting up when the Stuka entered the moist air lower down – aircraft in a formation of Ju 87Bs operating in Spain during the Civil war had hit the ground when dive-bombing in misty conditions. Finally, the pilot switched on the 'Screamer' and opened the dive brakes.

The attack signal was given by the formation leader starting his dive and it took about 8,000ft to reach the limiting speed of 350mph, after which the Stuka's velocity remained constant. It took about 30 seconds to dive from 15,000ft to reach the release altitude of 3,000ft,

Ju 87 B-1 Stuka Specifications	
Type:	Two seat dive-bomber and ground attack
Engine:	Junkers Jumo 211 Da 12 cylinder, inverted vee, liquid-cooled 1,100hp
Armament:	Two MG 17 machine guns in wings and one MG 15 manually aimed in rear cockpit
Top speed:	242mph at 13,000ft
Ceiling:	26,250ft
Range:	370 miles with full bombload
Wingspan:	45ft 3ins
Length:	36ft 5ins

Stuka Bombloads

Type and weight	Suitable target	Where carried
High Explosive SC50	troop positions or motor vehicles	Four under wings
High Explosive SC 250	ditto	One under fuselage
High Explosive SC500	field artillery positions	ditto
Semi-armour piercing SD 500	concrete fortifications	ditto
Armour piercing PC 1000	tanks	ditto

Notes:
SC stands for *Spreng Cylindrische* – viz: HE general purpose
SD stands for *Spreng Dickwand* – viz: HE thick-walled
PC stands for *Panzerbombe Cylindische* – viz: armour piercing
50, 250, 500 and 1000 are the bomb weights in kilogrammes
A typical load would be one SC 250 and four SC 50

Source: compiled from information contained in the *Luftwaffe Handbook* by A. Price (Ian Allan Ltd, 1977).

during which time the pilot endeavoured to hold his target in the centre of his reflector sight. Four seconds before passing the pull-out altitude (as set on the contact altimeter) a horn sounded and when it stopped, at the release height, the pilot pressed the button on his control column which actuated a powerful spring which returned the elevator tab to a neutral position. This caused the aircraft to become tail-heavy and it automatically pulled itself out of the dive. The pressing of the button also started the run-down on the bomb release mechanism and after a set time the bombs were released automatically. After pull-out the pilot regained control of his aircraft, opened the throttle and got away as quickly as possible.

Undoubtedly the Stuka struck terror in the early days of the war, but suffered heavy casualties in the Battle of Britain and had to be withdrawn. Thereafter, it continued to be used but only in areas where the Germans had air superiority. Total production by Junkers was over 5,700 of the Ju 87 A, B and D series.

Air to ground communication

Starting at the top, the Air Fleet HQ was sited close to the HQ of the Army Group they were supporting so that close co-operation was possible. At the 'sharp end' the Luftwaffe's Forward Air Controller was located with the forward troops, where he could send back requests for support to the squadrons at their airfields. He took charge of the aircraft when they approached the target area and talked them into their targets, sometimes with the aid of coloured smoke or ground markers. It was essential that friendly troops had suitable air recognition panels to prevent them being engaged.

Special Forces

The Germans also added a new dimension to warfare with the use of Special Forces – the *Brandenbergers*, who equated to Commandos and were trained to carry out sabotage and other special duties, and the *Fallschirmjäger* (paratroops), who were trained in aerial envelopment either by parachute or glider. Their subsequent actions in the battle for France were both dramatic and, more importantly, highly successful.

German paratroops were most effective during the early stages of the offensive, capturing vital bridges, fortifications and other strategic points. TM

FRANCE

Defensive war

France had ended the First World War in a blaze of glory, after a victorious offensive against Germany, but her losses were such that her leaders were determined they would never willingly go to war again. Strategically, the French had opted to fight a defensive war and their tactics reflected this strategy. They were prepared to stick to the tried and true tactics with which they had won the First World War and with so many old men in senior positions in the Army (they had raised the retirement age until promotion was literally only possible in 'dead men's shoes'!), there was little room for original thought. Later one French general was to write: 'If the French Army has succumbed, it was because our military thinking between 1919 and 1939 underwent a total eclipse without parallel.'[5] So the basic tactics depended upon maintaining a continuous defensive front through which the enemy could not penetrate. The French Army would stay put, in and behind this defensive line, while the enemy battered themselves to pieces trying to break through.

As a result of these tactics, forces had to be deployed all along the borders, and not even the French army was large enough for this to be done without dangerously over-stretching resources. For example, although French tanks outnumbered those of their opponents and were, in many cases, superior in firepower, protection and mobility, they were used merely as a supporting arm to the infantry. Consequently they were spread out 'in penny packets' all along the continuous front and proved easy meat to the *Schwerpunkt* of the *Blitzkrieg*.

This principle of dispersal was applied equally to the French Air Force. Gen D'Astier de la Vigerie noted in despair on 15 May 1940: 'My fighters are everywhere, sent without heed to our dislocated armies!'[6]

Pétain's 'Instructions'

In 1921 Marshal Pétain, the hero of the First World War and French C-in-C until 1931, issued regulations for the tactical handling of divisions and above. These regulations reflected his views on the inviolability of organised defensive lines and the need for massive defensive firepower. The policy was known in the French Army at the time as being 'lavish with steel, stingy with blood!' Revisions were made in 1936 but there were few, if any, changes to the basic tactics. Firepower was still pre-eminent, while manoeuvre was held to be the movement of fire rather than of units on the ground. In defence the enemy was to be halted by the lavish use of artillery fire and automatic weapons, covering carefully prepared defensive positions, at least some 2-4,000yds in depth. In the attack there was the essential requirement for massive, carefully arranged fire support, close detailed reconnaissance and, above all, extreme caution. The advantages gained from speed and surprise were discounted, as was the shock action of the tank.

Tank tactics

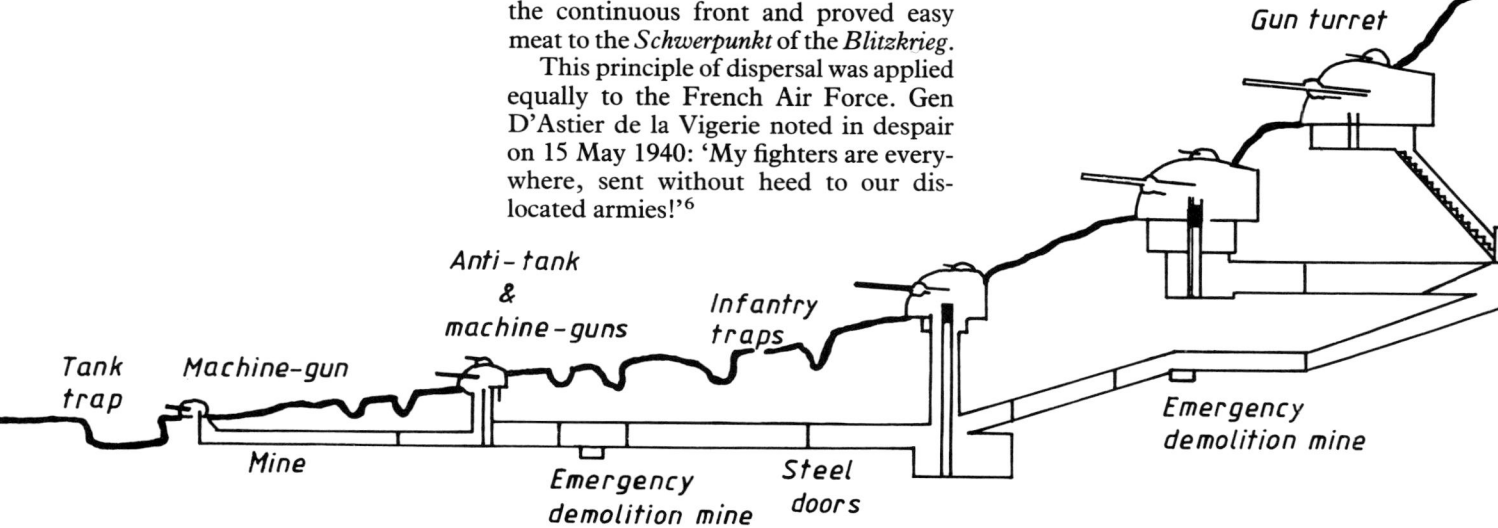

The French have always been excellent engineers, so the development of the French tank during the First World War was not very far behind the British. Their heavy tanks were not on a par with those of the Tank Corps, but light tanks – such as the Renault FT 17, the first tank to have a fully traversing turret – were excellent, and many survived to fight again in 1939-40 and to be captured and re-used by the Germans. In the French Army the tank was subordinated to the infantry and considered only as a means of assisting them to break through any difficult enemy positions. The French idea of mobile warfare was an advance at infantry pace, slow and cumbersome, with all the supporting arms geared to the speed of the slowest element.

It is only fair to say that there were a few French officers who thought differently, the foremost amongst them being Charles de Gaulle, a protégé of Pétain, whose ideas on the use of tanks and the way in which they should operate was far more akin to those of Guderian than the plodding French senior command. After the German armoured successes in Poland there was some attempt to organise proper armoured divisions but they were too few in number and came too late to have a major effect on the outcome of the battle.

The Maginot Line

The most revolutionary tactical decision taken by France was to build a long, costly line of defensive forts, and to tie down a large proportion of the army to man these static defences. This was done to eliminate the Franco-German frontier as a place where the enemy could attack. Undoubtedly this made sound sense for a nation much smaller in manpower than its old enemy, particularly after the horrific casualties they had suffered in the First World War. It was the intention to station mobile forces behind the line to take on any enemy who managed to penetrate, although it was considered highly unlikely that any such penetrations would be possible. Unfortunately there does not appear to have been any thought given to using the line offensively – in other words, to use it as a shield with a striking force (the 'sword') pivoting on it to smite the enemy.

It does not take hindsight to see that such a system of static defence could only have been viable had it been extended in one continuous front all along the French frontier, from Switzerland in the south to the North Sea. This objective was never achieved for a number of reasons. First were the building costs, which were placing an enormous burden on the French economy. These in turn created a climate of opinion in which it was possible to compromise and allow political considerations to override military requirements. Most crucial was the decision not to continue the line along the Belgian border. It was considered that as loyal allies of France, the Belgians would feel deep resentment at being 'shut out of the castle'. Furthermore, the old argument about the Belgian/German frontier being easier to defend than the longer border between France and Belgium was brushed down and given a fresh airing. So it became part of French policy that her forces should enter Belgium in the event of war – a policy which was completely thwarted when the Belgian King opted for neutrality. Another economy was achieved when it

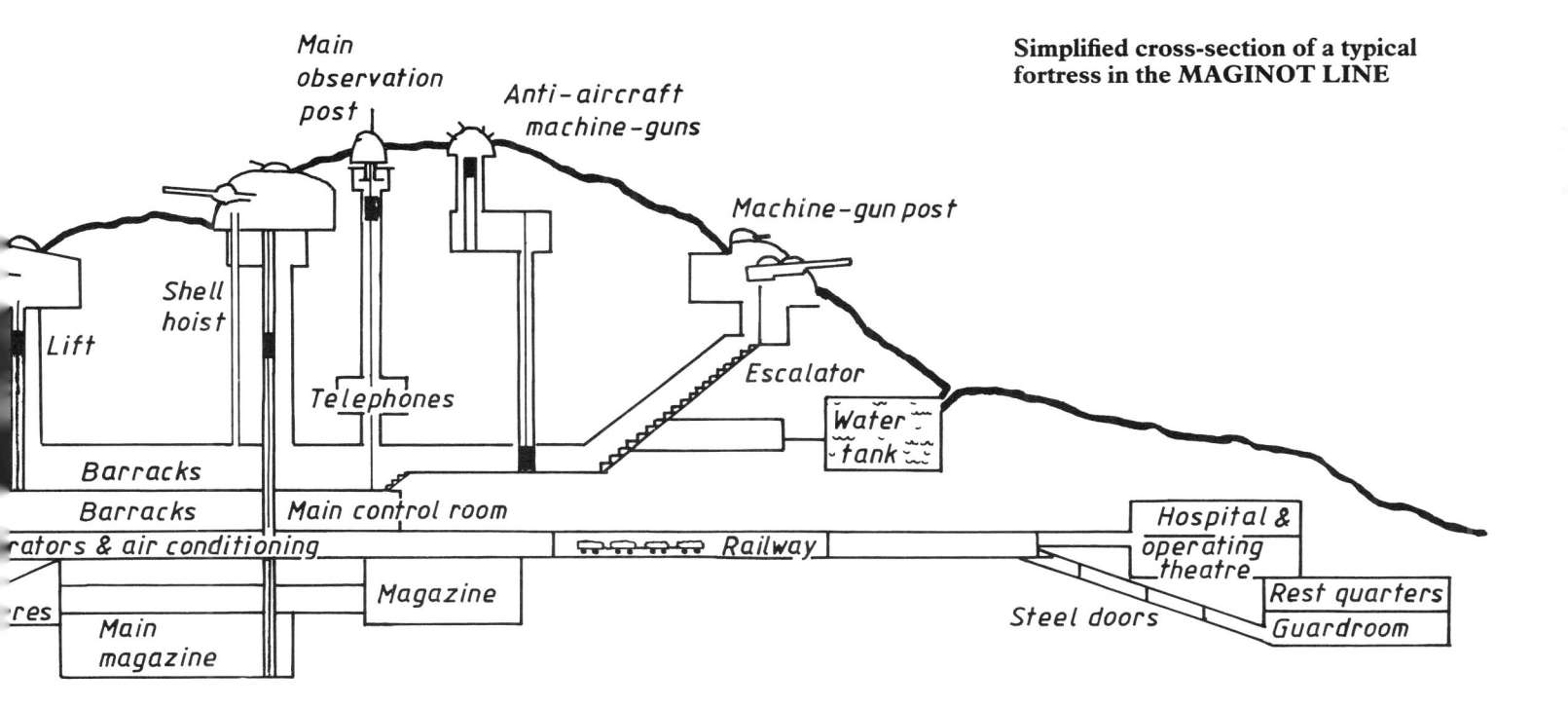

Simplified cross-section of a typical fortress in the MAGINOT LINE

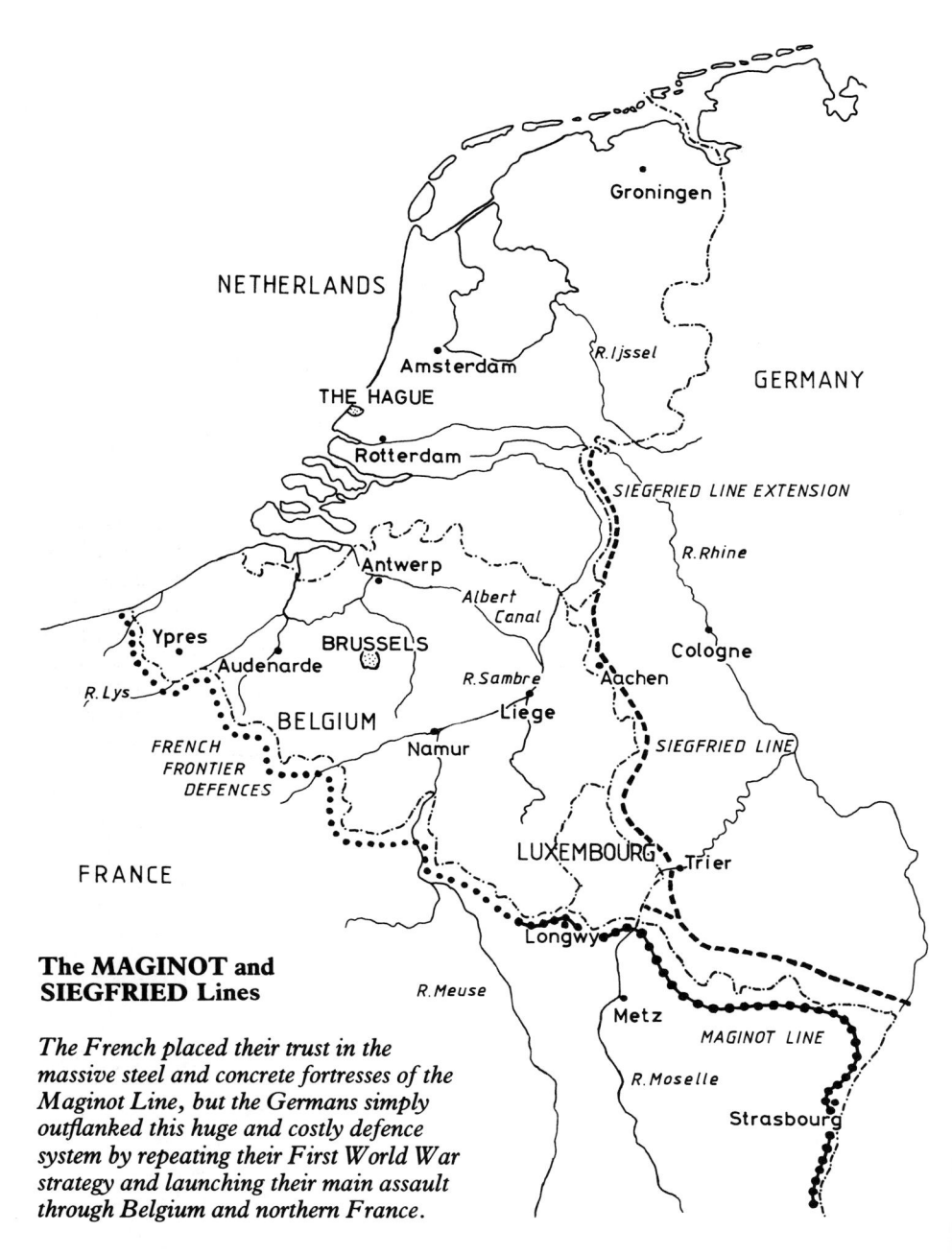

The MAGINOT and SIEGFRIED Lines

The French placed their trust in the massive steel and concrete fortresses of the Maginot Line, but the Germans simply outflanked this huge and costly defence system by repeating their First World War strategy and launching their main assault through Belgium and northern France.

have artillery, engineer and infantry commanders under him. From the call-up in the spring of 1939 until the surrender in June 1940 the Maginot Line was manned continuously. At the outbreak of hostilities there were eight sectors manned; from west to east these were: Crusnes, Thionville, Boulay, Faulquemont, Sarre, Rohrbach, Vosges and Haguenau. The Sarre section was actually known as the Sarre Gap (*la trouée de la Sarre*), because the planners hoped that the swampy terrain, streams, forests and artificially flooded areas would make a natural obstacle which would eliminate the need for any fixed defences.

In addition to the Maginot Line proper, other fortifications were built in the Alps, covering the passes and down to the sea at Menton. Finally, some more forts were built in Corsica to protect potential enemy landing places.

In 1938 the Germans started to build their own line of fortifications, the Westwall, dubbed by the British as the Siegfried Line. Although much was made of it by the Nazi propaganda machine, it did not compare either in size or in strength with the Maginot Line.

was decided not to build fortifications opposite the Ardennes: military experts were agreed that the terrain was far too difficult for enemy forces to achieve any significant degree of penetration.

On its completion the line extended only along France's southern borders, roughly from Strasbourg to Montmédy. Even so, the 87 miles of fortifications – called the Maginot Line after André Maginot, a French politician who managed to squeeze the necessary funds out of the Chamber of Deputies to build it – cost over seven billion francs. With the possible exception of the Great Wall of China, the Maginot Line is the longest and most complex system of fortifications ever built.

Work started in 1928 and the fortifications were first occupied in March 1936. However, many defects came to light and some were still being rectified in 1940. The '*Region Fortifée*' (RF) was divided into sectors, each commanded by a general, and the sectors were divided into sub-sectors, each held by a fortress infantry regiment. Each fort (*ouvrage*) had its own commander, who would

Facts and Figures on the Maginot Line		
Type of fort, etc	Number built	Remarks
a. NE frontier and Rhine		
artillery	23	) a total
infantry	35	) of 36 blocks
casemates & interval blockhouses	295	
interval shelters	70	
armoured interval OPS	14	
b. SE frontier and Corsica		
artillery	23	) a total
infantry	27	) of 146 blocks
interval casemates	17	mainly in Corsica
interval OPs	3	
interval shelters	11	
advanced post blockhouses	6	
Weapons and armoured turrets	Number installed	
artillery pieces		
135mm howitzers	43	
81mm mortars	132	
75mm guns (various)	169	
TOTAL	344	(half in north-east and half in the Alps)
armoured turrets		
retractable	132	
fixed	1533	

Source: compiled from information contained in *The Maginot Line Myth and Reality* by A. Kemp (Frederick Warne, 1981).

GREAT BRITAIN

Mechanisation

Of all the Allied armies which were destined to fight against the German *Blitzkrieg*, the most mechanised was the British Expeditionary Force. Although its infantry often had to march long distances, it is broadly true that the BEF was able to move on wheels when necessary. The RASC could carry troops and their equipment, but their transport was not armoured. A later chapter deals with their organisation and that of the mechanised cavalry regiments and tank battalions, but in general terms they operated tactically on their own and not as part of an all arms team. The cavalry were grouped into armoured reconnaissance brigades and operated more like the cavalry of old than their German equivalents, while the few tank battalions there were found themselves split up, operating in the same 'penny packets' as the French armour.

Modern tactics

In the 1937 Infantry Training pamphlet entitled *Infantry Training – Training and War* an attempt was made to extract all the lessons learned from open warfare in places such as the North-West Frontier. The aim was to get the best out of the capabilities of the new armoured fighting vehicles coming into service in increasing numbers as the Army became mechanised. In the advance to contact, mobile troops (light tanks or armoured cars) would operate in front of the infantry advanced guards in the same way as the horsed cavalry had operated. The leading infantry had to be ready to assist the mobile troops to deal with minor opposition and '. . .commanders of advanced guard battalions should be prepared to move forward without delay so that plans can be made and put into action at short notice.' The pamphlet went on to explain that as soon as contact

On one of the light railways in the Maginot Line General Gamelin takes HM King George VI on a tour of inspection. IWM

When Britain finally recognized the inevitability of war, a large programme of mechanization was embarked upon with considerable speed and determination. Here, mechanics of the Ordnance Corps are seen at work in a repair workshop. IWM

In the field, however, the infantry was still regarded as the backbone of the British army. These men on a training exercise are using the .55in Boys anti-tank rifle. Issued on the basis of one to each platoon, this weapon could only penetrate 21mm of armour at 300 metres and was therefore ineffective against all but the lightest armoured vehicles. IWM

had been made, infantry units were to deploy on a wider front, making full use of tracks and cross-country lines of advance. Speed was of the essence, so recce groups had to be available immediately. Some guidance was given as to how infantry should operate with tanks, but how the infantry on foot was expected to keep up with the mobile troops was never fully explained. Unfortunately, as Gen Farrar-Hockley comments in his book: 'Infantry Tactics 1939-1945': "...They either fell behind or held the latter back. Because there had been so few joint field exercises, the problem was not manifest."

In the defence
Sadly, not all the thinking in the manual was even as up-to-date as the 'advance to contact' section. Its words on the deliberate attack harkened back to the First World War tactics: 'In such cases,' it advised, 'to attack by day with any hope of success without excessive casualties requires deliberate and methodical preparations.' And the same applied to the defence. The manual could well have been written in 1914. Extensive digging was the order of the day, cover from fire being far more important than cover from view. As Farrar-Hockley explains: 'Developed fully, the defences repeated the pattern of those carried across Flanders and France from 1915 onwards. This did not train the army to meet the most likely threat; for the German concept was to break through on a narrow front with heavy fire power as a preliminary to passing numbers swiftly through the gap or gaps made to attack the foe in flank and rear.'

Communications
The most important failing the manual shows clearly is total lack of modern methods of communication. The section on 'Intercommunication', as it was called, within the battalion lists visual signalling, orderly, cable, patrols and brigade HQ, the companies and the flanking battalions, attached artillery, etc, consisted of motor bicycles, bicycles, Lucas lamps, heliograph, flags and six miles of cable, but no radios whatsoever. As far as tank co-operation was concerned, the manual explains that there were two simple flag signals used by tanks: (i) a green and white flag, which meant the opposition was crushed and

all was clear for the infantry to come on; (ii) a red and yellow flag, which meant the tank had broken down and should not be waited for. An additional signal, which varied from time to time, was also sometimes used to denote a friendly tank coming out of action. It is hardly surprising that the small number of radios in the German Army made such a dramatic difference to the speed at which orders could be passed.

British signallers during the 'Phoney War' used antiquated field telephone equipment in the front line, as did their French counterparts. One of the many ways in which the Allied forces lagged behind their common enemy. IWM

NOTES

1. M. Cooper *The German Army 1933-1945* London: Macdonald & James, 1978.
2. Ibid.
3. The 'Back to 1914' attitude was perhaps best typified by a remark made to Fuller by an officer of the old school on the day the Armistice was signed. 'Thank God', he said, 'we can now get back to some real soldiering!'
4. K. Macksey *Guderian, Panzer General* London: Macdonald & Co, 1975.
5. As quoted by Col A. Goutard in an article entitled 'The War of Missed Opportunites', in *The Fall of France 1940: Causes and Responsibilities*, edited by Samuel M. Osgood.
6. Ibid.

Chapter 4

German Organisation and Equipment

The three main branches of Germany's armed forces (*Die Wehrmacht*) were the Army (*Das Heer*), the Navy (*Die Kriegsmarine*) and the Air Force (*Die Luftwaffe*). They came under the Wehrmacht High Command (*Oberkommando der Wehrmacht OKW*), Germany's supreme command during the Second World War, which consisted of:

- The Wehrmacht Operations Office (later renamed the Wehrmacht Operations Staff)
- The Office for Foreign Affairs and Intelligence
- The Economics and Armaments Office
- The Office for General Wehrmacht Affairs.

The main task of the OKW was to correlate and supervise the individual strategy of the three Service Headquarters:

- The OKH (*Oberkommando des Heeres*), Army High Command
- The OKM (*Oberkommando der Marine*) Navy High Command
- The OKL (*Oberkommando der Luftwaffe*) Air Force High Command

Chief of the OKW was Field Marshal Keitel, who was involved in all of Hitler's strategic decisions. His fawning attitude towards the Führer earned him the contempt of many of his colleagues, who called him *Lakeitel* in a punning reference to the German word for footman or lackey.

Wehrmacht Operations Office
The WFA (*Wehrmachtführungsamt*) had three main branches: National Defence, Wehrmacht Communications, and Press and Propaganda. When war broke out in 1939 the WFA was headed by Alfred Jodl, then a major general. After Keitel, he was Hitler's closest adviser on all matters relating to top level Wehrmacht operations. It was his job to keep Hitler informed of military developments and to pass on the Führer's orders to the various operational commands. Inside the National Defence Branch were officers from the three main services (OKH, OKM and OKL) who were, in effect, Hitler's working staff. They had to produce the data on which the Supreme Commander could base his decisions, and then prepare his directives for the conduct of the war.

When Keitel and his adjutants, along with Jodl and one of his junior staff officers, joined the Führer's HQ on the

Front row
Brückner (personal aide), Keitel, Hitler, Jodl, Bormann, Below (Luftwaffe aide), Hoffmann (photographer).
Middle row
Bodenschatz (Luftwaffe Chief of Staff), Schmundt, Wolf, Dr Morell (Hitler's doctor), Schulze (Ordnance).
Back row
Engel (Heer aide), Dr Brandt (Hitler's surgeon), Puttkamer, Lorenz, Hewel (Foreign Office), ?, Schaube (personal aide), Wünsche.

outbreak of war, they found a formidable establishment already in operation. There were Colonel Schmundt, the Wehrmacht's Chief Adjutant to the Führer; three junior adjutants to represent each of the services; General Bodenschatz, liaison officer (LO) of the C-in-C Luftwaffe; *Obergruppenführer* Wolfe, LO of the C-in-C, SS; *Obergruppenführer* Brückner, SA Adjutant to the Führer; Martin Bormann, Chief of the Party Chancellory; Dr Dietrich, Chief Press Officer of the Reich; Ambassador Häwel, the Foreign Office representative; two SS *gruppenführers* responsible for Hitler's security and the internal routine of the HQ; Hitler's two personal physicians and, finally, the Reich photographer.

It was this entourage that accompanied Hitler when at 9pm on 3 September 1939 he left in a special train (*Führersonderzug*) bound for the Polish front. He had his own bodyguard battalion (*Führer-Begleit-Bataillon (FBB)*, which was a fully mechanised unit consisting of a rifle company, an armoured reconnaissance company, a panzer company and a combined motorised AA battalion. This unit was commanded at that time by *Generalmajor* Erwin Rommel, who later led 7 Panzer Division so brilliantly in France.

The National Defence Branch was left high and dry in Berlin under its chief, Col Warlimont. It took no part in preparing the Führer's 'Directives for the Conduct of the War' other than possible minor editing. The commanders-in-chief of the three Wehrmacht branches and their operations staff were also far removed from Hitler during this first campaign. OKH had its headquarters at Zossen, near Berlin, under the codename '*Zeppelin*'; OKM remained in the city of Berlin, while the OKL was at the Luftwaffe's officer cadet candidate school at Wildpark, near Potsdam, for which '*Kurfürst*' (Elector) was the codename.

Hitler and his staff returned to the new Reich Chancellory in Berlin on 26 September, and stayed there throughout the first winter of the war, apart from occasional visits to the Berghof at Berchtesgaten. A great deal of work was carried out building a new HQ for Hitler at Ziegenberg Castle, but he never used it. Other command posts were built in the Pfalz and the Black Forest. On the morning of 10 May 1940, the day on which the offensive against France was launched, Hitler occupied his first permanent HQ outside Berlin. This was the *Felsennest* (Rocky Nest), built in a copse on the top of a hill some 300m above the village of Rodert, west of Münstereifel and south of Bonn. Here he remained until 5 June, when the *Führerhauptquartiers (FHQu)* moved to Bruly de Pesche, a small Belgian village in a forest clearing north-east of Rocroi. The Todt Organisation[1] completed its construction in just eight days, after evacuating the entire civilian population.

Generaloberst (Field Marshal) Wilhelm Keitel, Chief of the OKW, briefs his Führer on the battle in France, inside the 'Felsennest'.   TM

The Army

The Commander-in-Chief of the German Army until 1938 was Gen Fritsch, but he strongly resented Nazi influence in Army affairs and was dismissed on a trumped-up charge of homosexuality. He was succeeded by Gen Walter von Brauchitsch, who was far more amenable to Hitler and his cronies and who held the post until 1941.

German infantrymen covered great distances on foot to consolidate the huge gains made by the fast-moving Panzer divisions. TM

But a few infantrymen were more fortunate than their comrades. The armoured fighting vehicles shown on the right each carried ten soldiers and two crew, and were armed with two MG 34. They were designated as Sd Kfz medium Armoured Personnel Carriers (mittlerer schutzenpanzerwagen). TM

On mobilisation in 1939 the OKH was divided into a field headquarters and a home command, the latter stationed in Berlin. The Commander of the Replacement Army (*Befehlshaber des Ersatzheeres*) was appointed to take control of the home command, with responsibility for the General Army Office, the Army Ordnance Office, the Army Administration Office, the Inspector of Officer Cadet Courses, the Inspectors of Arms and Services and the Chief of Army Judiciary. The field HQ comprised the Army General Staff and the Army Personnel Office, and was commanded by the Chief of the General Staff, with the *Oberquartier-Meister I (OQuI)* as his Deputy Chief of Staff. Subordinate to the OKW were the Army Groups, followed in turn by the Armies, Corps and Divisions.

Military Districts (*Die Wehrkreise*)

The *Wehrkreise* system was the basis upon which recruitment, drafting, induction and training was carried out in the German Army, as well as mobilisation of the Divisions and the provision of trained replacements. The Military Districts were set up in 1919 and worked directly under the OKH until 1938, when their functions were co-ordinated under the newly-created Replacement Army. In 1939, there were 18 *Wehrkreise* divided between six Army Groups.

Mobilisation

The German Army was mobilised in 'waves', a process which continued until late 1944. Between 1934 and April 1940 there were nine such 'waves', as the table shows.

The Field Army

The size and strength of divisions in the German Army varied considerably, as did their organisation and equipment. But the organisational principle was similar to that of larger formations, based as it was on three basic groups:

- the tactical group (*Fuhrungsabteilung*)
- the supply group (*Quartiermeister*)
- the personnel group (*Adjutantur*)

Outline Organisation of the Army (*Das Heer*)

OKH

ARMY GROUPS	(up to twelve)
ARMY	(up to four per Army Group) + GHQ troops
CORPS	(up to seven per Army) + organic or attached Army troops
DIVISIONS	(up to seven per Corps) + organic or attached Corps troops

German Mobilisation 1934-1940

Wave	Date formed	Number of Division	Comments
1	1934-1938	39	Peacetime army units
2	Aug 1939	15	From reservists
3	Aug 1939	22	*Landwehr* (older men)
4	Aug 1939	14	From reserve units
5	Sep 1939	11	Reservists
6	Oct 1939	6	All disbanded 1940
7	Dec 1939	13	From reserve units
8	Mar 1940	10+	Mostly older men
9	Apr 1940	10	Mostly 1940 draft

Source: Extracted from a table in *Hitler's Legions* by S. W. Mitcham (Leo Cooper, 1985).

- Regional headquarters
- /// Added in 1938 after Anschluss
- \\\ Added in 1939 after Polish Campaign

Notes: Wehrkreise XIV [motorised infantry divisions] XV [Light divisions] & XVI [panzer divisions] had no special territories

GERMAN INFANTERIE DIVISION

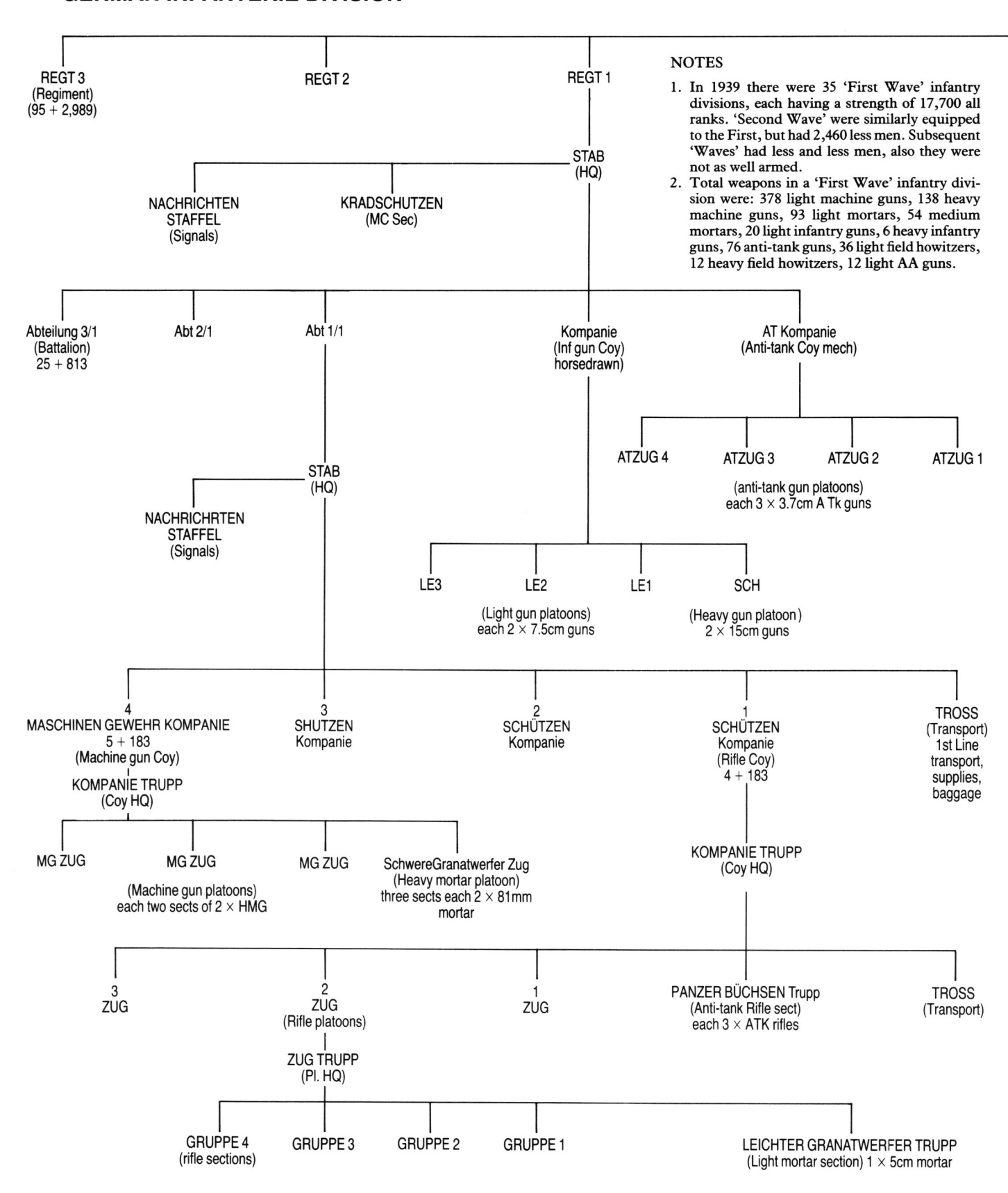

NOTES

1. In 1939 there were 35 'First Wave' infantry divisions, each having a strength of 17,700 all ranks. 'Second Wave' were similarly equipped to the First, but had 2,460 less men. Subsequent 'Waves' had less and less men, also they were not as well armed.
2. Total weapons in a 'First Wave' infantry division were: 378 light machine guns, 138 heavy machine guns, 93 light mortars, 54 medium mortars, 20 light infantry guns, 6 heavy infantry guns, 76 anti-tank guns, 36 light field howitzers, 12 heavy field howitzers, 12 light AA guns.

- REGT 3 (Regiment) (95 + 2,989)
- REGT 2
- REGT 1
  - STAB (HQ)
    - NACHRICHTEN STAFFEL (Signals)
    - KRADSCHUTZEN (MC Sec)
  - Abteilung 3/1 (Battalion) 25 + 813
  - Abt 2/1
  - Abt 1/1
    - STAB (HQ)
      - NACHRICHRTEN STAFFEL (Signals)
  - Kompanie (Inf gun Coy horsedrawn)
    - LE3, LE2, LE1 (Light gun platoons) each 2 × 7.5cm guns
    - SCH (Heavy gun platoon) 2 × 15cm guns
  - AT Kompanie (Anti-tank Coy mech)
    - ATZUG 4, ATZUG 3, ATZUG 2, ATZUG 1 (anti-tank gun platoons) each 3 × 3.7cm A Tk guns

- 4 MASCHINEN GEWEHR KOMPANIE 5 + 183 (Machine gun Coy)
  - KOMPANIE TRUPP (Coy HQ)
    - MG ZUG
    - MG ZUG
    - MG ZUG (Machine gun platoons) each two sects of 2 × HMG
    - SchwereGranatwerfer Zug (Heavy mortar platoon) three sects each 2 × 81mm mortar
- 3 SHUTZEN Kompanie
- 2 SCHÜTZEN Kompanie
- 1 SCHÜTZEN Kompanie (Rifle Coy) 4 + 183
  - KOMPANIE TRUPP (Coy HQ)
    - 3 ZUG
    - 2 ZUG (Rifle platoons)
      - ZUG TRUPP (Pl. HQ)
        - GRUPPE 4, GRUPPE 3, GRUPPE 2, GRUPPE 1 (rifle sections)
        - LEICHTER GRANATWERFER TRUPP (Light mortar section) 1 × 5cm mortar
    - 1 ZUG
    - PANZER BÜCHSEN Trupp (Anti-tank Rifle sect) each 3 × ATK rifles
  - TROSS (Transport)
- TROSS (Transport) 1st Line transport, supplies, baggage

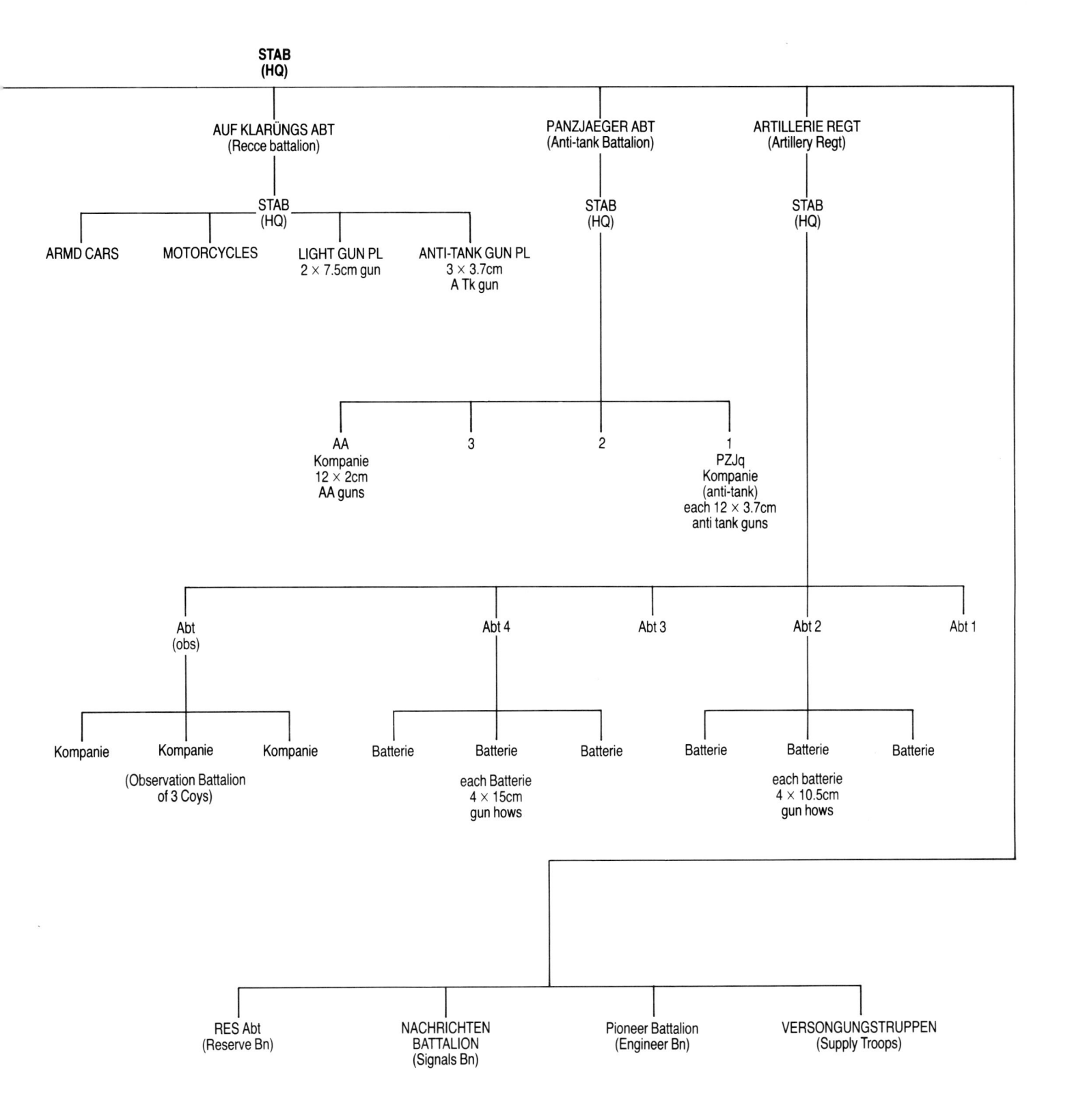

```
STAB
(HQ)
├── AUF KLARÜNGS ABT (Recce battalion)
│   └── STAB (HQ)
│       ├── ARMD CARS
│       ├── MOTORCYCLES
│       ├── LIGHT GUN PL — 2 × 7.5cm gun
│       └── ANTI-TANK GUN PL — 3 × 3.7cm A Tk gun
├── PANZJAEGER ABT (Anti-tank Battalion)
│   └── STAB (HQ)
│       ├── AA Kompanie — 12 × 2cm AA guns
│       ├── 3
│       ├── 2
│       └── 1 PZJq Kompanie (anti-tank) each 12 × 3.7cm anti tank guns
├── ARTILLERIE REGT (Artillery Regt)
│   └── STAB (HQ)
│       ├── Abt (obs)
│       │   ├── Kompanie
│       │   ├── Kompanie
│       │   └── Kompanie
│       │   (Observation Battalion of 3 Coys)
│       ├── Abt 4
│       │   ├── Batterie
│       │   ├── Batterie
│       │   └── Batterie
│       │   each Batterie 4 × 15cm gun hows
│       ├── Abt 3
│       ├── Abt 2
│       │   ├── Batterie
│       │   ├── Batterie
│       │   └── Batterie
│       │   each batterie 4 × 10.5cm gun hows
│       └── Abt 1
├── RES Abt (Reserve Bn)
├── NACHRICHTEN BATTALION (Signals Bn)
├── Pioneer Battalion (Engineer Bn)
└── VERSONGUNGSTRUPPEN (Supply Troops)
```

Flame throwers were used to great effect on defence bunkers although, as this photograph shows, the large canister was cumbersome to carry about. The man in the foreground is brandishing a Kampfpistolen, *the German equivalent of the British Very Light pistol.* TM

At the start of the Second World War there were the following basic types of division in the German Army:

Infantry Divisions. These were the most numerous and comprised three infantry regiments, each of three battalions with three rifle companies and a heavy weapons company; an anti-tank company of 3.7cm anti-tank guns, and an infantry gun company of 7.5cm guns. Other divisional units were an artillery regiment of three 10.5cm gun-howitzer battalions, one of 15cm gun-howitzers and an observation battalion, an engineer battalion, a reconnaissance battalion, an anti-tank battalion, a signal battalion, replacement battalion, plus the usual administrative units such as supply, repair and medical.

Panzer Divisions. At the start of the war there were only six panzer divisions in existence (Pz Divs 1 to 5 inclusive and Pz Div 10) and all took part in the Polish campaign. After that campaign the four light divisions (see following paragraph) became panzer divisions, so there were ten in existence by May 1940. The early panzer divisions, formed in 1935, had comprised of a panzer brigade of two regiments, a motor rifle (*Schutzen*) brigade also of two regiments, plus supporting arms and services, such as artillery, engineer and recce units. Each of the panzer regiments contained two battalions (*Abteilung*), with four companies (*Kompanie*) to each battalion. The total tank strength of the brigade was 561. On mobilisation, the fourth company of each battalion became the depot and reinforcement unit, while the remainder was reorganised into one medium and two light panzer companies, leading to a reduction in tank strength from 561 to around 300, although a fair proportion were more powerful tanks.

Light Divisions. At the same time as the original panzer divisions were forming, four light (*leichte*) divisions were raised by mechanising the German cavalry under a completely separate programme. The light divisions were small motorised formations containing just one battalion

Continued on page 53

46

Breakdown of Divisional Staffs

Tactical group
(Known as the Divisional Command Post)
Ia   Chief of Operations + staff
Ic   Chief of Intelligence + staff
Other combat staffs such as artillery and air liaison officers.
A senior artillery commander (Arko) would be attached to Div HQ if there were any higher formation artillery units allocated to the division for a particular operation. Otherwise the divisional artillery commander (*Artillerieführer* or *Arfu*) was the officer responsible for artillery matters.

Supply group
(Normally left to rear of Div CP)
Ib   Chief of Supply[a] + staff
IVa Chief Administrative Officer + staff
IVb Chief Medical Officer + staff
IVc Chief Veterinary Officer + staff
V   Chief of Motor Transport + staff

Personnel group
(Also left to rear)
IIa Chief of Personnel[b] + staff
IIb Deputy Personnel Officer[c] + staff
III Chief Judge Advocate
IVd Chaplain
and administrative staff to run the HQ, such as MT, security detachments, etc.

[a] also known as the Divisional Quartermaster, this officer commanded the supply group.
[b] also known as the Adjutant, he commanded the group and was responsible for officer affairs, including postings and promotions, etc.
[c] also known as Adjutant Two, this officer was responsible for administration involving other ranks.

Small inflatable boats were used by German combat engineers and infantry to cross small rivers and canals. Linked together they formed temporary footbridges over narrow waterways.   TM

German infantry on patrol during the bitter winter of 1939/40.   TM

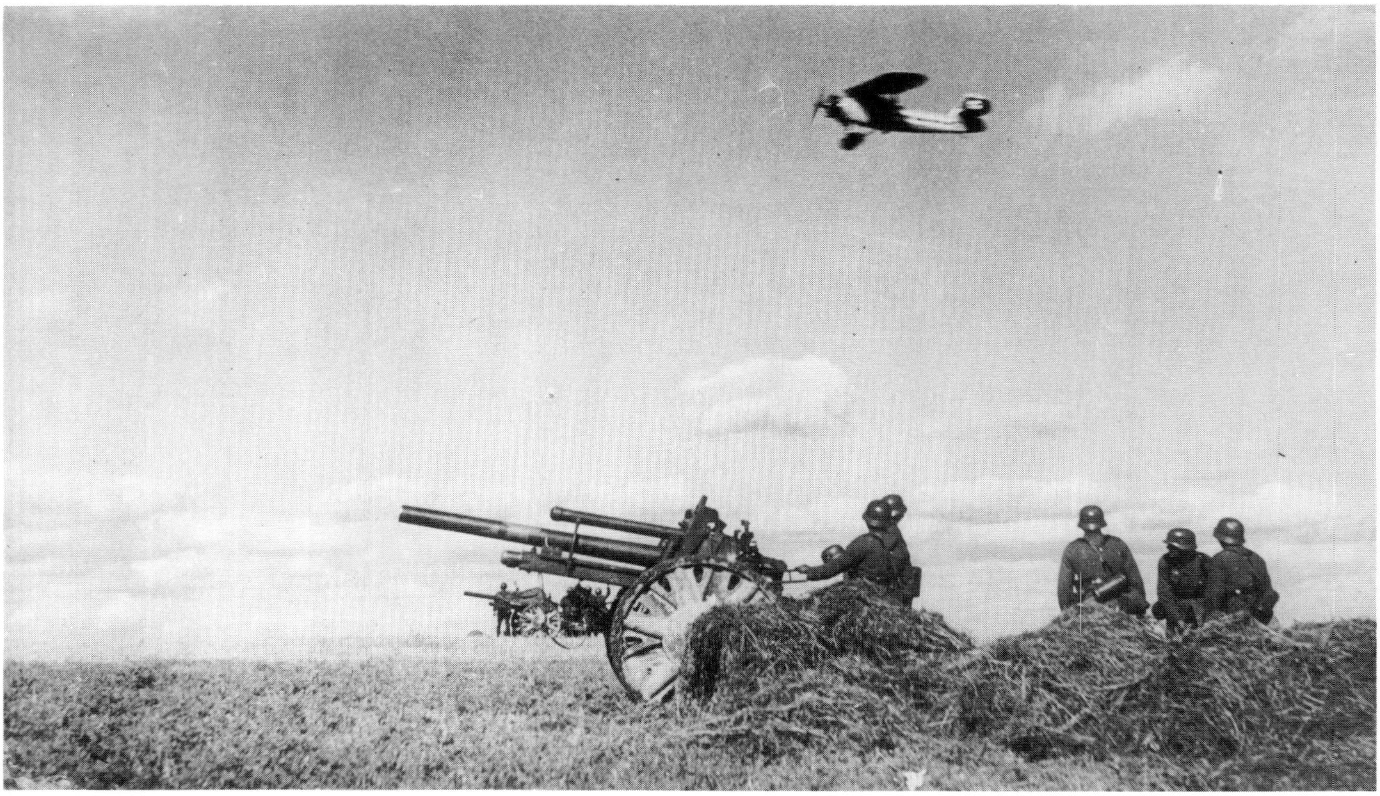

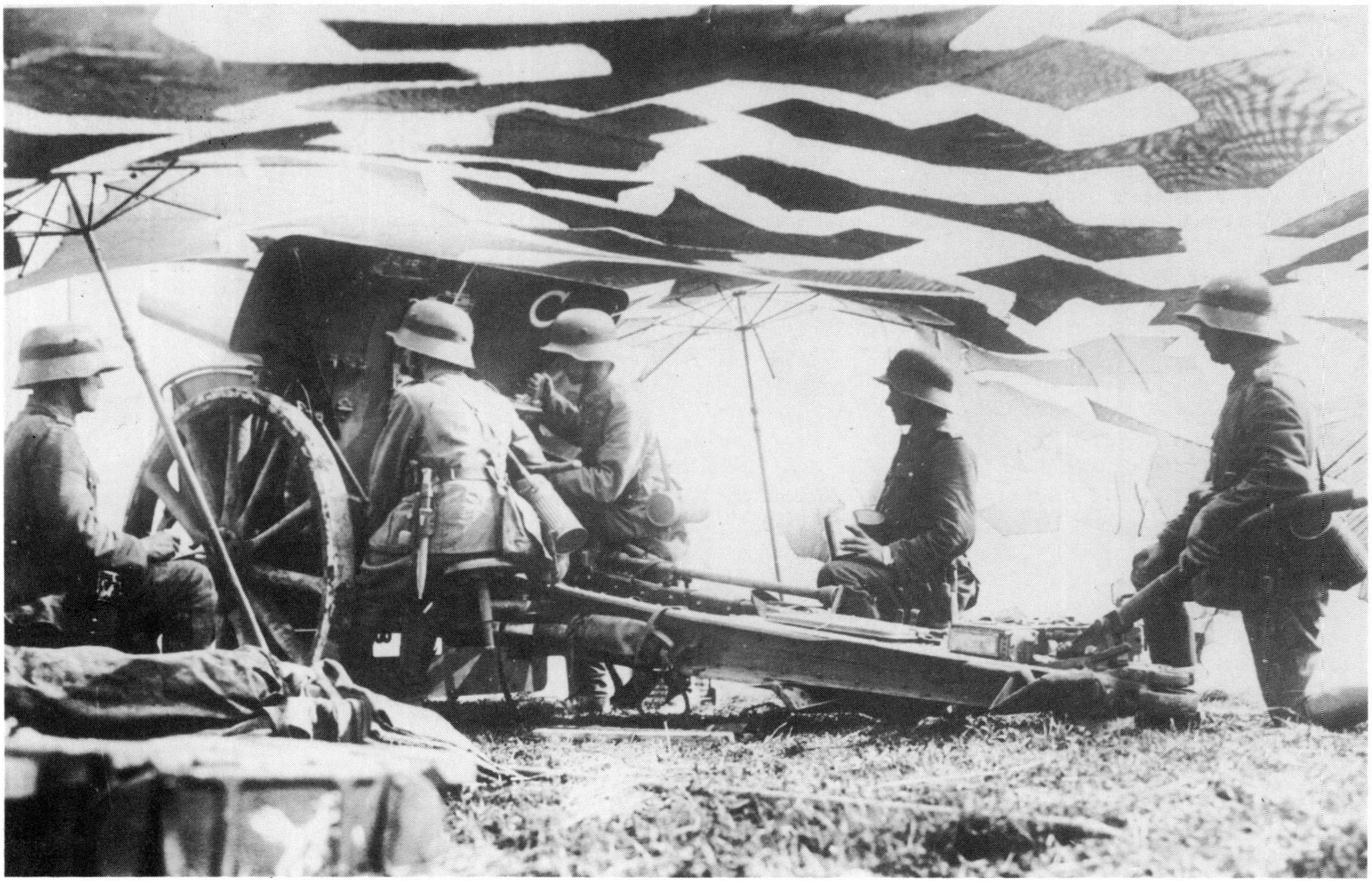

The backbone of German artillery was the 10.5cm leichte Feldhaubitze *(field howitzer) which was first put into service in 1935. It had a maximum range of just over 10½ miles.* TM

At the start of the Second World War the horse-drawn 7.5cm Feldkanone *(field gun) 16nA (neuer Artillerie) was used by the German army. It first came into service in 1934, but was soon relegated to the second line as it lacked both range (its maximum was 12,900 metres) and mobility. The weapon weighed 1,542 kg in action and 2,415 kg on the move. The large covering net has a design typical of those used for camouflage purposes during the pre-war period.* TM

The Panzer Divisions

Pz Div	Formation When & Where	Panzer Bde	Schutzen Bde	Artillerie Regt	Recce Bn
1	15 Oct 35 Weimar (Wkr IX) from elements of 3 Kavallerie Division	1 (Regt 1 & 2)	1 (Regt 1)	Regt 73	4
2	15 Oct 35 Würzburg (Wkr XIII) transferred to Vienna in 1938	2 (Regt 3 & 4)	2 (Regt 2)	Regt 74	NK
3	15 Oct 35 Wunsdorf (Wkr III) Manoeuvre Area with HQ in Berlin	3 'Berlin'	3 'Eberswalde'	Regt 75	3
4	10 Nov 38 Würzburg (Wkr XIII)	5 (Regt 35 & 36)	4 (Regt 12)	Regt 103	7
5	24 Nov 38 Oppein (Wkr VIII)	8 (Regt 15 & 31)	5 (Regt 13 & 14)	Regt 116	8
6	18 Oct 39 Wuppertal (Wkr VI) from 1 Leichten D Kavallerie Division	NIL-Regt 11	6 (Regt 4)	Regt 76	65
7	18 Oct 39 Gera (Wkr IX) from 2 Leichten Division	NIL-Regt 25	7 (Regt 6 & 7)	Regt 78	66
8	16 Oct 39 Cottbus (Wkr III) from 3 Leichten Division	NIL-Regt 10	8 (Regt 8)	Regt 80	67
9	3 Jan 40 Vienna (Wkr XVII) from 4 Leichten Division	NIL-Regt 33	9 (Regt 10 & 11)	Regt 102	9
10*	1 Apr 39 Prague then Stüttgart (Wkr V)	4 (Regt 7 & 8)	10 (Regt 69 & 86)	Regt 90	90

* When 10 Pz Div was first formed, there was no Panzer brigade, just 8 Pz Regt, and no Schutzen brigade, just 86 Mot Rifle Regt and 8 Recce Abt. The other units had joined the division by early 1940.

49

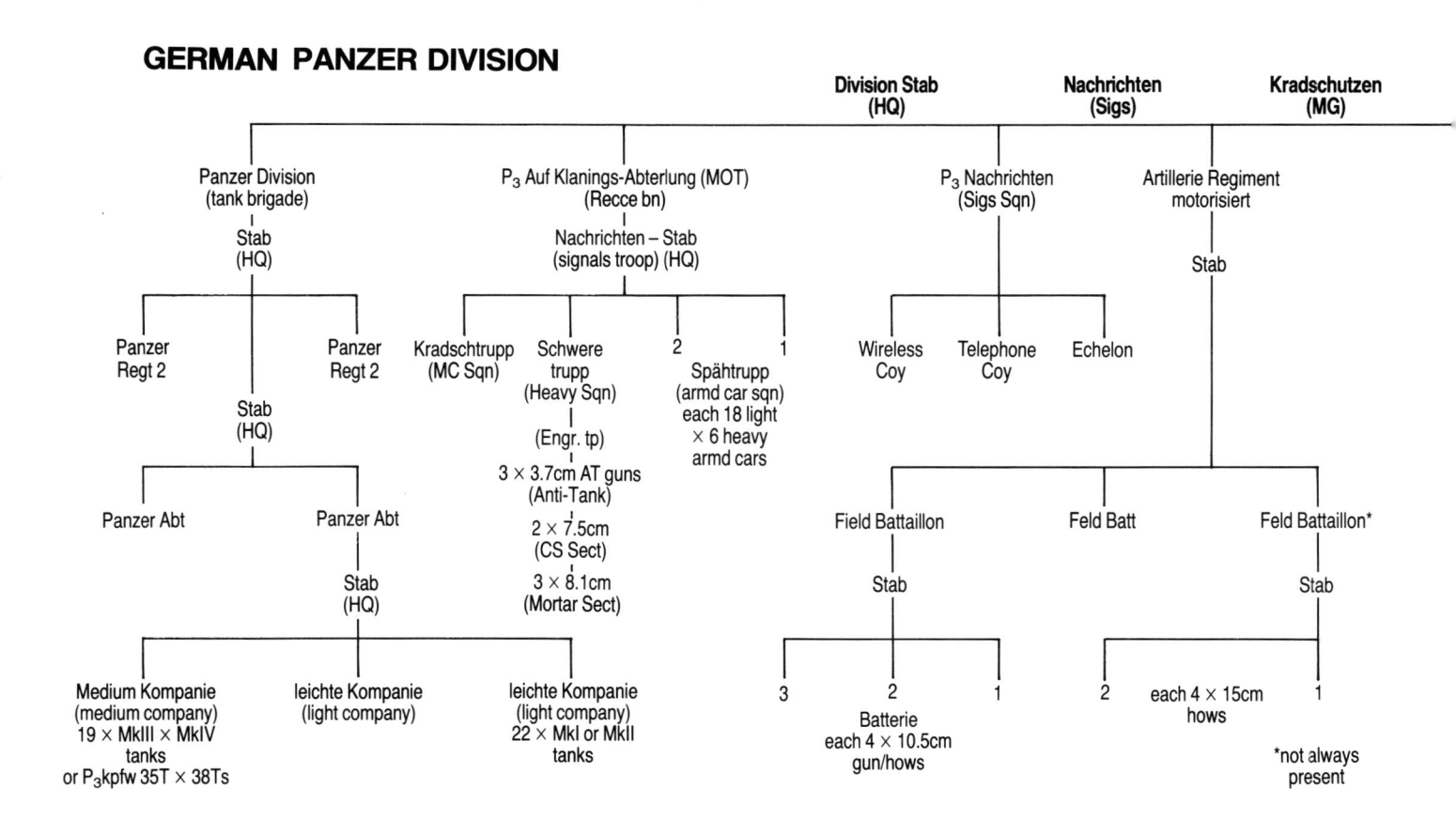

GERMAN PANZER DIVISION

- Division Stab (HQ)
  - Panzer Division (tank brigade)
    - Stab (HQ)
      - Panzer Regt 2
      - Panzer Regt 2
        - Stab (HQ)
          - Panzer Abt
          - Panzer Abt
            - Stab (HQ)
              - Medium Kompanie (medium company) 19 × MkIII × MkIV tanks or P₃kpfw 35T × 38Ts
              - leichte Kompanie (light company)
              - leichte Kompanie (light company) 22 × MkI or MkII tanks
  - P₃ Auf Klanings-Abterlung (MOT) (Recce bn)
    - Nachrichten – Stab (signals troop) (HQ)
      - Kradschtrupp (MC Sqn)
      - Schwere trupp (Heavy Sqn)
        - (Engr. tp)
        - 3 × 3.7cm AT guns (Anti-Tank)
        - 2 × 7.5cm (CS Sect)
        - 3 × 8.1cm (Mortar Sect)
      - 2
      - 1 Spähtrupp (armd car sqn) each 18 light × 6 heavy armd cars
- Nachrichten (Sigs)
  - P₃ Nachrichten (Sigs Sqn)
    - Wireless Coy
    - Telephone Coy
    - Echelon
  - Field Battaillon
    - Stab
      - 3
      - 2
      - 1 Batterie each 4 × 10.5cm gun/hows
- Kradschutzen (MG)
  - Artillerie Regiment motorisiert
    - Stab
      - Feld Batt
      - Feld Battaillon*
        - Stab
          - 2
          - each 4 × 15cm hows
          - 1
        - *not always present

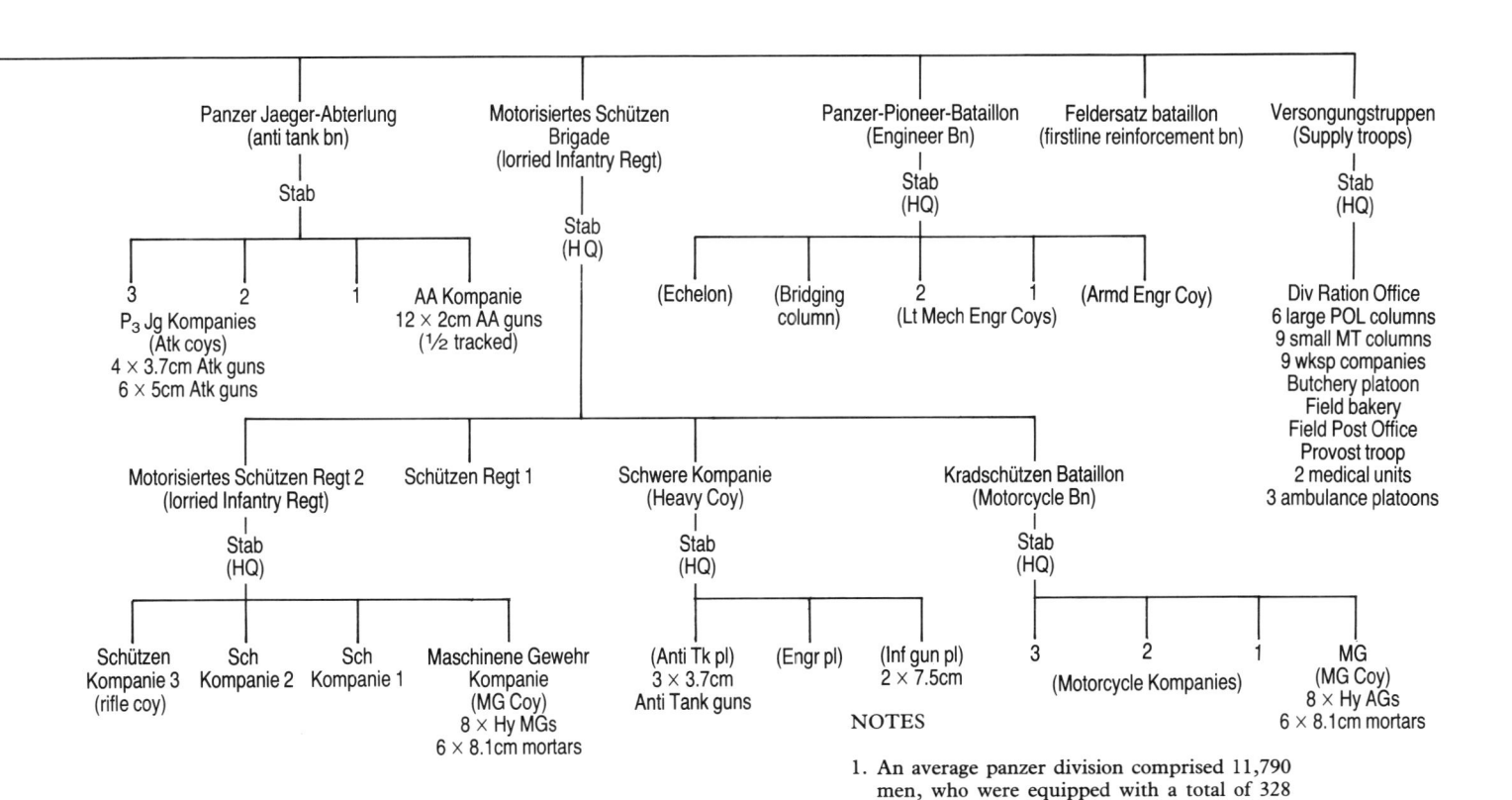

```
                    Panzer Jaeger-Abterlung      Motorisiertes Schützen         Panzer-Pioneer-Bataillon    Feldersatz bataillon           Versongungstruppen
                    (anti tank bn)                Brigade                       (Engineer Bn)              (firstline reinforcement bn)   (Supply troops)
                         |                       (lorried Infantry Regt)            |                                                         |
                        Stab                              |                        Stab                                                     Stab
                                                         Stab                      (HQ)                                                      (HQ)
                                                         (HQ)
      ┌──────┬────────┬──────────┐                                    ┌──────────┬──────────┬──────────┐
      3      2        1          AA Kompanie                       (Echelon)  (Bridging     2          1        (Armd Engr Coy)     Div Ration Office
    P₃ Jg Kompanies              12 × 2cm AA guns                              column)  (Lt Mech Engr Coys)                         6 large POL columns
      (Atk coys)                 (½ tracked)                                                                                        9 small MT columns
    4 × 3.7cm Atk guns                                                                                                              9 wksp companies
    6 × 5cm Atk guns                                                                                                                Butchery platoon
                                                                                                                                    Field bakery
                                                                                                                                    Field Post Office
                                                                                                                                    Provost troop
        Motorisiertes Schützen Regt 2     Schützen Regt 1       Schwere Kompanie              Kradschützen Bataillon                2 medical units
        (lorried Infantry Regt)                                  (Heavy Coy)                   (Motorcycle Bn)                      3 ambulance platoons
                |                                                    |                              |
               Stab                                                 Stab                           Stab
               (HQ)                                                 (HQ)                           (HQ)
   ┌──────┬──────┬────────┐                              ┌──────────┬──────────┐         ┌──────┬──────┬────────┐
 Schützen  Sch   Sch   Maschinene Gewehr              (Anti Tk pl) (Engr pl) (Inf gun pl) 3      2      1        MG
 Kompanie 3 Kompanie 2 Kompanie 1 Kompanie            3 × 3.7cm               2 × 7.5cm   (Motorcycle Kompanies)  (MG Coy)
 (rifle coy)                      (MG Coy)            Anti Tank guns                                             8 × Hy AGs
                                  8 × Hy MGs                                                                     6 × 8.1cm mortars
                                  6 × 8.1cm mortars                    NOTES

                                                                       1. An average panzer division comprised 11,790
                                                                          men, who were equipped with a total of 328
                                                                          tanks and 101 armoured cars.
```

51

Pz Kpfw I *light tanks of the 3rd Panzer Regiment on parade in the market-place of Kamenz, near Bamberg, on 2 October 1936.*
(author's collection)

The Pz Kpfw II Ausf A, *with its three-man crew, had a combat-loaded weight of 8.9 tons. It bore the brunt of the fighting on the Polish front but, like the* Pz Kpfw I, *it lacked the staying power needed to cope with modern battlefield conditions*
TM

of light tanks, while the main component was the motorised infantry element of four Schutzen battalions. Supporting units were very similar to those in the panzer divisions. In 1938, the four *leichte* divisions passed under control of Guderian's Inspectorate of Mobile Troops. Later, after the Polish campaign, they became the 6th, 7th, 8th and 9th Panzer Divisions. Their tank strength was increased by the addition of a three-battalion panzer regiment, except for 9th Panzer which only received a two-battalion regiment.

Motorised Divisions. Only four infantry divisions (2nd, 13th, 20th and 29th) were fully motorised and classified as *Infanterie Divisionen (Motorisiert)* at the outbreak of war. They each consisted of three motorised infantry regiments of three battalions initially, but in late 1940 lost their third regiment to help form more motorised divisions. Later in the war they were redesignated as *Panzer Grenadier Divisionen*.

Mountain Divisions. There were three mountain divisions at the start of the war and they formed a well-trained, élite force. Organised on the same lines as a normal infantry division, they normally had lighter equipment which could be broken down into loads for pack or horse transport. For example, their artillery regiments were equipped with 7.5cm guns instead of 10.5 howitzers, while the medium artillery was 10.5cm instead of the usual 15cm. Mountain divisions comprised three regiments of three battalions, each of which consisted of three mountain *Jaeger* companies, one machine gun company and one heavy weapons company.

On the other hand, the Pz Kpfw IV, *proved itself to be a highly effective weapon, and remained in production throughout the whole of the Second World War. At the start of the campaign in France there were only 280 of these fighting vehicles in divisional service: shown here is the* Ausf D *version.* TM

German Tank Details

Type	Date of origin	Weight tonnes	Crew	Main armament	Armour thickness (mm)	Max speed (km/h)	Range (km)
Pzkpfw I Ausf A	1934	5.4	2	2 x MG 13	Max 13 Min 6	35	145
Pzkpfw I Ausf B	1935	6.0	2	2 x MG 13	Max 13 Min 6	40	140
Pzkpfw II Ausf A, B, C	1937	8.9	3	1 x 2cm 1 x MG 34	Max 15 Min 5	40	200
Pzkpfw II Ausf D, E	1937	10.0	3	1 x 2cm 1 x MG 34	Max 30 Min 5	55	200
Pzkpfw 35 (tzech)	1934	10.5	4	1 x 3.7cm 2 x MG	Max 35 Min 8	40	200
Pzkpfw 38 (tzech)	1939	9.4	4	1 x 3.7cm 2 x MG	Max 25 Min 8	40	250
Pzkpfw III Ausf A to Ausf F	1937 to 1940	15.4 to 19.8	5	1 x 3.7cm 2/3 x MG 34 (dependent upon Ausfuhrung (Mark) of tank)	Max 15 to 30 Min 5 to 12	32	165
Pzkpfw IV Ausf A to Ausf D	1935 to 1939	18.4 to 20	5	1 x 7.5cm 2/3 x MG 34 (dependent upon Ausfuhrung)	Max 15 to 30 Min 5 to 10	32	150

The assault gun Sd Kfz 142 Ausf A *was developed primarily for infantry support. About 30 were built early in 1940 and used in the attack on France.* TM

Miscellaneous Divisions. There were a large number of special purpose divisions formed at various times during the war including Air Landing (*NB* paratroops were part of the Luftwaffe), Cavalry, Coastal Defence, Field Training, Fortress, *Jaeger*, Replacement, Reserve and Security, but it is not easy to pin down exactly which were in existence in May 1940. To the Army divisions must also be added the SS Divisions, of which 40 were used as ground troops during the war. Then there were various Luftwaffe units which included three types of ground divisions: parachute, field and AA (flak). Matthew Cooper in his book *The Germany Army 1939-45* estimates that the initial SS and Luftwaffe ground troops at the outbreak of war were:

a. *SS* Four motorised infantry regiments (including one in training), one artillery regiment, one independent battalion of each of the following: anti-tank, AA machine gun, pioneer, recce and signals, plus supply and replacement units, totalling 23,000 men.

b. *Luftwaffe* Flak Regiment Herman Goering, 1st Parachute (*Fallschirmjaeger*) Regiment and a number of field AA units.

Transport

At the start of the Second World War, and throughout the war, *das Heer* was not the highly mechanised army we may imagine. Whilst its administration and supply organisation was highly efficient, even up to the final months, its supply columns (*Kolonne*) depended more on horsedrawn (*fahrkolonne*) than on motorised (*kraftwagen kolonne*)units, although these did become more numerous. From the outset there was a grave shortage of motorised transport, even though in 1939 all civilian lorries were commandeered.

Most of these were not strong enough for military work and lacked four-wheel drive, so they did not last long. By early 1940 losses in action and bad roads in Poland, together with inadequate production from the factories, meant that many units were down to 50% of their establishment. Len Deighton states that Gen Franz Halder was so alarmed by the situation that he proposed a 'drastic and far-reaching demotorization programme which would at once start procuring horses, horse-transport vehicles and harnesses, so that the German Army could begin replacing some of its motor vehicles with horses.'

The fact that the normal infantry division had nearly 5,400 horses, yet under 1,000 motor vehicles of all types, showed the measure of German dependence upon the horse. It would require 2½ times the weight of its motor fuel requirements in hay and oats – a staggering 50 tons a day. Hours had to be spent looking after the horses, feeding, watering, grooming and exercising them, and a sophisticated veterinary service was needed to look after their health.

The Navy (*Die Kriegsmarine*)
Even before Hitler had decided to abrogate the Versailles Treaty, Germany had been secretly building ships in excess of the tonnages allowed by the Treaty for replacement vessels. As this table shows, these limits were very specific.

Versailles limits of German Warships, 1920-1935			
Type of warship	Number allowed	Age in years before replaced	Max tonnage per replacement ship
Battleship	6	20	10,000
Light cruiser	6	20	6,000
Destroyer	12	15	800
Torpedo boat	12	15	200
Submarine	Nil		

As early as the 1920s Germany started building light cruisers which, like all German warships built at that time, exceeded the displacement limits laid down in the Versailles Treaty. Hitler continued the deception, warning the Navy to keep quiet. As William Shirer quotes in his book *The Rise and Fall of the Third Reich*: 'In June 1934 Raeder had a long conversation with Hitler and noted down: "Führer's instructions: No mention must be made of a displacement of 25-26,000 tons, but only of improved 10,000 ton ships . . . the Führer demands complete secrecy on the construction of the U-boats."' By the time war was declared the *Oberkommando der Marine* had a formidable force to command.

'The Mission of the German Navy' – a propaganda poster issued in 1939. TM

The battle cruiser Scharnhorst, *armed with nine 11in (280mm) guns, was launched on 3 October 1936. With her sister ship* Gneisenau *and the* Prinz Eugen *she made a dramatic dash up the English Channel to regain her home port in February 1942.*   IWM

U-boats at Krupp's shipyard. Admiral Doenitz assured Hitler before the war that with 300 of these sinister vessels he could starve Britain into submission.   IWM

OKM organisation

Between 1920 and 1921 the Navy became a permanent service once again, carrying out regular exercises and making visits abroad. In 1925 the new cruiser *Emden* was launched and in 1928 the first of the 'pocket battleships' was laid down. Admiral Erich Raeder became C-in-C of the Navy in 1928 and was undoubtedly the main architect of the new *Kriegsmarine*, being responsible for its most rapid period of expansion, including the building of the 'pocket battleships', the new submarines and the build-up of a naval air arm.

The basic naval organisation did not require a great deal of change when war began. Under Raeder, the OKM was concerned with strategic and operational planning, keeping under its direct control the raiders plus their intelligence and supply systems. Below the OKM there were two commands: Group East and Group West, each of which was responsible for all naval operations in their respective areas and were responsible for the safety of coastal waters. Because most of the larger ships operated in the North Sea, Group West became the most important part of the navy and this inevitably led to some friction with OKM. Doenitz, later to become C-in-C in 1943 and Hitler's successor in April 1945, was then Flag Officer Submarines.

> **Disposition of the German Navy at the outbreak of war**
>
> **a. Under command C-in-C Western Area (HQ at Wilhelmshaven)**
> Pocket battleship *Admiral Scheer*
> Battle cruisers *Scharnhorst* and *Gneisenau*
> Cruisers *Admiral Hipper* and *Leipzig*
> Five light cruisers
> Three divisions of destroyers, three U Boat flotillas and one training flotilla (15 boats in total)
> Torpedo boats, MTBs, minelayers and fleet tenders
> Nine naval air squadrons (about 100 aircraft)
>
> **b. Under command C-in-C Eastern Area (HQ at Swinemunde, later Kiel)**
> Two old battleships *Schleswig Holstein* and *Schlesien*
> Seven destroyers
> Eight U Boats
> Torpedo boats, MTBs, minesweepers and minelayers
>
> **c. Under direct operational control of the Naval War Staff**
> Pocket-battleships *Deutschland* and *Admiral Graf Spee*
> Eleven U Boats
>
> **Ships under construction or refitting**
> Battleships *Bismark* and *Tirpitz*
> Aircraft carrier *Graf Zeppelin*
> Five heavy and one light cruisers
>
> The main German Naval bases were Wilhelmshaven, Brunsbuttel, Kiel, Hamburg, Swinemunde, Stettin, Pillau and Danzig.

Smaller vessels

Germany built a large number of motor torpedo boats – the *Schnellboot* (fast boat), which were rugged and seaworthy. Between 550 and 600 were built, lightly armed with two 21in torpedo tubes and two 20mm guns. They also designed a series of midget submarines, known as *Kleine Kampfmittel* (small battle units), some of which were little more than human torpedoes. The *Kriegsmarine* revived the very successful First World War strategm of using disguised merchantmen (*Hilfskreuzer*). They were sturdy cargo ships equipped with six to eight 5.9in guns in concealed places which were able to raid the trade routes, causing great confusion.

At the start of the Second World War the *Kriegsmarine* had far fewer ships than the Royal Navy, but this disparity in numbers was partly offset by the fact that most German vessels were more modern than the British in design, construction and armament.

The Schnellboot *was a fast and extremely effective motor torpedo boat.* TM

> **Die Kriegsmarine**
> (Only those ships afloat at the start of the war are shown)
>
> | Class of warship | Tonnage | Main Armament | Speed (kts) | Armour (ins) |
> |---|---|---|---|---|
> | **Battleships and Battlecruisers** | | | | |
> | Deutschland *a | 12,000 | 6 x 11in | 26 | 2½-3 |
> | Scharnhorst *b | 32,000 | 9 x 11in | 31 | 14 |
> | Bismark *c | 42,000 | 8 x 15in | 29 | 12½ |
>
> *a 3 in all: *Deutschland*, *Admiral Scheer* and *Admiral Graf Spee*.
> *b 2 in all: *Scharnhorst* and *Gneisenau*.
> *c 2 in all: *Bismark* and *Tirpitz*.
> In addition there were two old battleships: *Schleswig-Holstein* and *Schlesien*, both armed with 4 x 11in guns.
>
> | **Cruisers** | | | | |
> |---|---|---|---|---|
> | Emden | 5,600 | 8 x 5.9in | 29 | |
> | Koln | 6,650 | 9 x 5.9in | 32 | |
> | Leipzig | 6,700 | 9 x 5.9in | 32 | |
> | Nurnberg | 7,000 | 9 x 5.9in | 32 | |
> | Admiral Hipper | 14,000 | 8 x 8in | 32 | |
>
> There was a total of six light cruisers and one heavy cruiser afloat in 1939.
>
> | **Destroyers** | | | | |
> |---|---|---|---|---|
> | Z-1 | 2,400 | 5 x 5in | 38 | |
> | Z-23 | 2,600 | 5 x 5.9in | 38 | |
> | T-1 | 1,100 | 1 x 4.1in | 33 | |
> | T-22 | 1,300 | 4 x 4.1in | 33 | |
>
> The Germans had 34 destroyers in service in 1939.
>
> **Submarines** in service or approaching completion in 1939
>
> | | | | |
> |---|---|---|---|
> | Type IA | number built 2* | 850 | 6 tubes |
> | Type IIA | number built 6 | 250-300 | 3 tubes |
> | Type IIB, C & D | number built 44 | 250-300 | 3 tubes |
> | Type VII | number built 10 | 625 | 5 tubes |
> | Types VIIB | number built 24 | 750 | 5 tubes |
> | Type VIIC | number built 4 | 770 | 5 tubes |
> | Type IX | number built 8 | 1,030 | 6 tubes |
> | Type IXB | number built 14 | 1,110 | 6 tubes |
>
> * In addition to these 2 submarines, a further 567 Type IA were completed 1940-1944.
>
> Source: *The War at Sea Vol 1* by Capt. S. W. Roskill (HMSO, 1954).

Hermann Goering is greeted by his Führer after landing in a Fieseler 'Storch' Fi 156, a useful two-seater aircraft designed for light communications. TM

Four Messerschmitt Me 110 *two-seater fighters fly in formation over Paris. About 350 of these aircraft were used with considerable success in the French campaign, but they were outclassed by* Spitfires *and* Hurricanes *during the Battle of Britain.* TM

Die Luftwaffe
The Luftwaffe was directed by the Air Ministry (*Reichsluftfahrt Ministerium*) which was divided into two main parts: *Oberkommando der Luftwaffe (OKL)* which was concerned with the direction of the air force; the office of the Minister for Air (*Reichsminister der Luftfahrt*) which dealt with the purely administrative matters such as financial control and, at the start of the war, aircraft production. Heading both departments was the Reichsmarschall Hermann Goering, who was both C-in-C of the Air Force and Minister for Air. A hero of the First World War, Goering commanded the von Richthofen's fighter group in 1918 and was an early member of the NSDAP. He was responsible for building up the Luftwaffe and held the post of C-in-C from 1935, being promoted to Reichsmarschall in 1940.

The OKL was divided into a number of Directorates which were grouped under the Chief of the Operations Staff, the Chief of the General Staff or the Quartermaster General *viz*

Chief of Ops	CGS	QMG
Operations	Historical	Organisation
Training		Movements
Intelligence		Equipment
		Personnel

The Chief of the Ops Staff was responsible for the implementation of air strategy as laid down by the CGS as well as being responsible for operations. The CGS also controlled various Inspectorates, which dealt with flying subjects such as flight safety, fighter tactics, etc.

Luftflotten
In 1939 all operational flying units were divided between four *Luftflotten* (Air Fleets). Each was a balanced force of aircraft, comprising fighter, bomber, reconnaissance, ground attack, etc. More Luftflotten were formed as the war progressed. Each Luftflotte was divided into several Air Zones (*Luftgau*), with an HQ responsible for providing the men for

The man largely responsible for the creation of the Luftwaffe was Field Marshal Erhard Milch. Before 1935 much of the work had to be done in secret, but as German confidence grew the rearmament programme became plain for all to see. The first Luftwaffe pilots gained valuable combat experience during the Spanish Civil War.

Luftflotten as at the start of the war			
Luftflotte	Area covered	HQ location	Commander
1	Northern and Eastern Germany	Berlin	Kesselring
2	North-West Germany	Brunswick	Felmy
3	South-West Germany	Munich	Sperrle
4	South-East Germany, Austria and Czechoslovakia	Vienna	Loehr

At his Felsennest headquarters, Hitler poses with the heroes of Eban Emael after decorating each of them with a Ritterkreuz *(Knights Cross)*
Hans Teske

Main type of German aircraft at the start of the war						
Name and Type	Speed (mph)	Ceiling (feet)	Range (mls)	First flew	Armament	Crew
Fieseler Storch Fi 156 two seat, light multi-purpose communications aircraft with an excellent performance	165	16,050	205	NK	NIL	2
Heinkel He 111 medium bomber. Most effective in the world at start of war	258	25,600	745	1935	Bombload 4,410lbs	5
Junkers Ju 52 transport aircraft. Known affectionately as 'Iron Annie'	190	18,050	810	1930	1 x MG 131, 2 x MG 15	4
Junkers Ju 87 dive bomber	242	26,250	375	1935	Bombload 1,540lbs 2 x MG 117 in wings, MG 15 in rear cockpit	2
Junkers Ju 88 'schnell' (fast) bomber, also used for many other tasks (day/night fighter, dive bomber, recce, anti-tank, etc)	270	26,900	1,110	1936	Bombload 1,100lbs 2 x 20mm cannons & 3 x MG	2
Messerschmitt Bf 109E-3. One of the best fighters of the war, but not as good as the Spitfire	355	36,000	410	1935	3 x 20mm cannons 2 x MG 17	1
Messerschmitt Bf 110. Day and night fighter, but at its best by night	350	32,800	530	1936	2 x 20mm cannons 4 x MG 17 & 1 x MG 15	2

the technical and administrative tasks at the airfields in their zone. In parallel with the *Luftgau* organisation was the *Fliegerkorps* (Air Corps) which operated the aircraft. The basic flying unit was the Gruppe of 30 aircraft, which normally occupied one airfield. A Gruppe comprised three *Staffeln* (Squadrons), each with a nominal strength of nine aircraft, with air crews, technical and signal ground personnel.

Aircraft strength
At the start of the war the strength of the Luftwaffe was a total of 4,161 aircraft, divided as follows: recce: 604; fighters: 1,179; bombers: 1,180; dive bombers: 366; ground attack: 40; coastal: 240; transport: 466.[2]

Airborne forces
All parachute and glider borne troops were part of the Luftwaffe although army units could also be used for air-landing operations. From July 1938 they were formed into 7th Flieger Division with its HQ in Berlin. The divisional

At their best, the Germans achieved very high standards of aircraft design and construction. But some of their more workaday planes, such as these transport aircraft, were often ungainly and unreliable. IWM

Heinkel He III bombers seen through the nose of another He III. The nose-mounted machine gun is the 7.92mm MG 15. TM

A 2cm light Flak 30 protects German shipping at a Norwegian port after the 1940 invasion. TM

commander was Maj-Gen Karl Student, an energetic and able officer. The first army airlanding division was 22 (Airlanding) Division. Neither it, nor 7th Flieger Division were complete or fully trained at the start of the war but as the French and British had nothing comparable, this small force was to have a potent effect upon the battle.

The aircraft used for dropping paratroops and for towing gliders, was the Junkers Ju 52. The Gotha DFS glider was the only transport glider used by the Luftwaffe, and could carry a payload of 9 men or 1,000kgs of supplies, ammunition, weapons or equipment.

Anti-aircraft artillery
Almost two-thirds of the Luftwaffe's total manpower was serving in its 'Flak' arm at the start of the war. 'Flak' had two major tasks: to protect the Fatherland and to provide air defence to the field forces. The basic Flak unit was the battalion (*abteilung*), of which there were four basic types: heavy (*schwere*), light (*leichte*), mixed (*gemischte*) and searchlight (*scheinwerfer*).

Flak was either static – normally the *schwere* and *scheinwerfer abteilungen*, or mobile – motorised or semi-motorised. The types of Flak guns are shown below.

Flak guns			
Type	date introduced	engagement ceiling	shell
Schwere			
8.8cm Flak 18	1933 (used in Spain)	26,250ft	19.8lbs
(the Flak 36 and 37 were improved versions of the Flak 18)			
10.5cm Flak 38	1939	31,000ft	32.2lbs
12.8cm Flak 40	1940	35,000ft	57lbs
Medium			
3.7cm Flak 18 and 36		2,690ft	1lb 5oz
(Rate of fire 80rpm ammo in 6 round clips)			
Light			
2cm Flak 30 and 38		2,950ft	4oz
(Flak 30 – 120rpm, Flak 38 – 180rpm; the 2cm Flakvierling 38 comprised four 2cm Flak 38 in a quadruple mounting)			

The 10.8cm Flak 38 *was a larger version of the* 8.8cm Flak 41 *and was a very efficient weapon with a maximum ceiling of 12,800 metres.* TM

NOTES

1. Fritz Todt was a civil engineer responsible for most of the construction work demanded by Germany's war effort. The vast Todt Organisation, using an army of slave labour, built the Siegfried Line and a chain of concrete submarine bases on the French Atlantic coast, as well as converting the railway network in occupied Russia to the German gauge. Todt was appointed Armaments Minister in 1940, but was killed two years later when his plane crashed on take-off.
2. W. Murray *Luftwaffe* London: Allen & Unwin, 1985.

The searchlight most commonly used by the Luftwaffe was the Flackscheinwerfer 37. TM

Chapter 5

Allied Organisation and Equipment

FRANCE

The Hotchkiss Mle 1914 medium machine gun was so heavy and cumbersome that it frequently ended up as a static weapon, as in this AA post seen during the winter of 1939/40. TM

French chain of command

At the start of the war the Prime Minister, Edouard Daladier, was also Minister of National Defence. When, in March 1940, his government collapsed and Paul Reynaud took over, Daladier became War Minister in the new government.

French National Wartime Defence Organisation

General direction of the war	President Council of Ministers
Military direction of the war	War Committee C-in-C Armed Forces
Conduct of military operations	C-in-C Air Force C-in-C Army C-in-C Navy

The senior French military headquarters was the *Grand Quartier General* (GQG), commanded by Gen Maurice Gamelin, Chief of the General Staff of National Defence and Supreme Commander of all French land forces. Gamelin gave orders direct to all the armies in France (North-East and Alps), and abroad (Syria and North Africa). GQG was located at the Chateau de Vincennes on the eastern outskirts of Paris. It was divided into various staff *Bureaux* (eg *Deuxième:* Intelligence; *Troisième:* Operations; *Quatrième:* Transport and Supply).

Ground. Gamelin, as Supreme Commander, had a deputy, Gen Joseph Georges, who initially held the post of *Maj-Gen des Armées*. All orders to the ground troops on the North-East Front came through him. When it became clear that Gamelin could not effectively command the North-East armies and control overall French war strategy from one HQ, a separate HQ was formed to command the North-East Front, with Georges as C-in-C. This was located at La Ferté sous Jouarre, some forty miles east of Paris. At the same time, in early January 1940, a third HQ was established, GHQ Land Forces, under Gen Aimé Doumenec at Montry, roughly halfway between the others. This was not a sensible move as Alistair Horne comments in *To lose a Battle*: 'The new HQ, whose function was to prepare and elaborate orders, was created by fission chiefly from elements of Gen Georges's staff, and this breaking up of offices that had been working well together for several months had particularly lamentable effects.'

The Fusil Mitrailleur Mle 1924/29 *light machine gun was based on the Browning Automatic Rifle. One of the best of the French LMGs, it was unusual in that it had two triggers – one in the front for single rounds and the rear trigger for automatic fire.* TM

Sea. The French Navy was commanded by Admiral Jean Francois Darlan. The bulk of the French fleet (see below) were either located in the Mediterranean or operating in the North Atlantic out of Brest.

Air. The Chief of the Air Staff was Gen Joseph Vuillemin, an elderly ex-bomber pilot who had no new ideas on the handling of air power. His HQ was at Coulommiers, outside Paris. Under him came the OC of the Air Co-operation Forces (Gen Tetu) whose task it was to co-ordinate air activities with the Army's North-East Front HQ. The front was divided into zones of air operations. It is true to say that on the whole *L'Armée de l'Air* lacked any real driving force capable of clarifying doctrine or deciding what type and number of aircraft were needed to defend France. 'From this welter of confusion emerged an air force that was impossible to support logistically, that lacked the necessary mass of trained personnel, modern aircraft and ground organisation necessary to conduct sustained operations; and that had only an imperfect concept as to the role of airpower in modern war.'[1]

The French Army

'The French army is stronger than at any other moment in its history; it has top-grade equipment, first-class fortifications, excellent morale and a remarkable High Command. No one in this country wants war; but if we are compelled to achieve another victory, achieve it we shall.' So wrote one of France's most eminent military leaders just a few weeks before Germany invaded Poland. These reassuring words were patently untrue, as Paul Reynaud had pointed out a year earlier when he said: 'Just think! Since the armistice (of 1918) we have spent 372,000,000,000 francs – more than any other country. Yet today we find ourselves lagging behind in every field where there is genuine military rivalry: planes, AA, tanks. Why?

FRENCH DIVISION d'INFANTERIE (DI)

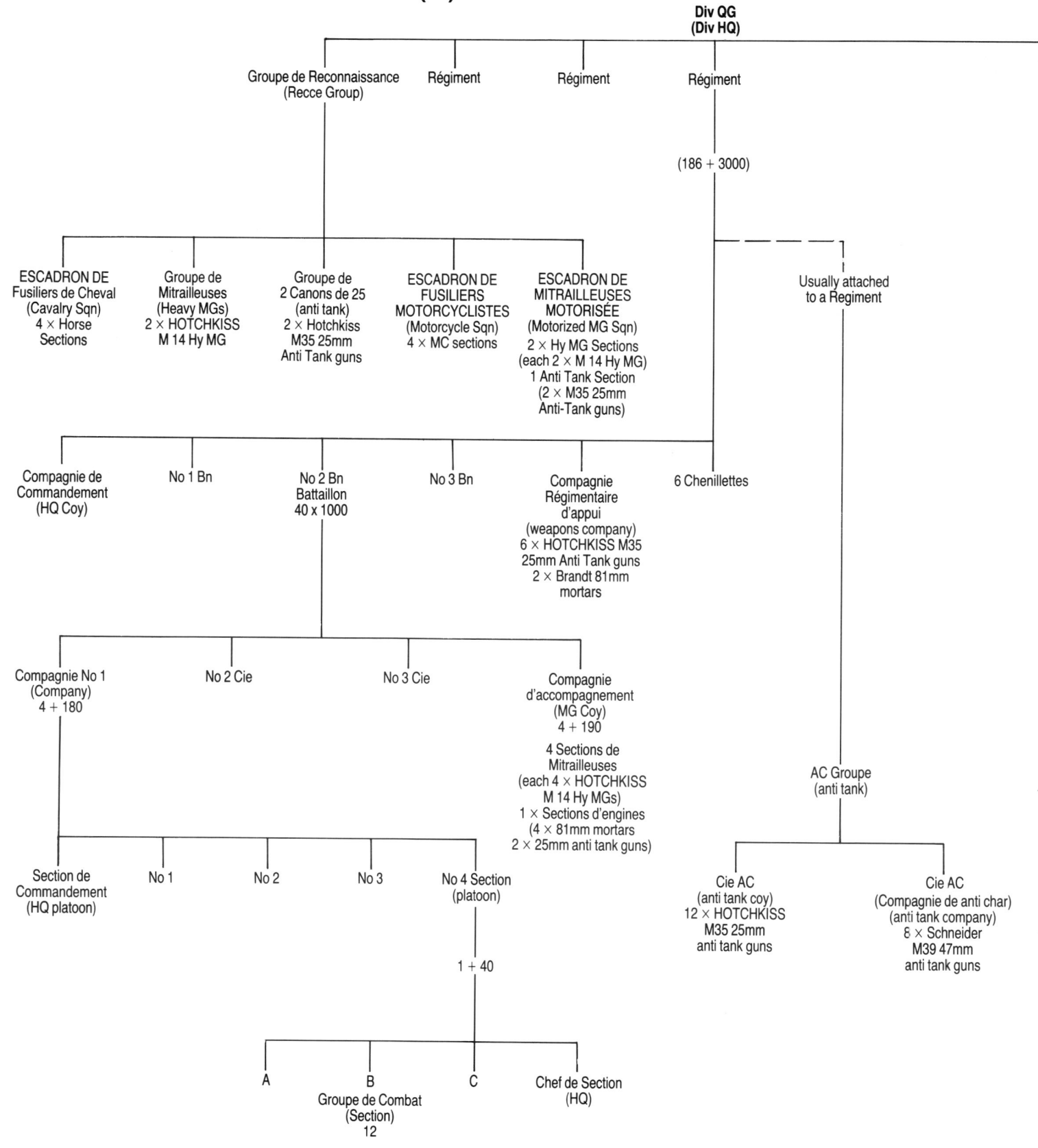

- **Div QG (Div HQ)**
  - **Groupe de Reconnaissance (Recce Group)**
    - ESCADRON DE Fusiliers de Cheval (Cavalry Sqn) — 4 × Horse Sections
    - Groupe de Mitrailleuses (Heavy MGs) — 2 × HOTCHKISS M 14 Hy MG
    - Groupe de 2 Canons de 25 (anti tank) — 2 × Hotchkiss M35 25mm Anti Tank guns
    - ESCADRON DE FUSILIERS MOTORCYCLISTES (Motorcycle Sqn) — 4 × MC sections
    - ESCADRON DE MITRAILLEUSES MOTORISÉE (Motorized MG Sqn) — 2 × Hy MG Sections (each 2 × M 14 Hy MG); 1 Anti Tank Section (2 × M35 25mm Anti-Tank guns)
  - **Régiment**
  - **Régiment**
  - **Régiment** (186 + 3000)
    - Compagnie de Commandement (HQ Coy)
    - No 1 Bn
    - No 2 Bn Battaillon — 40 x 1000
      - Compagnie No 1 (Company) — 4 + 180
        - Section de Commandement (HQ platoon)
        - No 1
        - No 2
        - No 3
        - No 4 Section (platoon) — 1 + 40
          - A
          - B — Groupe de Combat (Section) 12
          - C
          - Chef de Section (HQ)
      - No 2 Cie
      - No 3 Cie
      - Compagnie d'accompagnement (MG Coy) — 4 + 190
        - 4 Sections de Mitrailleuses (each 4 × HOTCHKISS M 14 Hy MGs)
        - 1 × Sections d'engines (4 × 81mm mortars, 2 × 25mm anti tank guns)
    - No 3 Bn
    - Compagnie Régimentaire d'appui (weapons company) — 6 × HOTCHKISS M35 25mm Anti Tank guns; 2 × Brandt 81mm mortars
    - 6 Chenillettes
  - Usually attached to a Regiment:
    - **AC Groupe (anti tank)**
      - Cie AC (anti tank coy) — 12 × HOTCHKISS M35 25mm anti tank guns
      - Cie AC (Compagnie de anti char) (anti tank company) — 8 × Schneider M39 47mm anti tank guns

66

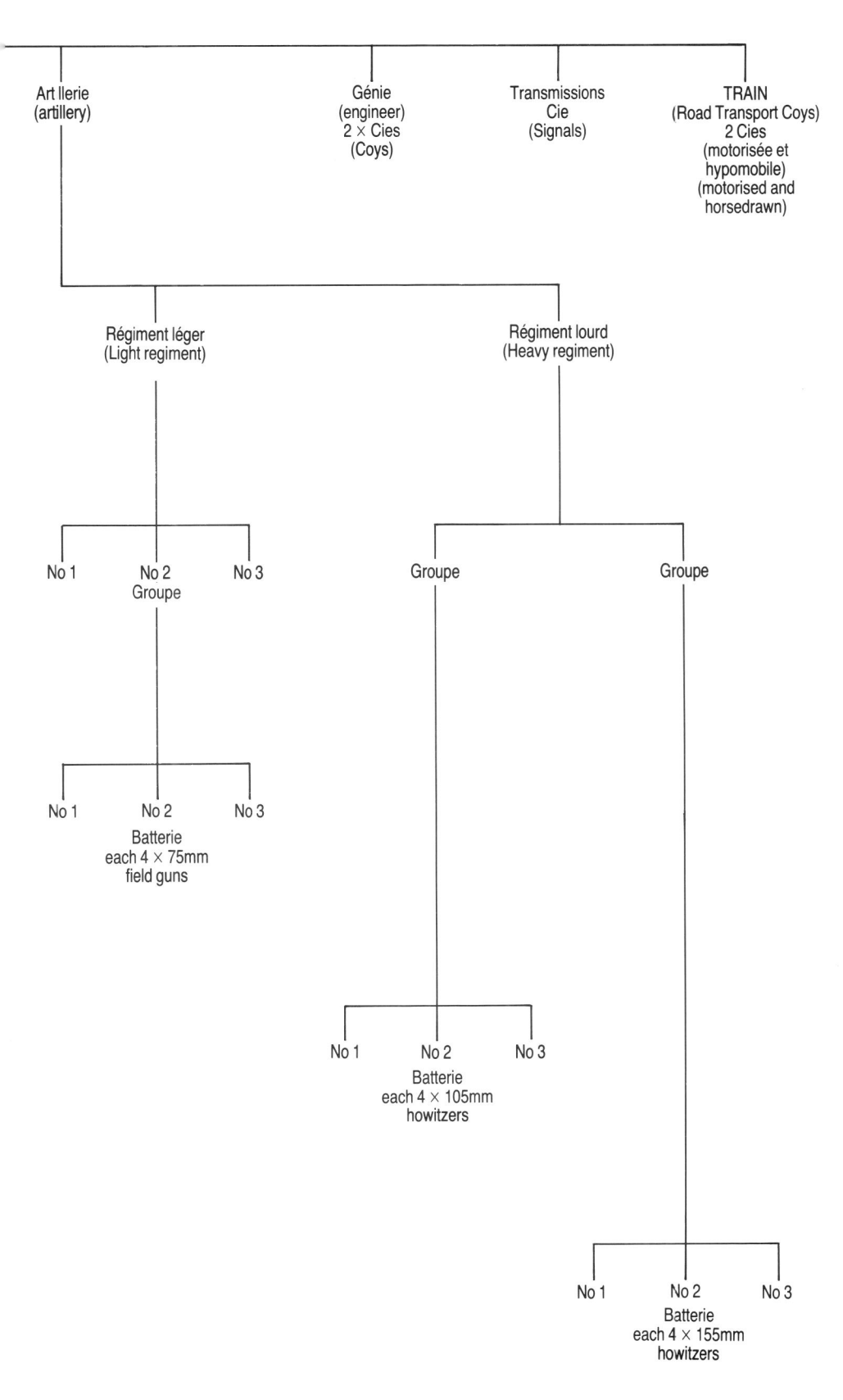

```
Artillerie          Génie           Transmissions      TRAIN
(artillery)        (engineer)            Cie        (Road Transport Coys)
                   2 × Cies          (Signals)         2 Cies
                    (Coys)                        (motorisée et
                                                   hypomobile)
                                                  (motorised and
                                                   horsedrawn)
```

```
     Régiment léger                    Régiment lourd
     (Light regiment)                  (Heavy regiment)

      |                                 |           |
    Groupe                            Groupe      Groupe

   |    |    |                        |    |    |
 No 1 No 2 No 3                     No 1 No 2 No 3
      Groupe
                                         Batterie
   |    |    |                          each 4 × 105mm
 No 1 No 2 No 3                          howitzers
      Batterie
     each 4 × 75mm                              |    |    |
      field guns                             No 1 No 2 No 3
                                                Batterie
                                               each 4 × 155mm
                                                howitzers
```

Because we have rashly pursued a policy of pure defence and of maintaining out-of-date equipment.'[2]

Between the wars, the French Army had 20 infantry divisions, 5 cavalry divisions and 5 tank brigades stationed in eighteen military areas in France, while overseas she maintained garrisons in North, West and East Africa, Madagascar and Indo-China. The North African element included five regiments of the famous French Foreign Legion.

As Europe began to rearm in the mid-thirties, the French followed suit, leading the field in mechanisation, especially as far as numbers of tanks were concerned. So much has been written about French armour and its poor showing in 1940 that it is not easy to separate fact from fiction or to arrive at true figures. One thing is very clear: while the French undoubtedly had more, better armed and better armoured tanks than the Germans, their tactical use of these AFVs was so old-fashioned as to negate this superiority.

At the time of the Munich crisis, the French Army comprised 84 divisions: 68 infantry, 2 light mechanised, 3 horsed cavalry and eleven fortress divisions. There were plenty of tanks in this force although most of them were spread in 'penny packets' within the infantry divisions. By May 1940 these figures had grown to the following:

82 infantry divisions (*Division d'Infanterie*)

7 motorised infantry divisions (*Division Infanterie Mécanique*)

13 fortress divisions (*Division d'Infanterie de Fortress*)

3 tank divisions (*Division Cuirassée*)

3 light mechanised divisions (*Division Légère Mécanique*)

5 light cavalry divisions (*Division Légère de Cavalerie*)

Before looking in detail at the various divisional organisations, a word about French armour. While there were only three French tank divisions facing the enemy on the Franco-German frontier in May 1940, they formed only one-fifth of the actual number of tanks ready for action. These tanks, were not old First World War leftovers, but rather modern, sophisticated armoured fighting vehicles.

FRENCH DIVISION Cuirassee Rapide (DCR) (Armoured Division)

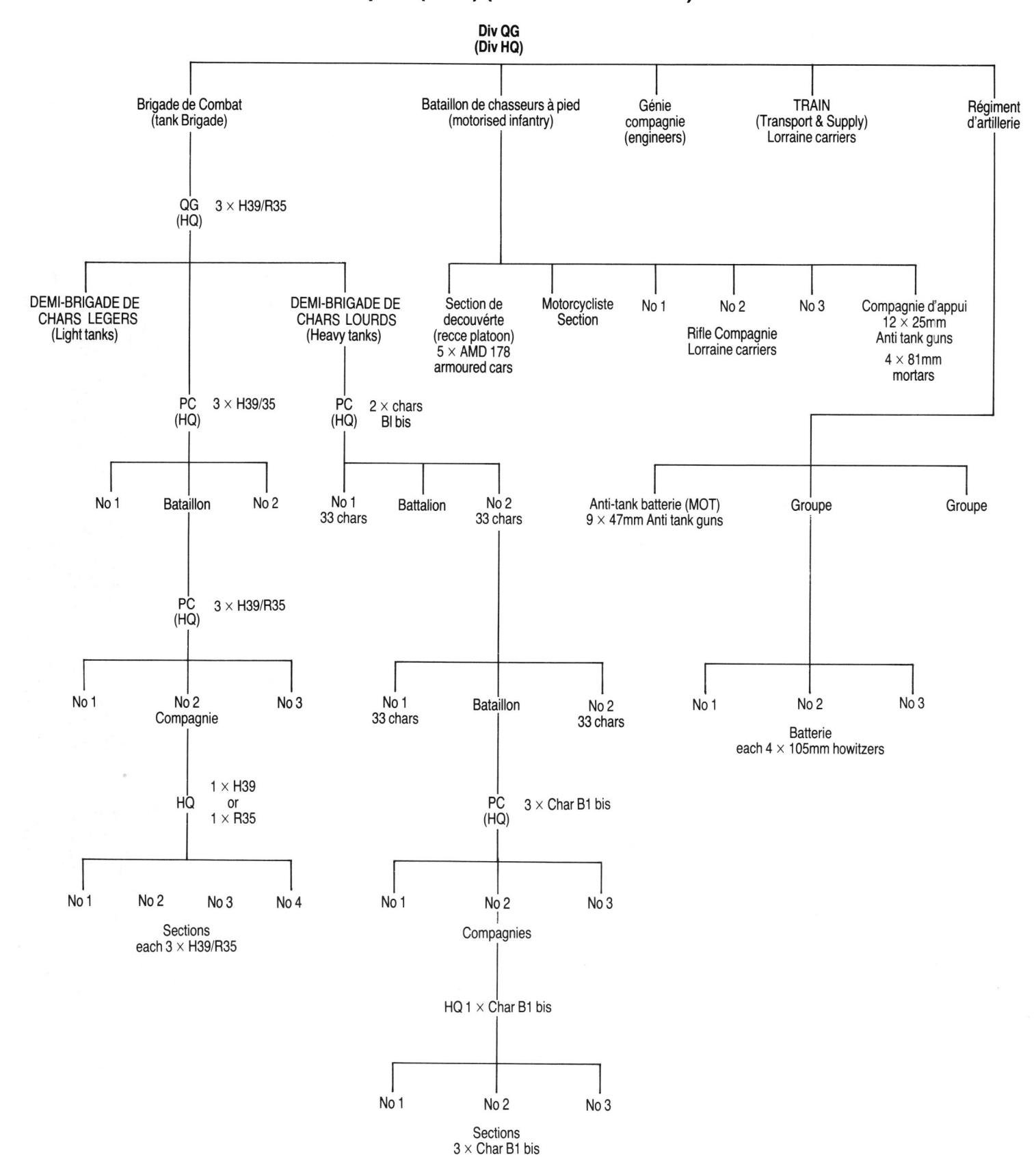

```
                                    Div QG
                                    (Div HQ)
    ┌───────────────┬───────────────────┬───────────────┬───────────────┬───────────────┐
Brigade de Combat   Bataillon de chasseurs à pied   Génie         TRAIN           Régiment
(tank Brigade)      (motorised infantry)            compagnie     (Transport      d'artillerie
                                                    (engineers)   & Supply)
                                                                  Lorraine carriers

    QG    3 × H39/R35
    (HQ)
    │
    ├──────────────────────┐                ┌──────────┬──────────┬──────────┬──────────┐
DEMI-BRIGADE DE      DEMI-BRIGADE DE    Section de    Motorcycliste  No 1      No 2      No 3    Compagnie d'appui
CHARS LEGERS         CHARS LOURDS       decouvérte    Section                                    12 × 25mm
(Light tanks)        (Heavy tanks)      (recce platoon)              Rifle Compagnie             Anti tank guns
                                        5 × AMD 178                  Lorraine carriers           4 × 81mm
                                        armoured cars                                            mortars

PC    3 × H39/35    PC    2 × chars
(HQ)                (HQ)  B1 bis
│                   │
├───────┬─────┐     ├──────────┬──────────┐    Anti-tank batterie (MOT)    Groupe          Groupe
No 1   Bataillon  No 2     No 1   Battalion  No 2    9 × 47mm Anti tank guns
                           33 chars          33 chars

PC    3 × H39/R35
(HQ)
│
├──────┬──────┐                    ┌──────┬──────────┬──────┐          ┌──────┬──────┐
No 1   No 2   No 3                 No 1   Bataillon   No 2           No 1   No 2   No 3
       Compagnie                   33 chars           33 chars                Batterie
                                                                              each 4 × 105mm howitzers

HQ   1 × H39                       PC    3 × Char B1 bis
     or                            (HQ)
     1 × R35                       │
│                                  ├──────┬──────┐
├──────┬──────┬──────┐             No 1   No 2   No 3
No 1  No 2   No 3   No 4                  Compagnies
      Sections
      each 3 × H39/R35              HQ 1 × Char B1 bis
                                    │
                                    ├──────┬──────┐
                                    No 1   No 2   No 3
                                           Sections
                                           3 × Char B1 bis
```

68

Twin 13.2mm Mitrailleuse Hotchkiss d 13mm 2 Mle 1930 *mounted on the back of a 1932 Berliet truck, with a sighting device alongside. Separate foot pedals were used to fire each of the guns, which were not really effective as anti-aircraft weapons at heights above 5,000m.* TM

The standard light anti-tank gun in the French Army was the 34 SA or, to give it its full title, the canon léger de 25 antichar SA-L Mle 1934, L/72. *It had a limited range of 1,800m and its small shell could penetrate only the lightest of armour. The British Army was issued with some of these weapons in 1939.* TM

FRENCH DIVISION LÉGÈRE MÉCANIQUE (DLM)

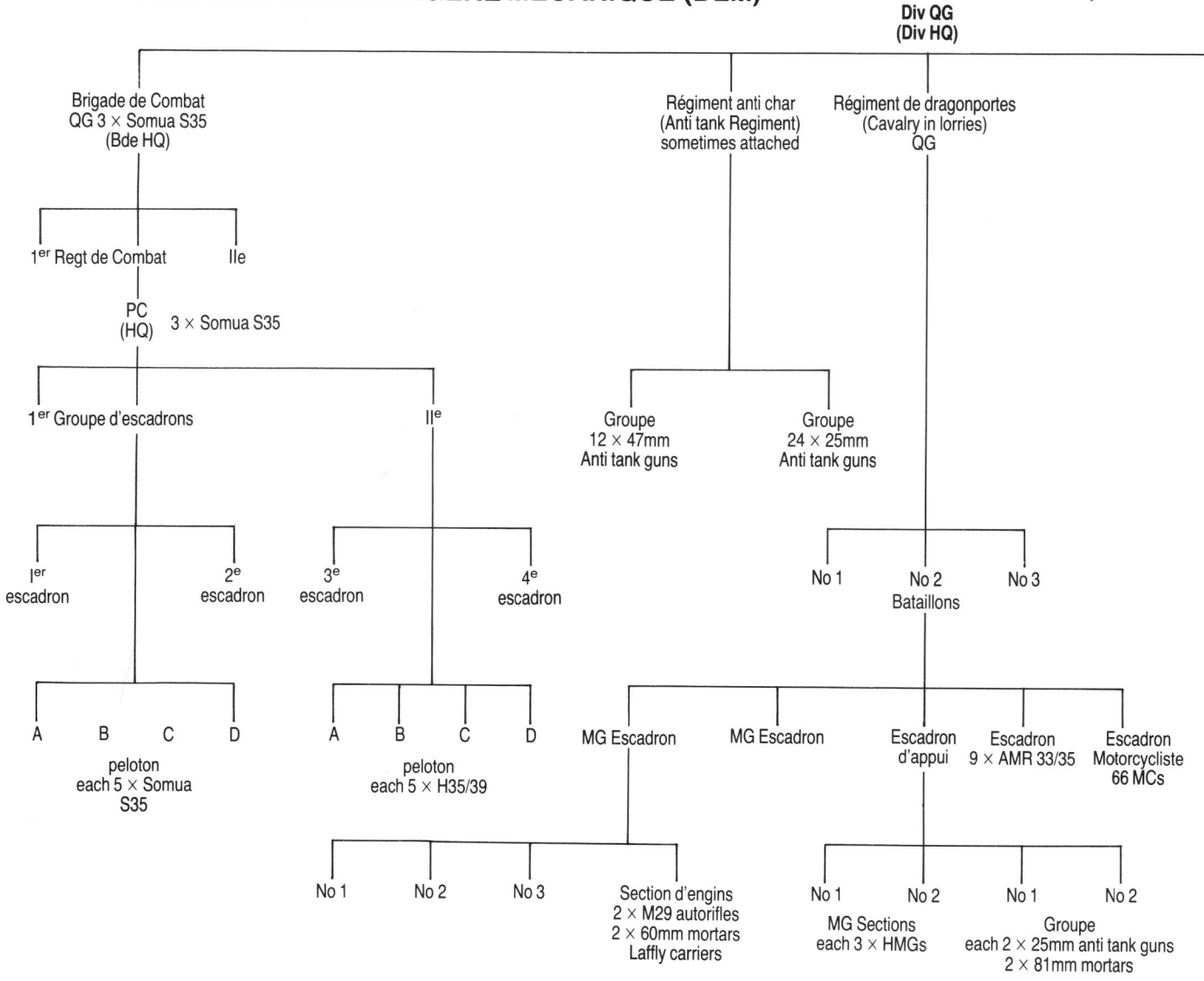

```
                                                                    Div QG
                                                                   (Div HQ)
        │                              │                    │            │
  Brigade de Combat              Régiment anti char    Régiment de dragonportes
  QG 3 × Somua S35               (Anti tank Regiment)  (Cavalry in lorries)
     (Bde HQ)                    sometimes attached         QG
        │                              │                    │
   ┌────┴────┐                    ┌────┴────┐
1er Regt de Combat  IIe         Groupe     Groupe
                               12 × 47mm   24 × 25mm
        │                      Anti tank   Anti tank
       PC     3 × Somua S35      guns        guns
      (HQ)                        │            │
        │                    ┌────┼────┐
   ┌────┴────┐              No 1  No 2  No 3
1er Groupe           IIe         Bataillons
d'escadrons
   │                    │
┌──┴──┐              ┌──┴──┐
1er   2e             3e    4e
escadron escadron    escadron escadron
   │                    │
┌─┬┴┬─┐              ┌─┬┴┬─┐
A B C D              A B C D
peloton              peloton
each 5 × Somua       each 5 × H35/39
   S35
```

- peloton each 5 × Somua S35
- peloton each 5 × H35/39

No 1, No 2, No 3 | MG Escadron | MG Escadron | Escadron d'appui | Escadron 9 × AMR 33/35 | Escadron Motorcycliste 66 MCs

Section d'engins
2 × M29 autorifles
2 × 60mm mortars
Laffly carriers

No 1 No 2 — MG Sections each 3 × HMGs
No 1 No 2 — Groupe each 2 × 25mm anti tank guns 2 × 81mm mortars

Basic French Divisions

Division d'infanterie. The basic infantry division consisted of three infantry regiments, each of a weapons company and three infantry battalions, plus a *Groupe de Reconnaissance de division d'infanterie*, an anti-tank group which was normally attached to one of the infantry regiments, two field artillery regiments (one heavy, one light), two engineer companies, a signal company, plus service and support.

Division de cavalerie. The three existing cavalry divisions were disbanded during the winter of 1939-40, and all but the 1st Cavalry Brigade were transferred to the new *Division Légère de Cavalerie* and partly mechanised.

Division Légère de Cavalerie. The DLC still contained a complete horsed brigade of two cavalry regiments, plus a *régiment de automitrailleuses* (RAM) containing a recce group (of one armoured car sqn of Panhard AMD 178, plus a motorcycle sqn (66 MCs)), and a combat group (of one light tank sqn of 13 Hotchkiss H35

French armour available May 1940

Formation	No	Type of tank	No available	Comment
Armoured Divisions (DCR)	3	Char B1/B1bis	198	4e DCR formed
		Hotchkiss H39/40	270	during May '40
Light Mech Divisions (DLM)	3	Somua S35	261	4th lt mech div
		Hotchkiss H35/H39	321	not yet formed
Light Cav Divisions (DLC)	5	Hotchkiss H35/H39	110	
Non-divisional tank battalions	25	Renault R35 (20bns)	900	
		Hotchkiss H35 (2bns)	90	
		FCM 36 (2bns)	90	
		Char D (1bn)	45	
		Total number of tanks available = 2,285		

70

Organization chart

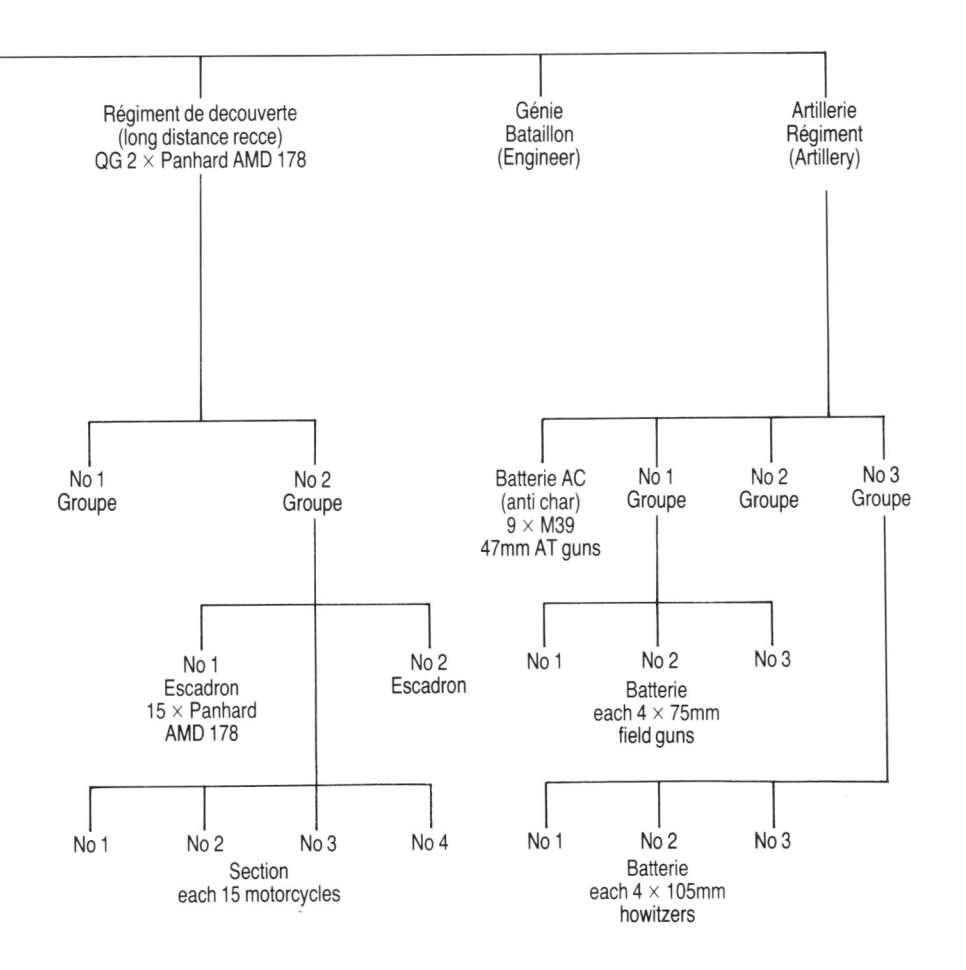

```
                    ┌──────────────────────┬──────────────────────┬──────────────────────┐
            Régiment de decouverte      Génie                 Artillerie
            (long distance recce)      Bataillon              Régiment
            QG 2 × Panhard AMD 178    (Engineer)             (Artillery)
                    │                                             │
         ┌──────────┴──────────┐            ┌──────────┬──────────┼──────────┐
       No 1                  No 2      Batterie AC   No 1       No 2       No 3
      Groupe                Groupe     (anti char)  Groupe     Groupe     Groupe
         │                                9 × M39
                                        47mm AT guns
   ┌─────┴─────┐                                    ┌──────────┬──────────┐
  No 1        No 2                                No 1       No 2       No 3
Escadron    Escadron                                         Batterie
15 × Panhard                                              each 4 × 75mm
  AMD 178                                                   field guns
   │                                                 ┌──────────┬──────────┐
┌──┬──┬──┐                                         No 1       No 2       No 3
No 1 No 2 No 3 No 4                                           Batterie
  Section                                                 each 4 × 105mm
each 15 motorcycles                                         howitzers
```

Main French tanks in service, May 1940

Type and Name	Date entered service	Weight (tons)	Crew	Main armament	Armour thickness (mm)	Speed (mph)	Range (mls)
Renault AMR 33	1933	6	2	1 x MG	Max 13 Min 5	31	125
Renault AMR 35	1935	6.5	2	1 x MG	Max 13 Min 5	34	125
Hotchkiss H35	1935	11.4	2	1 x 37mm	Max 34 Min 12	18	81
Hotchkiss H39	1939	12	2	1 x 37mm	Max 45 Min 12	22.5	94
Somua S35	1936	20	3	1 x 47mm	Max 55 Min 20	25	160
Char B1bis	1936	32	4	1 x 75mm how 1 x 47mm	Max 60 Min 14	17.5	87

and 23 MCs, plus a motorcycle sqn of 66 MCs), a battalion of *dragons portes* (one *automitrailleuse* sqn of nine Renault AMR 33, a rifle sqn, and a weapons sqn of 16 heavy MG, 4 x 81mm mortars and 2 x 25mm anti-tank guns), an anti-tank battery of 8 x 47mm, two artillery regiments (one light and one heavy) and an engineer company.

Division Légère Mécanique. The DLM comprised a tank brigade of two tank regiments (each of some 87 tanks divided equally between a light tank sqn of H35/H39 and a medium tank sqn of Somua S35), a motorised rifle brigade, a recce regiment, a towed artillery regiment, an engineer battalion and normal supporting units. The DLM's role was strategic reconnaissance and security.

Division Cuirassée. A DCR comprised two *demi-brigade de chars*, one of two light tank battalions of Hotchkiss H39s and the other of two heavy tank battalions of Char B1bis, a motorised infantry battalion of *chasseurs à pied* with three rifle companies (carried in Lorraine carriers) and a weapons company, an artillery regiment and an engineer company. 4e DCR had a much heavier *ad hoc* establishment when it was formed.

The French thus produced two different types of armoured division (cf German Panzer and *Leichte* divisions), although neither were capable of effective armoured action except within its highly specialised role. The DLM was well equipped to carry out recce on a wide front but lacked any real offensive power while the DCR had plenty of offensive power but lacked a recce potential or the capability for rapid independent movement.

Renault R35 *light tanks lead a column of marching infantry in mountainous country. The* R35, *which appeared in 1935, replaced all the earlier FT models built during the First World War, and became the standard French light tank. It weighed nearly 10 tons, and its main armament was a 37mm gun.*

Hotchkiss also built light tanks very similar in appearance, but because they could travel about 5mph faster than the Renault they were used as char de cavalerie. *It is interesting to note that both these models were better armoured and better armed than the German Pz Kpfw I and II.* TM

The Canon de 75 Mle 1897, *first produced by Schneider in 1897, was used by many countries as well as France and was still in service at the start of the Second World War. Later models were fitted with pneumatic tyres replacing the original wooden spoked wheels.* TM

This White-Laffy Automitrailleuse de Découverte AMD *of 1932 was one of a number of the original 1918 models that had been rebuilt and were still in service in 1940. There were about 230 such vehicles altogether: the side-mounted Hotchkiss MMG was for anti-aircraft use. The standard motor cycle and sidecar was widely used by the French Army for reconnaissance and communications work.*
TM

The French Char B1 *heavy tank was one of the most formidable tanks in the world in 1939. Weighing 35 tons, it carried a 75mm non-traversing gun in the hull, to the right of the driver, while the turret armament consisted of a 37mm gun (47mm in the* B1 bis*) together with a coax MG.* TM

The French Navy

Traditionally France has never been a strong maritime power, probably because throughout her history she has been engaged in a series of continental wars. She finished the First World War with a small number of worn out, obsolete vessels – a handful of dreadnoughts, some unimpressive cruisers and an outdated torpedo fleet. Although the French Navy received only 20% of the annual defence budget during the inter-war years, being out of the public eye – compared, for example, with the French Army – did have some advantages. For one thing the Navy did not have to depend on conscript sailors: the ships were manned by long term regulars or new volunteers. And for another, the authorities were able to get on quietly with the job of creating a small, but relatively modern fleet without too much outside interference.

But compared with the British or even the German Navy, it remained only a minor force, especially as so few vessels were ready for sea when the war began. For example, none of the new battleships (*Richelieu*, *Jean Bart*, *Clemenceau* and *Gascogne*) were ready, while the aircraft carrier *Bearn* was too slow to be used in a raiding group and had to be relegated to transport duty only. The new carrier *Joffre* was still only 25% complete in June 1940.

French naval strength 1939

Type of vessel	In commission	Under construction
Battleships	7	2
Aircraft carriers	2	1
Cruisers	19	—
Destroyers	71	8
Submarines	76	10

Source: *The Second World War: Europe & The Mediterranean.* T. E. Griess, Series editor (Dept of History, US Military Academy, West Point).

However, the French fleet did take on the major responsibility of looking after the western Mediterranean, so that the Royal Navy could be deployed elsewhere. The bulk of the French Navy were here – 3 battleships, a seaplane carrier, 10 cruisers, 48 destroyers and 53 submarines. In addition to this arrangement, the French Admiralty agreed to form and maintain a *Force de Raid* which comprised their two newest battleships (*Dunkerque* and *Strasbourg*), an aircraft carrier, 3 cruisers and 10 destroyers, all based on Brest. This force would operate against enemy raiders in the eastern Atlantic. Other small numbers of French naval vessels were operating in the Channel (7 destroyers), Bay of Biscay (3 large destroyers), South Atlantic (2 destroyers and 4 submarines) based on Morocco, and the Far East (2 cruisers, 5 or 6 destroyers and 2 submarines).[3]

Aeronavale. Attempts were also being made to modernise the French naval air arm when war came. Some modern carrier-borne bombers were in service but most of the remainder were outdated: replacements had been ordered from USA.

French Air Force

If the French Navy had been a neglected service then the French Air Force, which was only a little better funded, was certainly regarded as being of secondary importance to the Army. Unfortunately, by the time the authorities woke up to the need for more modern aircraft the war was already under way. New fighters were only just entering squadron service in May 1940, while France had gone to America to acquire new ground attack fighter-bombers (100 x Curtis Hawks). French air defence was very weak in the means of detecting enemy aircraft, short of anti-aircraft artillery and fighter-aircraft. In October 1939, they had only 549 fighters of which 131 were classed as *anciens*. The rest of the air force was just as badly off, with only 186 bombers, all of which were classed as *anciens* apart from 11; only 377 reconnaissance and observation aircraft of which 316 were *anciens*.[7] French weakness in the air led them to try to obtain more fighter aircraft from Britain and to advocate a policy of using all bombers to concentrate upon enemy military concentrations rather than bombing targets in Germany. The basic reason for this was to avoid retaliatory German attacks in view of their ill-preparedness to defend themselves against such a threat.

French battleships' specifications

Type	No built	Date built	Tonnage	Main armament	Speed	Armour
Battleships						
Courbet	2	1913-14	22,000	10 x 13.4in	20kts	10.5in
Provence (modernised 1933-36)	3	1915-16	23,000	10 x 13.4in	21kts	10.5in
Dunkerque	2	1937-38	26,000	8 x 13in	31kts	9.5in
Richelieu	2	1940	39,000	8 x 15in	33kts	13in

French Air Strength: May 1940

26	*Groupes de Chasse* (fighters)	700 planes
21	*Groupes de Bombardement* (bombers)	320 planes
5	*Groups de Bombardement d'Assaut* (light bombers)	80 planes
11	*Groupes de Reconnaissance*	170 planes
38	*Groupes Aeriens d'Observation*	420 planes
	Total	1,690 planes

French pilots were on the whole both experienced and well-trained.

French Aircraft

Type	First in service	Main armament	Max speed	Ceiling	Range
Morane-Sauliner MS 406 fighter	1939	1 x 20mm cannon 2 x MG in wings	300mph	30,850ft	500mls
Dewoitine D520 fighter	1940	1 x 20mm cannon 4 x MG in wings	330mph	36,090ft	775mls
(Best French fighter to reach squadrons before armistice)					
Potez 63 series light bomber	1938	1,323lb bombload	275mph	32,800ft	NK
Breguet 690-5 light attack bomber series	1939	880lb bombload 1 x 20mm cannon & 5 x MG	300mph	27,885ft	840mls
Farman F222/223 heavy bomber	1939	9,240lb bombload	250mph	26,250ft	1,490mls
Amiot 143 recce bomber	1935	1,764lb bombload	195mph	25,930ft	745mls
LeO 45 medium bomber	1938	4,440lb bombload	310mph	18,860ft	1,800mls

A French Amiot *five-seater reconnaissance bomber, with its remarkable view panels, dwarfs an RAF* Fairey *battle bomber in the background. The Amiot came into service in 1935, had an airspeed of just over 190mph and could carry 1,600kg of bombs, half of them inside the aircraft and the rest in external wing racks.* IWM

Of the 26 combat-ready fighter groups, 19 were equipped with Morane-Saulnier MS 406 *single-seater fighters. But French pilots found that they were too slow and poorly armed for effective combat in the air.* IWM

75

GREAT BRITAIN

Higher Command

The War Cabinet, which was set up by the Prime Minister, Mr Neville Chamberlain, met for the very first time on Sunday, 3 September 1939. It consisted of nine members: the Prime Minister, Chancellor of the Exchequer (Sir John Simon), Foreign Secretary (Viscount Halifax), Lord Privy Seal (Sir Samuel Hoare), Minister without Portfolio (Lord Hankey), Minister for the Co-ordination of Defence (Admiral of the Fleet Lord Chatfield), and the three Service Ministers – Mr Churchill (Admiralty), Mr Hore-Belisha (War Office) and Sir Kingsley Wood (Air). Other Ministers, officials and experts were invited to attend the War Cabinet from time to time, for the discussion of matters specially concerning them – in particular, Sir John Anderson (Home Secretary and Minister for Home Security) and Mr Anthony Eden (Secretary of State for the Dominions), were usually present, whilst the three Service Chiefs of Staff attended regularly for military business.

The Royal Navy

'Britain's Sure Shield' as the Senior Service was sometimes called, was undoubtedly the most important part of Britain's armed forces at the start of the Second World War. Its vital role in protecting Great Britain from blockade, and at the same time blockading the enemy, was essential to maintaining the very lifeblood of the country and the successful execution of the war. Wartime duties of the Royal Navy can be divided into three main groups:

- protection of the trade routes of the world's oceans;
- blockading the enemy's ports and coasts;
- defeating the enemy's fleet.

Bearing in mind the fact that the Navy had to operate by day and night over thousands of miles of ocean, the formidable nature of their duties can be well imagined.

Although the number of vessels had been reduced by various limitation treaties between the two World Wars, the Royal Navy in September 1939 was still the most powerful fleet in the world. In addition, Britain had excellent shipyard and dockyard facilities and adequate manpower (281,600 were serving in the RN as at 30 June 1940).

Naval supreme command. The supreme command of the Navy was vested in the Board of the Admiralty which had eleven members, of whom seven were naval officers, three were politicians and one was a civil servant.

The office of the Chief of Naval Staff was organised into seven divisions, responsible for: intelligence, plans, local defence, trade, operations, naval air, training and staff duties. These functions are self-explanatory except that 'plans' was not

Board of the Admiralty

Political Members	Naval Members	Permanent Member
First Lord*a	First Sea Lord*b (Chief of Naval Staff)	Permanent Secretary
Civil Lord	Second Sea Lord (Personnel)	
Financial Secretary	Third Sea Lord (Controller)	
	Fourth Sea Lord (Supplies and Transport)	
	Fifth Sea Lord (Air Services)	
	Deputy Chief of Naval Staff	
	Controller of Mercantile Shipbuilding	

*a First Lord at the outset of war was the Rt Hon Winston Churchill
*b First Sea Lord was Admiral of the Fleet Sir Dudley Pound

Source: *The War at Sea, Vol I* by Capt S. W. Roskill (HMSO, 1954).

concerned with the design of ships but with the planning of naval campaigns, while 'local defence' dealt with the protection of bases and harbours from enemy attacks, and 'trade' with the organisation of convoys and similar measures for the safety of merchant shipping.

Worldwide distribution
In September 1939 the Royal Navy served all round the world as well as in British waters. For example, a fleet of significant size was in the Mediterranean, another at the China Station, and others in the North and South Atlantic. Stations such as America and the West and East Indies were also manned, while the Royal Australian Navy, the Royal New Zealand Navy and the Royal Canadian Navy were all available to defend the Commonwealth. It was the Home Fleet, the Channel Force and the Humber Force who were to be concerned with the campaign in France. As well as these fleets, four naval shore commands were established – Portsmouth, the Nore (Chatham), the Western Approaches (Plymouth) and Rosyth – with responsibility for controlling coastal waters and for defending shipping entering home waters. Just before the war began, Orkneys & Shetlands Command was established, and in October 1939 Dover also became a separate command. During the campaign in France and the Low Countries the Nore, Portsmouth, Western Approaches and Dover were involved in guarding and carrying the British Expeditionary Force to France, in carrying out operations off Holland and Belgium and, finally, with the evacuation of our forces from Dunkirk and other French ports. The last of these operations was controlled from Dover.

The Fleet Air Arm
The Fleet Air Arm was established as a force, separate from the RAF, on 24 May 1939, to carry out reconnaissance for the fleet, extending the vision of the surface ships and thus enabling them to sight the enemy, then to shadow and maintain contact; to attack faster enemy ships trying to escape battle and thus enable them to be caught by our surface ships; to assist in protecting the fleet against submarine and air attacks, in particular the carriers themselves; spotting for the fleet during surface actions or shore bombardments.

Principal warships in commission, preparing for commission or building in September 1939

Type and name	No built	Displacement (tons)	Main armament	Max speed (knots)	Remarks
Battleships					
King George V class	5	35,000	10 x 14in guns	35	all building
Nelson class	2	33,900	9 x 16in guns	23	
Royal Sovereign class	5	29,150	8 x 15in guns	21	
Queen Elizabeth class	5	31,000	8 x 15in guns	24	3 modernised extensively
Battle cruisers					
Hood	1	42,100	8 x 15in guns	31	
Renown	1	32,000	6 x 15in guns	29	extensively modernised
Repulse	1	32,000	6 x 15in guns	29	
Aircraft carriers					
Illustrious class	6	23,000	35/40 or 50/55 aircraft carried	30	all building
Ark Royal	1	22,000	60 ac carried	31	
Courageous class	2	22,500	48 ac carried	30	converted to
Furious	1	22,450	33 ac carried	30	aircraft
Eagle	1	22,600	21 ac carried	24	carriers
Hermes	1	10,850	15 ac carried	25	

Additional vessels
34 heavy cruisers (including 9 building and 2 Australian)
42 light cruisers (including 10 building and 5 Australian)
6 anti-aircraft cruisers
5 minelayers (4 building)
184 destroyers (including 6 Canadian and 5 Australian)
69 submarines
Numerous escort vessels, patrol vessels, minesweepers, monitors and netlayers
Source: *The War at Sea, Vol I* by Capt S. W. Roskill (HMSO, 1954).

There were four aircraft types in service at the start of the war:
Fairey Swordfish – torpedo bomber/spotter/reconnaissance
Blackburn Skua – two-seater fighter/dive bomber
Blackburn Roc – two-seater fighter
Gloster Gladiator (sea version) – single-seater fighter.

(opposite)
The British battle-cruiser HMS Hood, commissioned in August 1920, was lost in May 1940 during the pursuit of the Bismark *and* Prinz Eugen.

From the Royal Yacht, His Majesty King George V reviews ships of the Home Fleet during the Silver Jubilee celebrations of 1935. IWM

77

The British Army
The Supreme Command of the Army was vested in the Army Council. Like the Board of the Admiralty it was composed of political, civil and military members, numbering seven in all.

The Army Council		
Political Members	Military Members	Civil Service Member
Secretary of State for War*a	Chief of the Imperial General Staff (CIGS)*b	Permanent Under-Secretary of State for War
Under-Secretary of State for War	Adjutant-General to the Forces	
Parliamentary and Financial Secretary	Quartermaster-General to the Forces	

*a Mr Leslie Hore-Belisha
*b Gen Sir Edmund Ironside

During a visit to the BEF General Georges inspects a 3in mortar detachment at Orchies. By 1939 this 3in mortar had replaced the 3.7in howitzer as the standard infantry support weapon. At a rate of five rounds a minute, it could fire a 10lb HE or smoke projectile up to 1,600yds or, with modified propellants, as far as 2,750yds if necessary. IWM

The British Expeditionary Force
Like the Navy, the Army was responsible for both Home defence and Empire defence. This was initially carried out by the Regular Army, until the men who were called up for wartime service under the National Service (Armed Forces) Act could be trained and sent out to join their units. In addition, Expeditionary Forces were formed as and when required – such as during the Crimean War and in the First World War. In March 1939 it was decided to increase the military strength of the Army by doubling the Territorial force and on 27 April conscription was introduced.

Before the Second World War it had been agreed that the British contribution to any Allied war effort would be restricted to naval and air forces so that we could avoid sending an expeditionary force to the Continent. This proposal was dropped in mid-1939, and Britain then undertook to provide a sizeable expeditionary force together with an air component. By the time of the declaration of war the size of this force was increased to over 160,000 men, all of whom were safely transported to France by 27 September 1939, without a single casualty.

The Commander-in-Chief of the BEF was Gen The Viscount Gort who commanded a force of three Corps, together with GHQ troops, Lines of Communication troops, plus the various reinforcements which arrived during May and June 1940. The outline organisation of the BEF in May 1940 is shown in this Table:

Outline organisation of British Expeditionary Force (as at 10 May 1940)

GHQ Troops

Royal Armoured Corps
1st Light Armoured Reconnaissance Brigade — each two
2nd Light Armoured Reconnaissance Brigade — regiments
1st Army Tank Brigade (4th and 7th RTR)
plus four cavalry regiments not brigaded.

Royal Artillery
Two RHA regiments, four field regts, eight medium regts, three heavy regts and thee super heavy regts
1st AA Brigade (three AA regts)
2nd AA Brigade (one AA and two LAA regts)
4th AA Brigade (one AA regt and one LAA bty)
5th Searchlight Brigade (two searchlight regts).

Royal Engineers
Five field coys, one field park, one army field survey and three chemical warfare companies
Thirty-eight general construction companies, two road construction, one excavator, four tunneling and one workshop and park company
One field survey depot and two water-boring sections.

Infantry
One infantry battalion   Seven pioneer battalions
Four machine gun battalions   One garrison battalion.

I Corps
1st Division (1st Guards Brigade, 2nd Brigade, 3rd Brigade, each three battalions)
2nd Division (4th, 5th and 6th Brigade each three bns)
48th (South Midland) Division (143rd, 144th and 145th Brigade each three bns)
(Each division had three field regiments and an anti-tank regiment, RA, three field companies and a field park company RE).

Corps troops
Two field regts, two medium regts, an LAA regt, an LAA bty and a survey regt, RA
Three field coys, a field park and a field survey coy RE
Three machine gun battalions.

II Corps
3rd Division (7th Guards Brigade, 8th and 9th Brigade)
4th Division (10th, 11th and 12th Brigade)
5th Division (13th and 17th Brigade) in GHQ reserve on 10th May
50th Division (150th, 151st and 25th Brigade)   (Divisional troops as for I Corps).

Corps troops
Two field regts, two medium regts, an LAA regt and a survey regt, RA
Three field coys, a field park and a field survey coy, RE   Three machine gun battalions.

III Corps
42nd (East Lancashire) Division (125th, 126th and 127th Brigade)
44th (Home Counties) Division (131st, 132nd and 133rd Brigade)   (Divisional troops as for I Corps).

Corps troops
One RHA and one field regt, two medium, one LAA and one survey regt, RA
Three field coys, a field park and a field survey coy, RE   Three machine gun battalions.

Other troops

Formation	Comprised
12th (Eastern) Division	35th, 36th and 37th Brigade
23rd (Northumberland) Division	69th and 70th Brigade
46th (North Midland & West Riding) Division	137th and 138th Brigade
51st (Highland) Division	152nd, 153rd and 154th Brigade
1st Armoured Division	2nd and 3rd Armoured Brigade
52nd (Lowland) Division	155th, 156th and 157th Brigade
20th Guards Brigade	
30th Brigade	

These troops served under a variety of higher formations, *viz*:

Formation	Task
12th Division	Lines of Communication, BEF
23rd Division	GHQ, BEF, II Corps, then II Corps
46th Division	L of C, BEF, then III Corps
51st Division	GHQ, BEF, then II Corps, II Corps, 3 French Army, CQG (French), 9 Fr Corps
1st Armd Division	GHQ, BEF, then 7th and 10th French Army
52nd Division	GHQ, BEF
20th Gds Brigade	defence of Boulogne
30th Brigade	defence of Calais

Source: *The War in France & Flanders 1939-1940*, Appendix I by Major F. L. Ellis (HMSO, 1953).

Organisations

Before looking at the basic organisations of the infantry and armoured divisions, it is as well to understand certain points about the units that made up the BEF.

Owing to shortages in 1940, not all units were fully up to strength or fully equipped. Manpower shortages in the Regular Army also meant that units contained a fair proportion of reservists, as some of those on home establishment were little more than cadres.

However, they were probably the most mechanised force the British Army had produced to that date. Although the infantry did, on occasions, have to march long distances, it is broadly true to say that the BEF was a mobile force.

Apart from unit vehicles, transport was provided by the Royal Army Service Corps (RASC). To quote from the official history:

> 'They carried troops and their equipment, they carried and distributed ammunition, stores, rations, petrol and mail; they provided transport alike in back areas and at the front for most every purpose, driving often under most difficult conditions and at times in danger. The Army could not have existed without them.'

The history goes on to praise the work of all the other Corps, making special mention of the work of the Royal Corps of Signals and the Royal Army Medical Corps.

GHQ Troops. The troops shown in this category were a 'pool' of troops at the disposal of GHQ. They were allocated to corps or other formations on a permanent or temporary basis, or used for special tasks. The light armoured reconnaissance brigades, for example, were usually employed as divisional cavalry, while most of the artillery shown was permanently allocated to corps and disposed to cover their fronts.

Armoured Division. The 1st Armoured Division was the *only* armoured division ready for despatch to France in May 1940. It never fought as a complete division. Armoured units in the BEF consisted of mechanised cavalry regiments or Royal Tank Regiment battalions. Cavalry were either armoured car regiments, divisional cavalry regiments or light tank regiments, while RTR battalions were either armoured regiments or army tank battalions.

BRITISH INFANTRY DIVISION

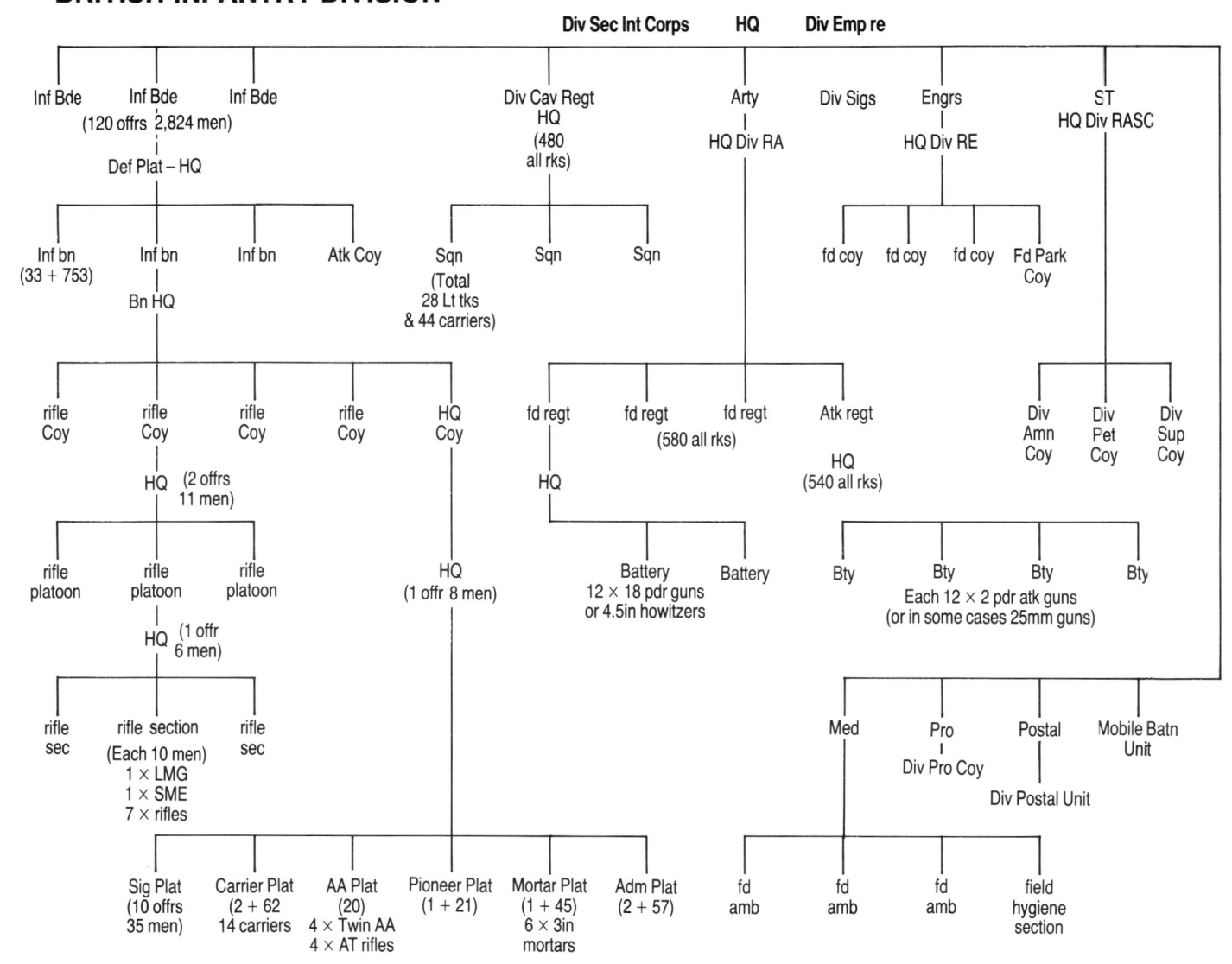

```
                                              Div Sec Int Corps    HQ      Div Emp re
                                                     |              |           |
  ┌──────────┬──────────┬──────────────────────┬─────┴──────┬──────┴──────┬──────────────┐
Inf Bde    Inf Bde    Inf Bde              Div Cav Regt   Arty        Div Sigs   Engrs         ST
        (120 offrs 2,824 men)                  HQ           |             |        |      HQ Div RASC
           Def Plat – HQ                     (480        HQ Div RA    HQ Div RE
                                            all rks)
  ┌────────┬────────┬─────────┐         ┌─────┬─────┬─────┐                ┌──────┬──────┬──────┐
Inf bn   Inf bn   Inf bn   Atk Coy     Sqn   Sqn   Sqn                  fd coy fd coy fd coy Fd Park
(33 + 753)  |                          (Total                                                   Coy
         Bn HQ                       28 Lt tks
                                    & 44 carriers)
  ┌──────┬──────┬──────┬──────┐            ┌──────┬──────┬──────┐            ┌──────┬──────┬──────┐
rifle  rifle  rifle  rifle   HQ          fd regt fd regt fd regt Atk regt    Div    Div    Div
 Coy    Coy    Coy    Coy   Coy                   (580 all rks)               Amn    Pet    Sup
         |                                    |                    |          Coy    Coy    Coy
        HQ  (2 offrs                          HQ                   HQ
            11 men)                                           (540 all rks)
  ┌──────┬──────┐                        ┌────────┬────────┐    ┌──────┬──────┬──────┬──────┐
rifle  rifle  rifle                   Battery   Battery         Bty    Bty    Bty    Bty
platoon platoon platoon               12 × 18 pdr guns         Each 12 × 2 pdr atk guns
         |                            or 4.5in howitzers       (or in some cases 25mm guns)
        HQ  (1 offr
        HQ (1 offr 8 men)
            6 men)
  ┌──────┬──────┐
rifle  rifle  rifle                                        ┌──────┬──────┬──────┬──────┐
 sec  section  sec                                        Med    Pro   Postal  Mobile Batn
      (Each 10 men)                                        |      |      |      Unit
      1 × LMG                                             fd    Div Pro Div Postal
      1 × SME                                             amb    Coy    Unit
      7 × rifles
                                                           ┌──────┬──────┬──────┐
                                                          fd    fd    fd    field
                                                          amb   amb   amb   hygiene
                                                                              section
  ┌──────┬──────┬──────┬──────┬──────┐
Sig Plat Carrier Plat AA Plat Pioneer Plat Mortar Plat Adm Plat
(10 offrs  (2 + 62   (20)     (1 + 21)    (1 + 45)   (2 + 57)
 35 men)  14 carriers 4 × Twin AA          6 × 3in
                      4 × AT rifles        mortars
```

TOTAL all ranks – 13,863

BRITISH ARMOURED DIVISION

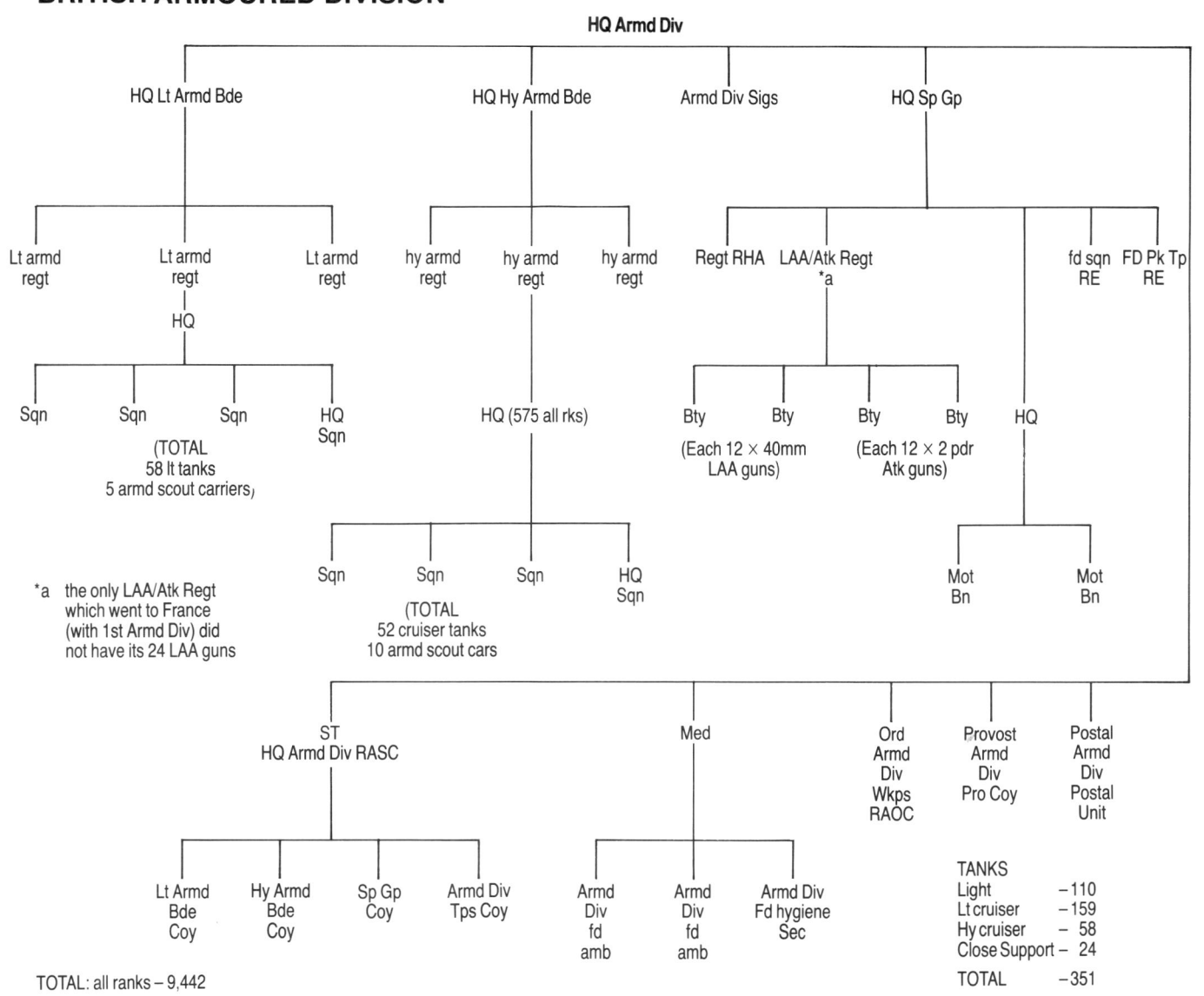

```
                                    HQ Armd Div
        ┌──────────────────┬──────────────┬──────────────┐
   HQ Lt Armd Bde     HQ Hy Armd Bde  Armd Div Sigs   HQ Sp Gp
        │                  │                              │
   ┌────┼────┐         ┌───┼───┐              ┌─────┬─────┼──────┬────┐
 Lt  Lt  Lt         hy   hy   hy          Regt RHA  LAA/Atk     fd sqn  FD Pk Tp
armd armd armd     armd armd armd                    Regt        RE      RE
regt regt regt     regt regt regt                    *a
      │                  │                    ┌────┬────┬────┐   │
      HQ                 │                   Bty  Bty  Bty  Bty  HQ
  ┌──┬──┬──┐         HQ (575 all rks)      (Each 12 × 40mm  (Each 12 × 2 pdr
 Sqn Sqn Sqn HQ                             LAA guns)        Atk guns)
             Sqn                                                  │
(TOTAL                                                         ┌──┴──┐
58 lt tanks                                                   Mot   Mot
5 armd scout carriers)                                        Bn    Bn
                        ┌──┬──┬──┐
*a the only LAA/Atk Regt Sqn Sqn Sqn HQ
   which went to France              Sqn
   (with 1st Armd Div) did       (TOTAL
   not have its 24 LAA guns      52 cruiser tanks
                                 10 armd scout cars
```

```
        ┌──────────────────┬──────────┬──────────┬──────────┐
       ST                 Med        Ord        Provost    Postal
   HQ Armd Div RASC                  Armd       Armd       Armd
                                     Div        Div        Div
                                     Wkps       Pro Coy    Postal
                                     RAOC                  Unit
   ┌────┬────┬────┐    ┌────┬────┬────┐
  Lt Armd Hy Armd Sp Gp Armd Div  Armd  Armd  Armd Div
  Bde Coy Bde Coy Coy   Tps Coy   Div   Div   Fd hygiene
                                  fd    fd    Sec
                                  amb   amb
```

TANKS
Light   – 110
Lt cruiser   – 159
Hy cruiser   – 58
Close Support – 24
TOTAL   – 351

TOTAL: all ranks – 9,442

Illustrations on the previous spread show a British gun crew in action at St Maxent during the German attack, manning a 25pdr Mark 1. This was the main equipment of field artillery regiments in 1939. Many of these guns were lost at Dunkirk and taken into German service. IWM

Below the Armoured Division Chart is an A 10 Cruiser Tank Mk IIA, also used by 1st Armoured Division in France. The A 9 was similar in appearance but was less well protected, with only 14mm armour compared with 30mm. TM

		Artillery	
Unit	Basic organisation	Type of weapon	Number held
Field Regiment	HQ and two btys 580 all rks	Armament varied – 18pdr 4.5 howitzer or converted 18/25pdrs	24
Medium Regiment	HQ and two btys 650 all rks	Armament either 6in howitzer or 60pdr guns	16
Heavy Regiment	HQ and four btys 700 all rks	Armament 6in guns plus 8in or 9.2in howitzers	4 12
Anti-tank Regiment	HQ and four btys 540 all rks	Armament 2pdr or 25mm guns	48
AA Regiment	HQ and 3/4 btys	Armament 3.7in AA guns	24/32
LAA Regiment	HQ and 3/4 btys	Armament 40mm Bofors	36/48

Infantry

There were three different types of infantry battalion in the BEF, the normal infantry battalion, the machine-gun battalion and the motor-cycle battalion. The normal infantry battalion had a total strength of some 780 all ranks, equipped with the short magazine Lee-Enfield .303 rifle (734 riflemen), 50 LMGs, two 3in mortars, twelve 2in mortars and 22 anti-tank rifles. The main equipment of the machine-gun battalion was the Vickers .303 heavy machine gun, belt-fed and tripod mounted, 48 in total, divided into four companies. The motor-cycle battalion comprised three motor-cycle companies, and was equipped with 11 scout cars, 99 motor-cycle combinations (with sidecar) and 43 motor-cycles.

The best tank in service with the BEF, commonly known as the Matilda II, was the A 12 Infantry Tank Mk II. With armour plating up to 78mm thick in places, it was a fighting vehicle that considerably impressed the German opposition. TM

Types of British tanks in service in the BEF

Type	Date of production	Weight tonnes	Crew	Main armament	Armour thickness (mm)	Max speed (mph)	Range (ml)
Light Mk VI, A to C	1936	4.8-5.24	3	1 x Heavy MG 1 x MG	14 Max 4 Min	35	130
Cruiser Mk I (A9)	1937	12.8	6	1 x 2pdr 3 x MG	14 Max 6 Min	25	150
Cruiser Mk II (A10) * 1 x 3.7in howitzer in close support model)	1938	14.15	5	1 x 2pdr* 2 x MG	30 Max 6 Min	16	100
Cruiser Mk III (A13)	1938	14	4	1 x 2pdr 1 x MG	14 Max 6 Min	30	90
Cruiser Mk IV (A13 Mk II) * 1 x 3.7 howitzer in CS model)	1939	14.75	4	1 x 2pdr* 1 x Hy MG 1 x MG	30 Max 6 Min	30	90
Infantry tank Mk I Matilda I (A11)	1937	11	2	1 x Heavy MG 1 x MG	60 Max 10 Min	8	80
Infantry tank Mk II Matilda II (A12)	1938	26.5	4	1 x 2pdr 1 x MG	78 Max 13 Min	15	160

The Vickers Light Mark VI was the standard British light tank when war broke out in 1939. The Mark VIA, shown here, was one of many variations to be found in divisional cavalry regiments and in the cavalry light tank regiments of 1st Armoured Division. TM

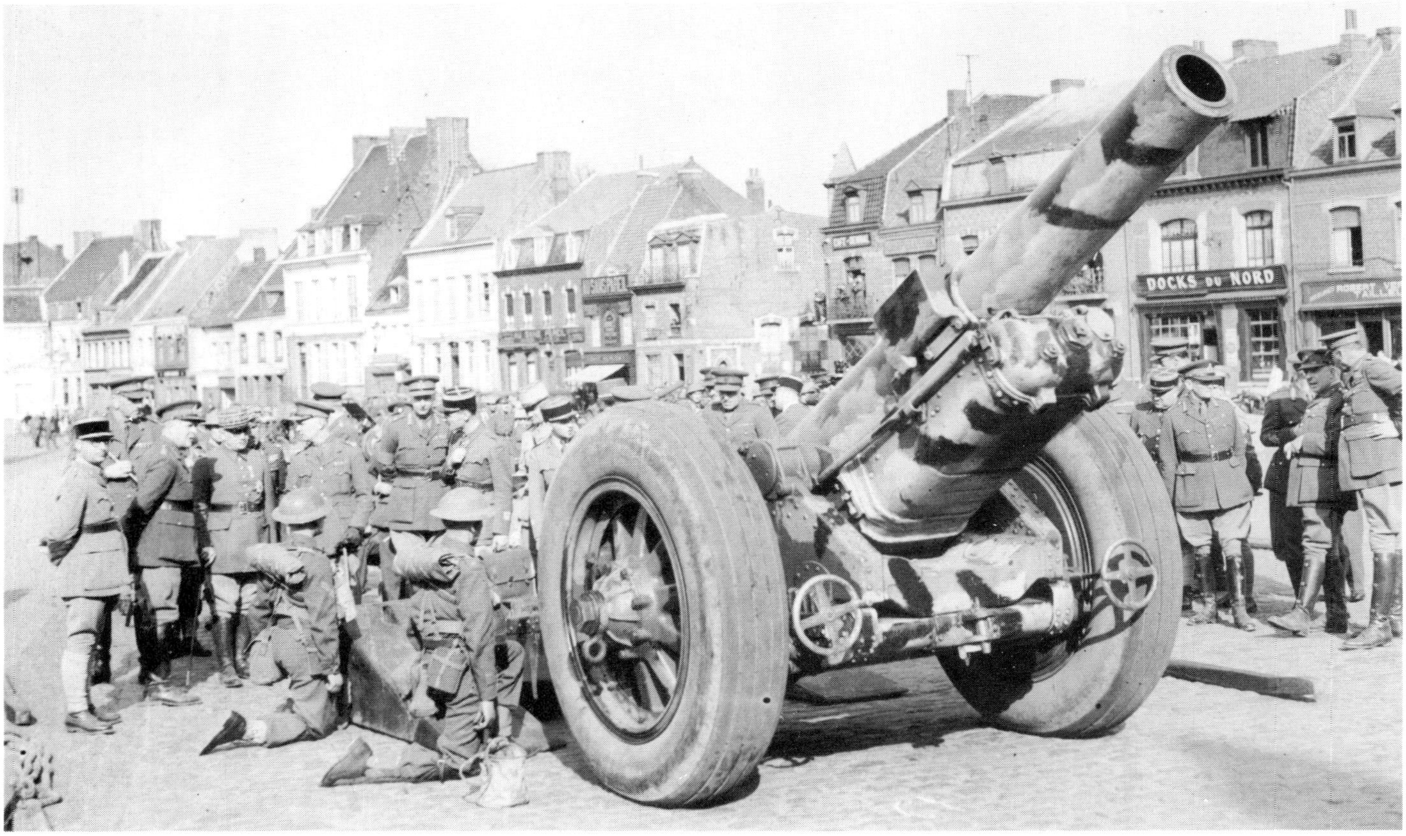
DOCKS DU NORD

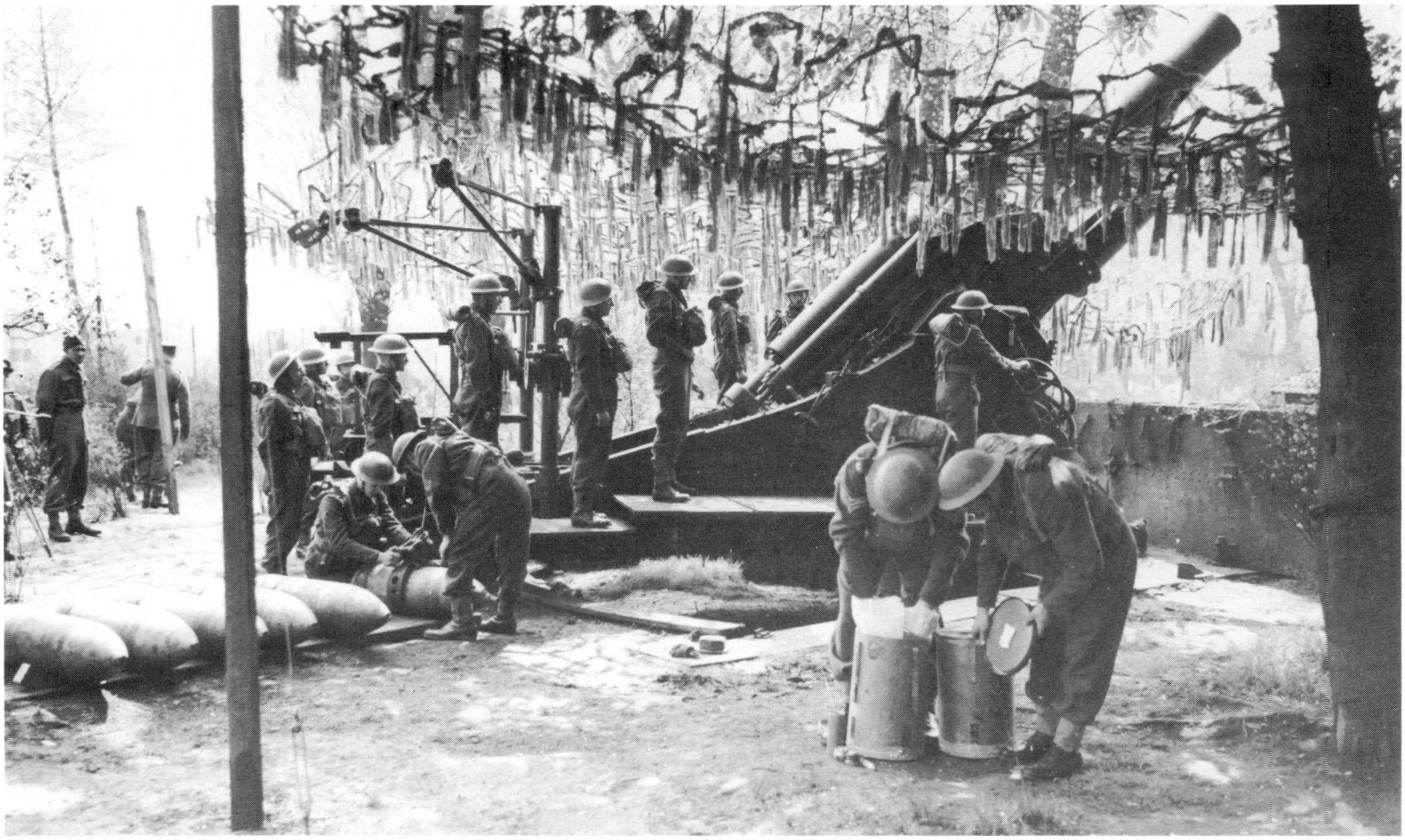

General Georges and Lord Gort inspect an 8in howitzer and its British crew. This powerful gun had a maximum range of 12,400yds and fired shells weighing 200lbs. All artillery in the BEF was tractor-drawn: no horses were used. IWM

One of the largest of all the BEF guns was this 12in howitzer near Lille. It weighed 47 tons, fired 750lb shells to a range of 14,000yds and belonged to 2nd Super Heavy Regiment of the Royal Artillery, attached to 2nd Corps. IWM

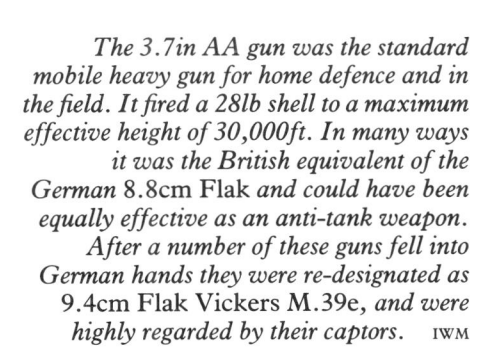

The 3.7in AA gun was the standard mobile heavy gun for home defence and in the field. It fired a 28lb shell to a maximum effective height of 30,000ft. In many ways it was the British equivalent of the German 8.8cm Flak and could have been equally effective as an anti-tank weapon.
After a number of these guns fell into German hands they were re-designated as 9.4cm Flak Vickers M.39e, and were highly regarded by their captors. IWM

The Air Council

Secretary of State for Air*a
Parliamentary Under-Secretary of State for Air
Chief of the Air Staff*b
Air Member for Personnel
Air Member for Supply and Organisation
Air Member for Training
Air Member for Development and Production
Permanent Under-Secretary of State for Air

*a Rt Hon Sir Samuel Hoare (until 10 May 1940, when Rt Hon Sir Archibald Sinclair took his place).
*b Marshal of the RAF Sir Cyril Newall (until 24 October 1940, when Air Chief Marshal Sir Charles Portal took his place).

The Royal Air Force

Compared with the Navy and Army, the Royal Air Force was a very young Service, celebrating its twenty-first birthday on 1 April 1939. The chief feature of its control was flexibility. It was headed by an Air Council composed of eight members, to whom additional members were added as required.

Below the Air Council was the Air Ministry, divided into four main departments (1) plans, operations, intelligence, signals, etc; (2) personnel; (3) development and production; (4) supply and organisation; and below it eight commands: fighter, bomber, coastal, army co-operation, balloon, flying training, maintenance and technical training.

British Air Forces in France

As with the Army we will concentrate upon those elements of the RAF involved in France. The plans took account of the need for two distinct formations:
- the Air Component, intended to supply reconnaissance and protection for the BEF,
- the Advanced Air Striking Force of Bomber Command, stationed in France so as to be nearer to Germany and the probable scene of operations.

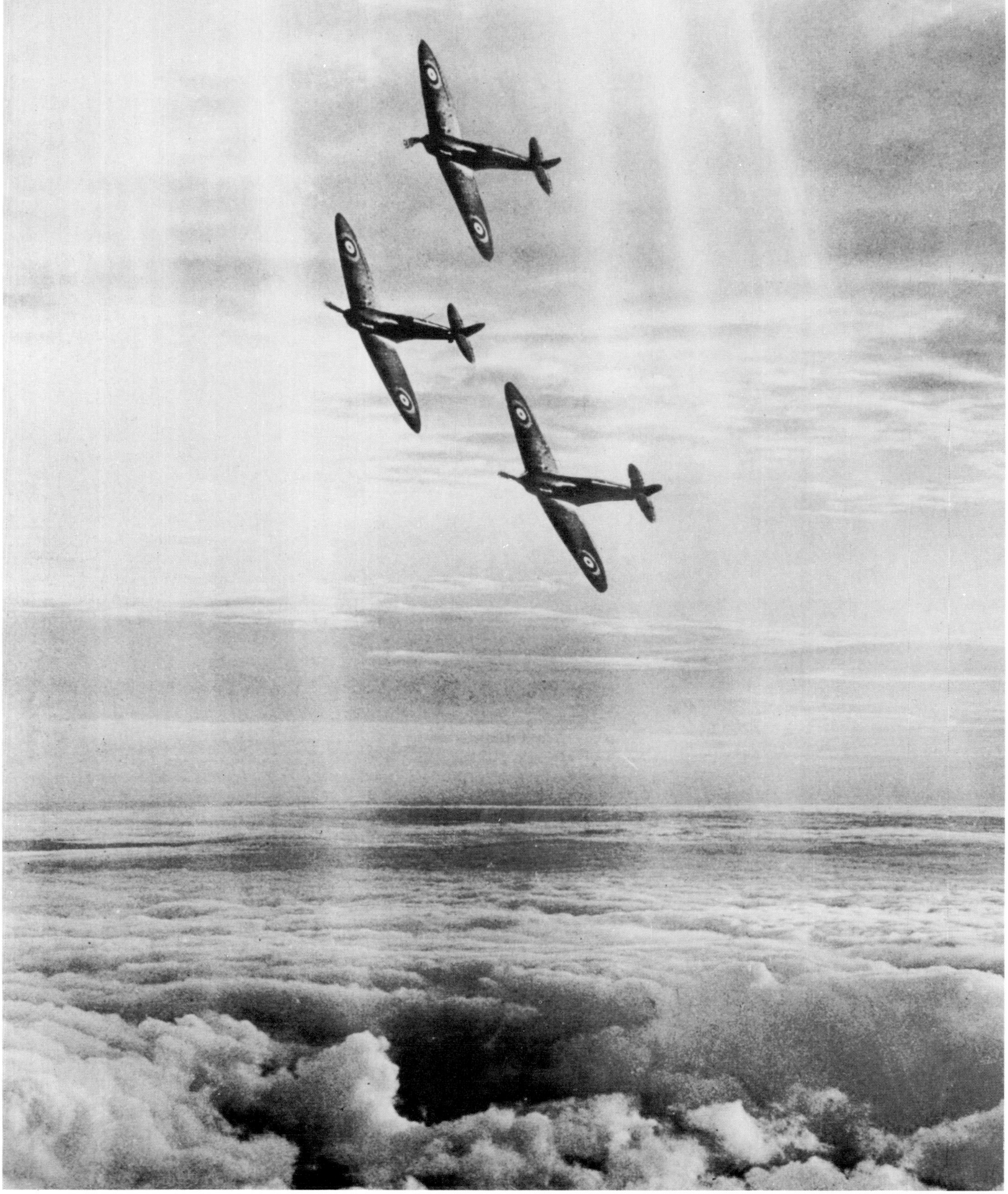

In addition to the fighting formation shown below, there were also in the British Air Force in France signals, balloon, maintenance and servicing units and medical and other services.

The Air Component thus had five squadrons of Lysanders, responsible for tactical reconnaissance and photographic survey on the BEF front; four Blenheim squadrons for strategic recce beyond the British and Belgian lines as far as the Rhine; its four Hurricanes (up to six under the reinforcement plan) for protecting the British troops, bases and recce aircraft.

The Advanced Air Striking Force had much wider responsibilities. The AASF had to serve the needs of the whole Allied front because the French had so few modern bombers. Its ten squadrons of Battle and Blenheim bombers were to attack the advancing German columns at such natural bottlenecks as bridges and road junctions; its two squadrons of Hurricanes (increased to four when the German attack was launched) were there to support the bombers and help defend the Rheims area where the AASF was based.

Home Commands

The main Home Commands involved in the campaign were Fighter Command (No 11 Group, plus squadrons from Nos 12 and 13 Groups for some time), Bomber Command (Nos 2, 3, 4 and 5 Groups) and Coastal Command (No 16 Group, plus squadrons from Nos 17 and 18 Group and the Fleet Air Arm).

A force of metal monoplanes

To quote from the official history: 'The Royal Air Force in 1934 was a force of wooden bi-planes. By 1939, with a few exceptions at home and rather more overseas, it was a force of metal monoplanes . . . The expansion of the RAF between 1934 and the outbreak of war is not a story without imperfections. It is not even a story without gross and palpable faults. But it is a story in which the merits far outweigh the defects.'[4] The RAF would need all the 'merits' it could muster when the Phoney War came to its sudden end.

Main RAF aircraft involved in campaign						
Type and name	Speed (mph)	Ceiling (ft)	Range (mls)	First	Main armament	Crew
Light Bombers						
Fairy Battle	241	25,000	900	1936	1,000lb bombs	3
Bristol Blenheim	266	31,500	1,950	1935	1,000lb bombs	3
Heavy Bombers						
Vickers Wellington	235	22,000	2,200*	1936	4,500lb bombs	6
* carrying 1,500lb, less with full load.						
AW 38 Whitley	222	21,000	1,650*	1936	7,000lb bombs	5
(On 19 March 1940, Whitleys dropped the first bombs of the war onto Germany.)						
* carrying 3,000lb, 470mls with full load.						
Fighters						
Supermarine Spitfire Mk 1/1A	362	34,000	395	1936	4 MGs on Mk 1 / 8 MGs on Mk 1A	1
Hawker Hurricane Mk 1	316	33,200	460	1935	8 MGs	1
Army co-operation						
Westland Lysander	237	26,000	600	1936	3 MGs (one in rear cockpit)	2

A trio of Supermarine Spitfires on lone patrol above the evening clouds – one of the best-known photographs of the Second World War. IWM

Hawker Hurricanes of No 73 Squadron seek out enemy aircraft over the Western Front. IWM

British Air Forces in France
AOC-in-C Air Marshall Barratt
Snr Staff Offr AVM Evill

Air Component
AVM Blount
No 14 Group
No 60 (Fighter) Wing (two sqns)
No 61 (Fighter) Wing (two sqns)
No 70 (Bomber Recce) Wing (two sqns)
No 52 (Bomber) Wing (three sqns)
No 50 (Army Co-op) Wing (three sqns)
No 51 (Army Co-op) Wing (two sqns plus one communication sqn)

Advanced Air Striking Force
AVM Playfair
No 71 (Bomber) Wing (four sqns)
No 75 (Bomber) Wing (three sqns)
No 76 (Bomber) Wing (three sqns)
No 67 (Fighter) Wing (two sqns plus one photo recce sqn)

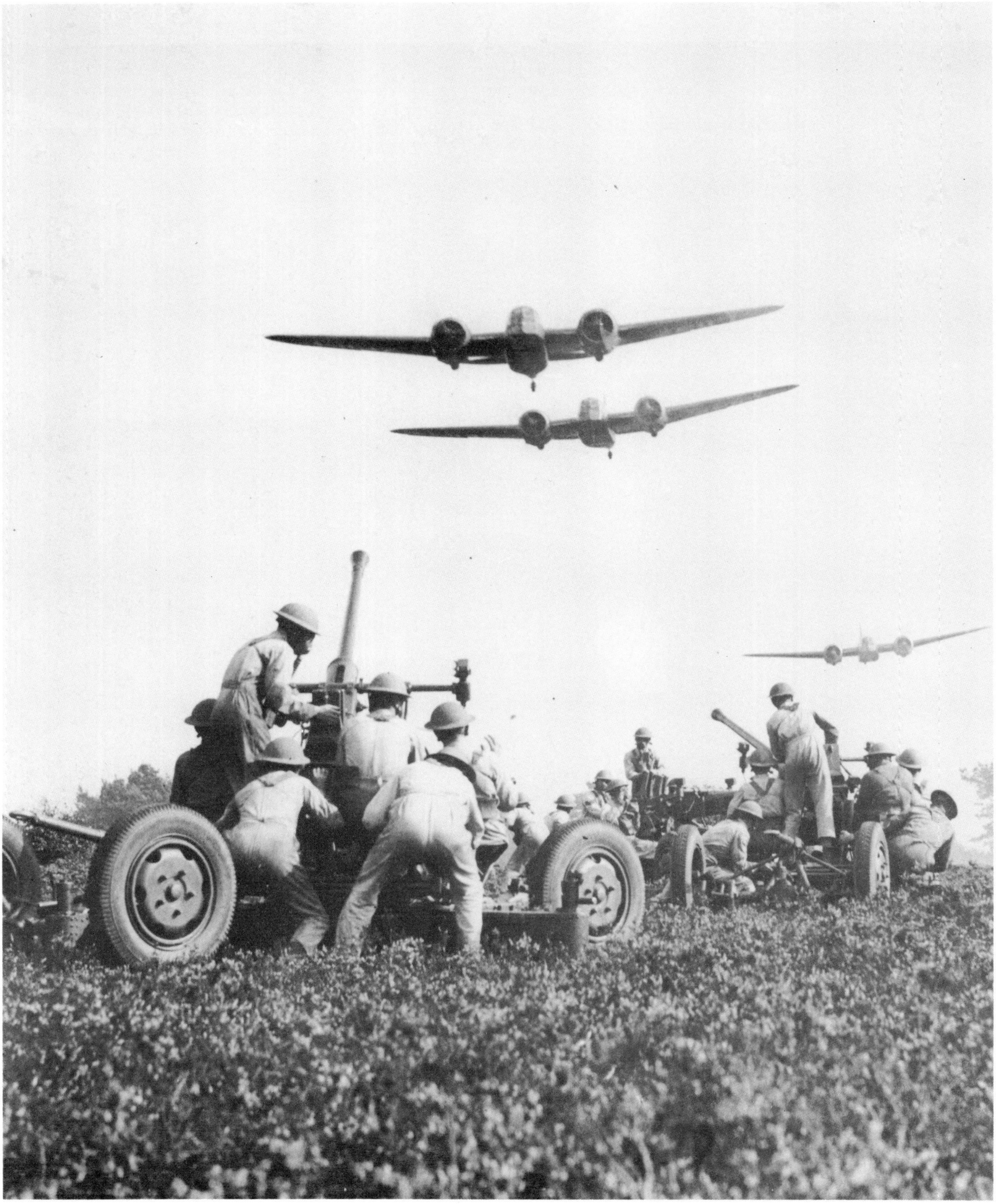

On a realistic training exercise Bofors LAA gun crews engage a flight of Bristol Blenheim bombers. IWM

BELGIUM

After the First World War Belgium signed defence agreements with Britain and France and maintained a sizeable twelve-division strong conscript army until 1923. Thereafter, it was steadily reduced until by 1926 there were only two active and two reserve divisions left. Neutralism was the byword and it was taken for granted that Britain and France would come to the rescue if Germany attacked. The rise of the Third Reich led to an increase in the level of funding for the forces, general conscription was re-introduced and a ceiling of 500,000 for the army was set in 1935. By the time the war began six active and twelve reserve infantry divisions had been raised plus a corps of two divisions of the *Chasseurs Ardennais*.

When Britain and France declared war on Germany, King Leopold III re-affirmed Belgium's neutrality. This unfortunately prevented the Allies from taking up realistic defensive positions within Belgium. Belgium's army was now some 600,000 men – stronger than it had been before, but the call-up created massive problems in industry and the public services because so many key men were taken away from their jobs.

The Belgian Army

In May 1940 the Belgian Army consisted of five regular and two reserve *Corps d'Armée* (numbered from I CA to VII CA, plus a *Corps de Cavalerie*, which were divided into:

- *Infantry Divisions*. There were six regular and twelve reserve infantry divisions, numbered consecutively from 1 Di to 18 Di, each containing three *régiments d'infanterie*, one *régiment d'artillerie* and one *bataillon du génie*. In addition, there were two divisions of the famous *Chasseurs Ardennais* each with a company of 19 *Bataillon du Génie*.
- *Cavalry Divisions*. There were two *divisions de Cavalerie*: 1DC – *1er Guides, 3e & 3e Lanciers, 1er & 3e Carabiniers Cyclistes, 17 Régiment d'Artillerie* and *25 Bataillon du Génie*. 2DC – *1er Lanciers, 1er & 2er Chasseurs à Cheval, 2e & 4e Carabiniers Cyclistes,* 18 A and 26 Gn. *Brigade de Cavaliers Portes* (motorised) – *2e Guides & 4e Lanciers*.
- *Corps artillery and engineers*. Five of the seven corps had an artillery regiment and an engineer battalion: V or VI *Corps d'Armée* were the exceptions.

The 7.65mm Maxim machine gun had a variety of mounts, but none more novel than this wheeled version drawn by dogs in service with the Belgian Army during the 1930s. The Mitrailleuse 'Maxim', *the main heavy machine gun used by the German Army during the First World War, was produced by the Deutches Waffen und Munitionsfabriken at Spandau. It proved to be so reliable and powerful a weapon that it was adopted by the armies of many other countries between the two wars. The crew shown in the photograph carry* Mauser *rifles dating back to 1889.* TM

Belgian infantry parade with Utility B *small infantry carriers, which were British Carden-Lloyd light tractors built under licence. Each carried a driver and six men.*

Georges Mazy

- *Miscellaneous*. In addition to the eight corps described above, there were the following other military units:

Gendarmerie – 1er & 2er Regiments Légèrs.

Frontier guards – *1er & 2er Régiments Cyclistes-Frontière*, and a *Bataillon Cycliste-Frontière du Limbourg.*

Fortress troops – two *Régiments d'artillérie de forteresse* (one for Liège and one for Namur); a *Régiment Unites Speciales de Forteresse (USF)* comprising *Ier-Ve battailons a Anvers, VIe à Namur* and *VIIe à Liège.*

Anti-aircraft – *Ier and 2e Régiments de Defense terrestre contre Aeronefs (DCTA).*

Army troops – basically five army artillery regiments, three engineer battalions plus a pontoon bn, medical, supply and transportation units.

Static units – 45 *Bataillons de Gardes-Voies, Communications et Establissements*, nine territorial battalions, various training and recruitment centres, plus military hospitals, arsenals and depots.

Equipment. The Belgian Army was organised and equipped for defensive operations, nevertheless they had modern, serviceable weapons in their active units. Infantry divisions, for example, had 48 × 47mm anti-tank guns, plus grenade launchers, excellent FN rifles and 75mm mortars. The anti-tank guns were towed by Utility B tractors built under licence in Belgium, but designed by Vickers Armstrong. The cavalry had 150 × T-13 tanks and 45 × T-15s. The former were Vickers Carden Loyd Type 1 or Type 111 light tractors, which had been fitted with a turret mounting a 47mm gun. The superstructure was made up of armoured steel

The T 13 light tank which carried a 47mm gun in a hooded mantlet, was also built in Belgium by Fabrique Nationale under licence from Britain. Similar arrangements applied to some French tank designs. TM

The T 15 was the Carden-Lloyd M1934, armed with either a heavy machine gun or a 37mm gun. It weighed 4 tons, and was no match for the heavier German panzers.
Georges Mazy

Men of the Battalion de Cyclistes de Frontière, Compagnie de Henri Chapelle *man a* T 13 *light tank.*   Georges Mazy

sheets. In the case of the Type 1 the gun faced rearwards, while the Type 111 had an open turret with all-round travese. The Vickers Carden Loyd T-15s were built in UK, but spare parts were of local manufacture.

The cavalry had been mechanised in 1937 with 23 Renault *Auto-Mitrailleuses de Combat*, some of which were fitted with a turret about two years later, which mounted a 47mm gun and a Hotchkiss 12.7mm machine gun. Most of the light troops were motorised, but the reserve divisions were very badly armed, with out-dated equipment.

The Belgian Navy
Belgium did not have a proper navy. They took over some 14 MTBs, abandoned by the Germans when they evacuated Flanders in 1918 and these became the basis of a coastal defence force. Despite purchasing the British sloop *Zinnia* in 1920, they quickly lost interest in the new force and it was disbanded. Some of the vessels were retained for fishery protection work, but were captured by the Germans in 1940. Belgium did, however, maintain a *Corps de Marine* which contained the *1er, 2e* and *3e Escadrilles*.

The Belgian Air Force
Although small, the Belgian Air Force was reasonably well-equipped and efficient. Its operational status as at 10 May 1940 shows that *L'Aviation Militaire* was composed of three *Régiments d'Aeronautique*:
- *1st Regiment (Army Co-operation)* was based at Bierset, Deurne and Gossoncourt and was equipped with 40 Fairey Fox and 10 Renard 31.
- *2nd Regiment (Fighters)* was based at Schaffen and Nijvel with 30 Fairey Fox, 25 Fiat CR 42 Falco, 15 Gloster Gladiator, and 11 Hawker Hurricane.
- *3rd Regiment (Recon and bombers)* was based at Evere with 27 Fairey Fox and 13 Fairey Battle.

The total operational strength of the Belgian Air Force on 10 May 1940 was 180 aircraft. All three Regiments had significant numbers of Belgium's main fighter-bomber, the obsolescent Fairey Fox, which had first flown in 1925 and was still in production in 1939! Up until March 1940 the even older Fairey Firefly was in first-line service but was then replaced by the CR 42 Falco.

HOLLAND

Dutch Hussars manning their Austrian manufactured 8mm MO8 Schwarlose MG on an AA mount.   TM

Main Belgian Aircraft involved in Campaign			
Name & Type	First flew	Performance	Armament
Fairey Fox I to VI light day bomber	1925	max speed 230mph, ceiling 29,000ft, range 465mls	3×MG and 528lb bombload
Fairey Battle 3 man light bomber	1936	max speed 140mph, ceiling 25,000ft, range 900mls	2×MG and 1,000lb bombload
Fiat CR 42 Falco single seat fighter	1936	max speed 265mph, ceiling 34,500ft, range 480mls	4×MG and 440lb bombload

The Dutch Army (*Landmacht*)

The Netherlands were neutral during the First World War, so there was little incentive to spend money on the armed forces between the wars. By the 1930s the army was run down and badly equipped. It was also organised on a militia basis, some 20,000 men being called up for military training. They continued to be liable for refresher training over a period of six years. In 1938 the government at long last authorised funds to cover new weapons and equipment. 73,000 men were declared liable for military service that year, but only 19,500 were actually called up. The Netherlands were determined to remain neutral once again, so their *Landmacht* was strictly a home defence force.

The Dutch Field Army in 1939 was composed of an HQ, four field corps, a light division, a regiment of coastal artillery, additional field artillery, a brigade of engineers, plus specialised engineers (such as bridging and pontoon

A Dutch artilleryman, with his officer, sets into position a Wonsstelling 33 RI 6cm *gun.* S-MG

Major Dutch Units (Corps & Divisions)

Corps	Division	Infantry	Artillery
1st Leger korps	1st	Regiment Grenadiers Regiment Jagers 4th Infantry Regt	2nd Field Regt
			10th Regt motor artillery
	2nd	10th Infantry Regt 15th Infantry Regt 22nd Infantry Regt	6th Field Regt
2nd Leger korps	3rd	1st Infantry Regt 9th Infantry Regt 12th Infantry Regt	4th Field Regt
			12th Regt motor artillery
	4th	8th Infantry Regt 11th Infantry Regt 19th Infantry Regt	8th Field Regt
3rd Leger korps	5th	2nd Infantry Regt 13th Infantry Regt 17th Infantry Regt	3rd Field Regt
			11th Regt motor artillery
	6th	3rd Infantry Regt 6th Infantry Regt 14th Infantry Regt	7th Field Regt
4th Leger korps	7th	7th Infantry Regt 18th Infantry Regt 20th Infantry Regt	1st Field Regt
			9th Regt motor artillery
	4th	5th Infantry Regt 16th Infantry Regt 21st Infantry Regt	5th Field Regt

Source: *Samenstelling van de koninklijke landmacht op voet van vrede No 82.*

Main Dutch Aircraft in Campaign

Name & Type	First flew	Performance	Armament
Fokker CX two seat biplane bomber & recce	1934	max speed 200mph, ceiling 27,230ft, range 515mls	2×MG on top of front fuselage 1XMG rear cockpit 884lb bombload
Fokker D XXI single seat fighter	1936	max speed 285mph, ceiling 36,090ft, range 590mls	4×MG two in fuselage, two in wings
Fokker G1 three seat heavy fighter	1937	max speed 295mph, ceiling 30,500ft, range 945mls	8×MG in nose one in tail 880lb bombload
Fokker T5 medium bomber	1937	max speed 260mph, ceiling 26,575ft, range 1,025mls	5×MG 2,200lb bombload

units). Each Corps contained two divisions and one regiment of motorised artillery while divisions comprised three infantry regiments and a field artillery regiment. The light division contained two regiments of bicycle troops, four regiments of cavalry, two cavalry motor cycle regiments, two squadrons of tanks and the Corps motor artillery.

By the time war came to the Netherlands a further two infantry divisions had been added, and the total home defence force numbered about 400,000 men.

The Dutch Air Force

The Dutch had considerable interest in aeroplanes, the great Fokker firm being a very famous name in the history of

During the Phoney War, vigil is kept near Scheveningen, one of the many vulnerable points on the Dutch coast. N. Schimmelpenningh

In the 1930s Holland purchased a number of Swedish Landswerk *armoured cars – the L180, which became the M36 under Dutch designation, and this L182, otherwise known as the M38. It weighed about 7 tons, carried a crew of five, a 20mm Madsen cannon and a coax machine-gun.* TM

flying. They produced many excellent aircraft, some of which were to fight against the Germans. These included the Fokker DXXI single-engined fighter and the twin-engined Fokker G1. In May 1940 the Dutch Air Force had 29 DXXIs and 41 G1s. All fought well; many were destroyed or ran out of ammunition after two furious days of continuous activity. Only one type of light bomber was in service, the elderly Fokker CX biplane, and all of these were destroyed. The Fokker T series of medium bomber/seaplane (T4, T5 and T8W). The T4 seaplane mainly operated in the Dutch East Indies, the T5 medium bomber fought to the last in May 1940 (there were some 12 in service), while 8 surviving T8W seaplanes escaped to Britain.

The Dutch Navy
The major portion of the naval strength of the Netherlands was built to protect the Dutch East Indies, largely on account of its importance as an oil producer (seventh in the world league in the 1920s) and the likely threat to its sovereignty from Japan. Dutch policy was to build a small but high-quality fleet capable of delaying an enemy attack until help arrived either from USA or Great Britain. Holland itself needed litle naval defence as any attack would obviously come from the land. Therefore its European naval force was limited to a number of minelayers, MTBs and gunboats, although some submarines were built. At the time of the German invasion some Dutch forces in home waters were able to escape to Britain. These included two cruisers, one destroyer, nine submarines, two gunboats, one sloop and six MTBs. The remaining vessels of the Royal Dutch Navy were either captured or destroyed.

NOTES

1. T. E. Griess *The Second World War: Europe and the Mediterranean* Department of History, U.S. Military Academy, West Point.
2. J. Benoist-Mechin *Sixty Days That Shook The West* London: Jonathan Cape, 1963.
3. Figures quoted from Capt S. W. Roskill's *The War at Sea 1939-1945, Vol. I* London: HMSO, 1954.
4. D. Richards *Royal Air Force 1939-1945, Vol. I: The Fight at Odds* London: HMSO, 1953.

Chapter 6

Morale in Peace and War

The French C-in-C Northeast Front, Gen Georges, accompanied by Lord Gort, C-in-C of the BEF, inspect a guard of honour mounted by men of the Royal Inniskilling Fusiliers. Smart uniforms, reliable weapons and sound discipline all contributed to the excellent morale of British troops in northern France. IWM

Every successful military commander at every level of command knows how essential it is to create and sustain good morale among fighting men. The reason is very simple: good morale often tilts the scales between victory and defeat. It is an elusive quality more easily recognized than described, although in his autobiography Field Marshal Lord Montgomery spelt out some of the ingredients, as he saw them, in his usual crisp manner:[1]

> The morale of the soldier is the greatest single factor in war, and the best way to achieve a high morale in war-time is by success in battle. The British soldier, when properly led, reponds to a challenge and not to welfare benefits. Man does not

live by bread alone. The soldier has to be kept active, alert and purposeful all the time. He will do anything you ask of him, so long as you arrange that he gets his mail from home, the newspapers and, curiously enough, plenty of tea.

Other things, such as proper uniforms, reliable equipment with plenty of ammunition, regular food and pay go towards building good morale. Yet not one of them is essential, as was shown by many a ragged, underfed and badly-equipped partisan group during the Second World War. Indeed, there are those who say that if you cosset soldiers, which was a fault many Europeans found in America's treatment of her GIs, you run the risk of undermining their morale and weakening their fighting spirit.

Sound training and good leadership, another elusive quality, also help to foster positive attitudes. So does physical fitness. The old Latin motto *mens sana in corpore sano* (a healthy mind in a healthy body) is as valid today as it was in Caesar's time. Fighting for King and Country, fighting to protect loved ones at home, fighting for a cause that is seen as just, or in defence of personal values and beliefs, can all be powerful forces in creating good morale, or providing the right kind of motivation as modern jargon would

Another important ingredient in the maintenance of good morale was a regular supply of mail from home. This was especially important in the long periods of inactivity during the 'Phoney War'. IWM

For the great majority of the British people, and for supporters of the Allied cause throughout the world, Winston Churchill with his familiar cigar became a symbol of those qualities most necessary in war – courage, determination and a bulldog tenacity. This photograph was taken while he watched a demonstration of anti-aircraft guns in action. With him, hands over her ears, is his wife, Clementine. His daughter Mary leans over his shoulder to point out targets. IWM

have it. Loyalty to the colours and to the regiment, a sense of *esprit de corps*, pride in one's own unit and in one's fellow soldiers are also of great importance. Good morale fosters a spirit of comradeship and a readiness to share hardship, deprivation and danger, best summed up by expressions such as 'we're all in the same boat, so we'd better make the best of things'.

Nil Carborundum

To accept the inevitable was characteristic of the British serving soldier in both World Wars. Such acceptance, or resignation in the face of adversity, was shown in many different ways: in the irrepressible cheerfulness of the London Cockney, the sharp-witted banter of the Geordie, the dour, often incomprehensible, humour of the Scot, the adenoidal wisecracks of the Liverpudlian, the open good nature and warm-heartedness of the West countryman. These were just some of the characteristics and qualities the British serving soldier brought to bear upon the disagreeable tasks of waging war.

'Cheer up mate, you'll soon be dead!', 'Don't yer know there's a war on?' and '*Nil Carborundum*' (this latter from the lips of men who laid no claim to any kind of education, classical or otherwise) were among the many phrases and catchwords that caught the spirit of the men, and the times in which they lived and died. T. S. Eliot may have been right when he talked of a stoicism born not of conviction, but of a certain kind of arrogance; a refusal to be humbled before God or one's fellow man. But whatever their origins, such attitudes produced a steely resolve to survive under intolerable conditions, and a most powerful determination to 'do one's duty' and 'not to let your mates down', whatever the cost.

If this is the stuff of heroism, so be it. It has little to do with idealism or any notions of chivalry, and owes nothing to the romantic view of war. But it does help to explain the steadfastness of ordinary British soldiers under fire, their countless feats of endurance in the front line and their acts of great courage, as well as great compasion, in the heat of battle.

Few tanks for the BEF
The British Expeditionary Force that went to France a week after war broke out in September 1939, and the support units of the RAF who went with them, consisted mostly of regular soldiers with regular reservists to make up strengths where necessary. So they were all professional soldiers, one way or another, who had been well-trained in the basic skills of soldiering. With the exception of armoured vehicles, they were also reasonably well equipped. Furthermore, the BEF was a highly motivated force, quietly confident of its own abilities.

It has to be said that this confidence was not always shared by its senior officers. Field Marshal Lord Montgomery was later to declare that 'in September 1939 the British Army was totally unfit to fight a first-class war on the Continent of Europe'. He advanced in evidence the facts that no large-scale exercises had been carried out in the years immediately before the war, that the Field Army had a totally inadequate signals system, that forces in the field had little or no administrative backing and that a high command structure simply did not exist. All this was indisputable, so Montgomery may not have reached his conclusions entirely with the benefit of hindsight. He was highly critical of the lack of anti-tank weapons of suitable calibre, and of the almost total absence of tanks:

> There was somewhere in France, under GHQ, one Army Tank Brigade. For myself, I never saw any of its tanks during the winter or during the active operations in May. And we were the nation which had invented the tank and were the first to use it in battle in 1916![2]

But such deficiencies seem not to have had any adverse effect on British morale, partly because soldiers of the BEF were not used to seeing large tank formations and did not, therefore, mark their absence, and partly because by temperament and training they made the best of whatever came to hand. In his book *Assignment to Catastrophe* the Prime Minister's personal representative during

Mess tins at the ready, these British soldiers with the BEF 'somewhere in France' have formed an orderly queue ready to receive their main meal of the day. Good, hot food, with plenty of tea, was a high priority in helping to maintain the morale of our fighting men. IWM

A welcome brew-up for the crew of a British tank standing well camouflaged at a roadside in northern France. IWM

In the days before commercial radio and television, and with severe restrictions on newsprint, posters were widely used to promote the national war effort in Britain.

the battle of France, General Sir Edward Spears, makes two observations on the state of morale within the BEF. In the first of these he compares attitudes and behaviour during the 'Phoney War':

> Front-line observers said the conditions of the British and French forces behind the front line were completely different. In our sector the forces were ceaselessly working and training. The men were occupied. On the French front the soldiers were listless, *désoeuvrés* (unoccupied and idle). Little seemed to be going on either in the front or the rear areas.[3]

Later, after the fighting had begun in earnest, General Spears had this to say.

> As I look back now it is satisfactory to recall that never for a moment did I have any doubts about the BEF. I was absolutely certain that the troops would do what one expected. They might be decimated, but those who were left would bob up cheerful and unaffected to fight again till the war was won.[3]

Those two quotes tell us as much about the attitudes and assumptions of the British military establishment as they do about the rank-and-file.

There was one significant difference between the young men of serving age in 1914 and their counterparts in 1939. At the outbreak of the First World War a great wave of patriotic fervour swept the country. There was much flag-waving, marching up and down, and dancing in the streets during that heady August of 1914. The most ardent jingoism was evident throughout the land, and volunteers came forward eagerly in their many thousands in a spirit of jubilation and celebration. Women shared this fever of excitement no less than men. 'Oh, we don't want to lose you, but we think you ought to go', they sang, and sent white feathers to those they thought were failing in their duty. The men, in their turn, assured their wives, their sweethearts, their families and their friends that 'It'll all be over by Christmas'. Words whose hidden truth was soon revealed by the grim irony of many an unmarked grave in the muddy fields of Flanders.

Not Such A Lovely War

But when war came again in 1939, no hats were thrown in the air. There was no elation, no euphoria, no exultation, only a sense of relief that the days of uncertainty were over at last. The prevailing mood of the British people, serving men and women and civilians alike, was one of quiet determination, tinged with fear about the massive air attacks everyone expected. 'It'll all be over by Christmas' was heard again, only now the words were usually spoken in slightly rueful manner and without conviction.

Civilian morale corresponded almost exactly with that of front-line troops in the BEF. Most men and women buckled down to the various tasks in hand, and responded cheerfully enough to the many directives from above. The training in such matters as Air Raid Precautions paid off, and administrative challenges such as the distribution of home shelters and the evacuation of women and children from congested urban centres were met with considerable flair and efficiency. Perhaps the greatest of these challenges was the issue of gas masks to every man, woman and child in the country. This precaution, and the fear of retaliation, convinced the Germans that any gas attack against the civilian population was bound to fail. As Norman Longmate explains in his splendidly evocative book *How We Lived Then*:

> The humble gas mask, the subject of endless jokes and criticism and never used, proved after all to have justified its existence, though most ended their lives ingloriously as salvage, or were packed with earth and transformed into hanging plant pots.[4]

Vox Pop

The songs of the period also tell their own story. 'Extraordinary how potent cheap music is,' says one of the Noel Coward's characters in *Private Lives*. There is certainly no better way of evoking the flavour of the period than by recalling the songs whistled in the streets and broadcast on the wireless, as it was still called at the time. They had none of the jaunty confidence of the songs of 1914. One of the most popular tunes during that long, hot summer of 1939 was *South of the Border (Down Mexico Way)*: not the sort of music to encourage men to march to war. A rather better marching tune was *Roll Out the Barrel*. Some rather feeble attempts were made to write songs with patriotic feeling, but they failed to catch on, especially with the troops. The sentimental songs of Vera Lynn came later in the war, as did the most famous of all, *Lili Marlene*. This serenade to a street whore was first broadcast by the German authorities to undermine the morale of the British fighting men presumably by inducing nostalgia, home-sickness and envy. But as a piece of propaganda it badly misfired, for the song was cheerfully taken up with equal enthusiasm by both the British and the German armies; it became, and remains, the theme-song of all those who fought in North Africa.

Just as popular music turned its back on patriotic and martial sentiments in the years between the wars, so did mass-circulation newspapers and magazines. Edward Hulton's well-remembered weekly *Picture Post*, modelled on *Life* magazine in the USA, published many powerful war photographs taken during the fighting in Spain, Abyssinia and China. Like most of its contemporaries, it was passionately anti-war in its editorial policy. 'The common man in Britain does not want war,' *Picture Post* declared not long before September 1939. 'The common

BACK THEM UP!

By stimulating national savings and presenting the armed forces in a visually dramatic way a useful double purpose was served – large sums of money were raised, and civilian morale was boosted. TM

At the time it was estimated that 30,000 civilians were killed and wounded in the German air attack on the city of Rotterdam. It is now known that this figure was greatly exaggerated. Nevertheless, so great was the fear of further raids that the Dutch government was forced to surrender on 14 May 1940, four days after the Germans launched their attack on Holland.

Royal Netherlands Army and Arms Museum

man in France does not want war. The common man in Germany does not want war. This is the age of the common man. Therefore there will be no war.' In expressing such ideas it was certainly not alone. Nearly all newspapers and magazines reflected the view of the overwhelming majority of British people, certainly up to the time of the Munich Agreement in 1938, that war should be avoided at all costs – which is, of course, another way of saying 'peace at any price'.

Moves towards total disarmament, deep cuts in military expenditure, a dependence on sanctions and the League of Nations, the Peace Campaign and the growth of pacifism, even the shameful Oxford Union resolution of 1933 'that this House will in no circumstances fight for King and Country',[5] have to be seen in the light of the appalling blood-letting of the First World War. Most of those who devoutly worked for peace were not traitors, or cowards or dishonourable men and women. Far from it. They believed with the greatest sincerity that war could no longer be used as an instrument of national policy. The only people to be despised are those who, for most of the 1930s, called loudly for peace and opposed every move for Britain's rearmament and then denounced the Rt. Hon. Neville Chamberlain, later in the decade and in the bitterest of terms, as an appeaser and near-traitor. Theirs is the disgrace, not his.

Winston Churchill, who had consistently warned his fellow-countrymen about the growing menace of the Axis powers, was more generous to his predecessor. Speaking in the House of Commons on 12 November 1940, three days after Chamberlain's death, he said:

> Whatever else history may or may not say about these terrible, tremendous years, we can be sure that Neville Chamberlain acted with perfect sincerity according to his lights and strove to the utmost of his capacity and authority, which were powerful, to save the world from the awful, devastating struggle in which we are now engaged.[6]

A formation of Heinkel He III *bombers* IWM

Fear of gas attack was the other major anxiety felt by civilian populations in the main cities. Three weeks after the start of the war, people in a London bus queue can be seen carrying their gas masks carefully packed in the cardboard boxes provided for the purpose. IWM

The Luftwaffe was deliberately used in attacks on civilian populations to create refugee problems and further dislocate road communications ahead of advancing German land forces. This photograph, taken in Belgium in May 1940, shows just how effective these tactics could be in practice. IWM

The Oxford Union resolution attracted more attention abroad than it did at home. Both Hitler and Mussolini took it as clear evidence that the British had become decadent and had lost their will to fight. The German Embassy in London fed Berlin with plenty more 'evidence' of this kind at the time, but after Hitler tore up the Munich agreement they repeatedly warned their masters in Berlin that Britain would stand by her pledge to the Poles.

By then, of course, the damage had been done. Hitler had not been impressed by Chamberlain and, surrounded by henchmen who told him exactly what he wanted to hear, he completely misread the British national mood in the final crucial months. He did not understand that the image presented by Britain to the world in 1914 and in 1939 were simply opposing facets of the same national character. The jaunty confidence that belonged to the brilliant days of post-Edwardian splendour and golden imperial power, was now replaced by a quiet determination to 'save the whole world from the pestilence of Nazi tyranny and in defence of all that is most sacred to man,' to quote from Churchill's speech to the House of Commons on the outbreak of war.

The significant change of mood in Britain after Hitler's contemptuous disregard for the Munich agreement seems not to have been shared by the French. As an island race Britons felt more secure than their allies. There was still great pride and confidence in the Royal Navy, and in the belief that 'the old country always pulls through in the end'. And although the British are less aware of their past history than many people, deeply ingrained in their consciousness are stories about Drake and the King of Spain, wars against the French culminating, of course, in Wellington's victory over Napoleon at Waterloo, the Crimea, the Boer War and the defeat of the Kaiser – all of them wars in which the British muddled through but finally emerged victorious. French memories, on the other hand, had much more to do with German invasions. Another factor was, curiously enough, patience. Often in his blustering rhetoric Hitler would say, on one issue or another, that his 'patience was exhausted'. But in the end, it was the patience of ordinary British men and women that finally gave way. 'That man 'itler's got to be stopped' they told each other in London's East End. And they were right.

Morale in France
Like the British, the French did not go to war in 1939 with the élan of the 1914 generation. Their mood seems to have been one of resolve mixed with some doubt and even dread – dread of enduring once more the horrors and losses of the earlier war, dread too of bomber and tank attacks (what was soon to be called 'blitzkrieg') and even of gas. The doubt concerned the sense of going to war to save Poland, a country too far away to be saved, no matter what her allies did.

Between the wars France enjoyed the status of a Great Power. The extent of her colonial empire was second only to that of the British. Her glorious army, emerging victorious from the First World War, had never seemed stronger. The Maginot Line on her eastern frontier was deemed to be impenetrable. Although the huge and growing cost of its construction placed a heavy burden on the French economy, in other respects France was well able to support the rearmament needed to deal with the Nazi menace in the late Thirties. Her security was further reinforced by a series of alliances and treaties, particularly with nations bordering on her late enemy, Germany.

Yet in a few weeks in the summer of 1940 France suffered at German hands the most complete and humiliating defeat in her history. Her armies were broken and her government destroyed, to be replaced by a puppet regime in that half of the country the Nazis did not then deign to occupy. How to explain this incredible reverse? All contemporary accounts and later inquests point to the same conclusion – failure of morale. Faced with devastating and apparently unstoppable attacks by tanks, motorised units and dive-bombers, French leaders lost their nerve. Most of the generals and senior government ministers were defeatist and unable to cope. Her soldiers and citizens were bewildered, divided and plain frightened. Clearly, poor morale was not the only reason for the fall of France, but it is hard to deny that it was the most significant factor.

The morale of a nation's fighting men does not depend solely on their personal qualities, training and leadership, important as these things are. The crucial element in modern war is the spirit of the nation as a whole. A strong army is not produced by a weak-spirited nation – as Hitler noted. Between the wars of France seemed strong, but was in fact weak, divided, defensive and lacking in the will to fight – as Hitler also noted.

This defensive attitude had its roots in the carnage of the First World War when France suffered more than her allies and her enemies. Some 1,385,000 men were killed and a further 3,500,000 were wounded, posted missing or taken prisoner. The war was fought mostly on French soil, and the consequent destruction of houses, public buildings, factories, farmland, forest and livestock was beyond calculation. These losses affected every family in France. They go a long way to explain the French obsession with squeezing out of Germany as much as they could by way of reparations, and the intense national longing for security. The attitude to war after 1918 (as in Britain) was 'Never again!'. This made every Frenchman – politicians and generals, peasants and *poilus* – question the need for any kind of action that might lead France to armed conflict. Only a strictly defensive war could be contemplated, and then only as a last possible resort.

There was also a powerful demographic reason for not wanting to become involved in another major European confrontation. The loss of virtually an entire generation of young men during the First World War made far worse a problem that already existed, namely a steadily declining and ageing population. There were now fewer Frenchmen than there were Germans. The military consequence of this uncomfortable fact was graphically described by Paul Reynaud, the then Prime Minister of France, to Winston Churchill in April 1940. He pointed out that it was only with the arrival of the American that Allied strength had equalled that of Germany in the First World

If smartness of appearance is a true indication of the state of military morale, there are perhaps some conclusions to be drawn from this photograph of British and French soldiers drawn up on parade at a medal presentation ceremony during the Phoney War. IWM

Sieg Heil! Huge crowds greet their Führer at a rally in Berlin on 6 June 1940, after the fall of France. TM

War. 'How much worse is the position today,' he went on. Against Germany's 150 divisions available for the Western Front, the Allies had 100, of which 10 were British. But the German population was now 80 million, from which she could raise 300 divisions. 'We must therefore face a large and increasing numerical superiority . . .'[7]

Three years earlier, in 1937, Churchill had already declared that having regard to the disparity of populations, the construction of the Maginot Line 'must be regarded as a wise and prudent measure'. But he pointed out that it absorbed a very large number of highly-trained soldiers, and 'exercised an enervating effect both upon military strategy and upon national vigilance.' He went on to warn that '. . . it engendered a defensive mentality. Offensive action was associated in French minds with the initial failures of the French onslaught in 1914 . . . with the long agonies of the Somme and Passchendaele and above all with the sense that the fire-power of modern weapons was devastating to the attacker.[8]

Political Divisions in France
After the First World War France was probably more bitterly divided and at war with herself than at any time since the French Revolution, and certainly more so than her British allies, notwithstanding the General Strike of 1926. The Right and the rich tended to applaud Hitler and his Nazis because they had forcibly united their nation, dealt with the unions, put down the Communists and the Jews and generally followed all the policies dear to right-wing hearts. The Left and the poorer classes, on the other hand, were opposed to 'imperialist' and 'capitalist' wars for any purpose. Pacificism and support for the Disarmament movement were widespread, as in Britain. Most of the grand old men of the First World War (Clemenceau, Briand and the like) had gone, and in their places were forgettable men of no stature leading 'a cascade of Cabinets'. Small wonder that France's foreign policy, and her reaction to the growing German menace, was usually so hesitant and defensive.

As a result, in every international crisis between 1933 and 1939, Hitler outmanoeuvred and defeated the French in diplomatic terms. They were forced to accept German rearmament, German reoccupation of the Rhineland, German Anschluss with Austria, German dismemberment and then occupation of her ally Czechoslovakia, and lastly the Molotov-Ribbentrop Pact of August 1939 – all of which left France's carefully-built system of mutual defence pacts in total ruin. It must have done little for national self-esteem.

The one thing that rallied most Frenchmen was the conviction that the army could beat off all and any attacks. 'I believe that the French Army is a more

Behind the safety of a mobile crash barrier Hitler talks to one of his mountain troops, readily identified by an edelweiss worn in his peaked field cap (gebirgsmuetze). TM

effective force than at any moment in its history', declared General Weygand in July 1939[9], seemingly unaware that the High Command was still thinking in terms of the strategy and tactics of 1914-1918, still wedded to the concept of the 'unbroken line', still believing that the horse was a valuable asset in warfare, still seeing tanks as no more than supports for the infantry. So when their glorious army collapsed under the German hammer in May 1940, the whole of the French nation collapsed with it. There was nothing left.

Morale in Germany

In *Mein Kampf* and in his many public speeches, and from the moment he came to power, Adolf Hitler used the language of a war leader. Nazi policies were based on the assumption that sooner or later Germany would have to fight in order to achieve her objectives. Indeed, like all tyrannies, there would come a time when the Nazis would need a war to retain their iron grip on the nation. But when war did come in September 1939, ordinary Germany people greeted the news with no greater enthusiam than their British and French opposite numbers. An American observer[10] in Berlin wrote:

> I was standing in the Wilhelmstrasse . . . when the loudspeakers suddenly announced that Great Britain had declared herself at war with Germany. Some 250 people . . . listened attentively to the announcement. When it was finished there was not a murmur. They just stood there. Stunned. It was difficult for them to comprehend that Hitler had led them into a world war.

Unlike the British and the French, the Germans had little or no opportunity to display any doubts, disagreements or fears as the international situation worsened the report suggests, they were led, uncomprehending, by their Führer. The Nazis strictly controlled all media of expression, and all other political parties had been suppressed. Critical views and attitudes were only too likely to lead to a concentration camp. Doubts were not an option for Germans, at least in public.

Nonetheless Germany's morale in September 1939 was certainly high, and her people displayed a confidence and fighting-spirit lacking in the French and the British. While the latter remembered the First World War as a bloodbath but also a victory sealed by a Peace Treaty that, if kept, would preserve peace indefinitely, the Germans, as we have seen, remembered it as a time of defeat and humiliation in which they had been deprived of their honour, their armed forces, much of their territory and all their colonies, and had been condemned to pay for much of the cost of the war they had just lost. During the twenties, Germany's democratic governments had almost completely failed to restore the nation to the place most Germans felt it deserved in the world, failed to undo the burdensome terms of the Peace Treaties, and failed to cope with the problems of inflation, unemployment and economic depression.

Hitler's achievement

Then came Adolf Hitler and the Nazis. In a remarkably short time, unemployment and inflation had disappeared, the nation was united, her lost European territories regained, with advantage, her army and navy restored and more powerful than ever, a mighty air force built up, the hated treaties torn up, and Germany was once again a Great Power in the world. All this was well described by Hitler himself in a speech to the Reichstag on 28 April 1939, in which he answered an appeal from the American President for a guarantee of non-aggression.

> Mr. Roosevelt, . . . I once took over a State which was faced by complete ruin, thanks to its trust in the promises of the rest of the world and to the bad regime of democratic governments . . . I have conquered chaos in Germany, re-established order and enormously increased production . . . developed traffic, caused mighty roads to be built and canals dug, called into being gigantic new factories and at the same time endeavoured to further the education of our people.
> I have succeeded in finding useful work once more for the whole of the seven million people unemployed . . . Not only have I united the German people politically, but I have also rearmed them. I have also endeavoured to destroy sheet by sheet that treaty which in its four hundred and forty-eight articles contains the vilest oppression which peoples and human beings have brought back to the Reich provinces stolen from us in 1919. I have led back to their native country millions of Germans who were torn away from us and were in misery . . . and, Mr. Roosevelt, without spilling blood and without bringing to my people, and consequently to others, the misery of war . . .'

William Shirer,[11] commenting on this speech, described it as Hitler's greatest masterpiece in hoodwinking the German people, but made it clear that it failed to impress people and governments outside Germany. What Shirer seems to have overlooked was that for Germans much of what Hitler said had a basis in truth, and what *they* overlooked was that Nazi achievements were based on unparalleled terror and naked aggression, and that Hitler had skilfully avoided giving the assurance the President had asked for.

But the triumphs Hitler outlined in his speech, however they had been won, laid the foundations on which German confidence at the outbreak of war rested. They had come to believe that their Führer could achieve anything for them, without a war. So that when war came they were, as we have seen, stunned, but they were not dismayed or defeatist. They had none of the doubts and fears that beset the French. After the war a former German Chief of Staff wrote a book called *The Year of Destiny, 1939-40* in which he said:

> The German nation accepted the outbreak of war in a mood of solemn gravity. Their was no trace of that jubilant enthusiasm which had been so marked in 1914. In silence the men of military age obeyed their mobilization orders and reported to their units. It was as though the whole country, men and women, soldiers and civilians, was aware of the fatal nature of what was now beginning.

In June 1940 a 19-year-old cadet officer Fabian von Bonin-von Ostau, serving as a car commander in the Panzer Division, made some comments on German morale which could surely have been made by hundreds of his fellow-officers.

> The morale of the German soldiers was then as high as in May, especially when the final success in France became a reality. The morale of our Nation was also very high. People were remembering our defeat in 1918 and the consequences of the Versailles Treaty. That was an extremely hard burden for the whole nation to bear and was the main reason for Hitler's political success.

These somewhat naive comments appear to overlook – but perhaps they reflect – what were possibly the most powerful elements in the build-up of German morale: the success of Nazi propaganda and terrorism. 'No regime in history has ever paid such careful attention to psychological factors in politics,' wrote Alan Bullock in his masterly study of Hitler.[12]

> To attend one of his meetings was to go through an emotional experience, not to

One of the tasks of the dreaded SS in Nazi-occupied territories was to crush all resistance and destroy civilian morale by the systematic use of terror. TM

108

Even though this is a propaganda shot, there was nothing bogus about the exuberant high morale of young German veterans as they sang their marching songs on their way to the western front, confident in their leaders, their equipment and their own fighting prowess. TM

listen to an argument or a programme... Hitler had grasped as no one before him what could be done with a combination of propaganda and terrorism. For the complement to the attractive power of the great spectacles was the compulsive power of the Gestapo and the SS.'

From the moment Hitler came to power in 1933, his infamous Minister of Propaganda, Dr. Josef Goebbels, brought all media of expression under the complete control of the Nazi State. In the words of William L. Schirer:

Every morning the editors of the Berlin daily newspapers and the correspondents of those published elsewhere in Germany gathered at the Propaganda Ministry to be told by Dr. Goebbels or one of his aides what news to print or suppress, how to write the news and headline it... what editorials were desired for the day... Radio and motion pictures were also quickly harnessed to serve the propaganda of the Nazi State. Goebbels had always seen in radio... the chief instrument of propaganda in modern society.'

All this never-ceasing propaganda was directed towards making the German people, in Hitler's words, 'ripe for the domination to which we are called'.

There was, too, a more technical reason for the high morale of Germany's armed forces in 1939. All the evidence goes to show that, at least in the early years of the war, they were well-trained – a number of army and air force units having gained battle experience in the Spanish Civil War – well equipped and

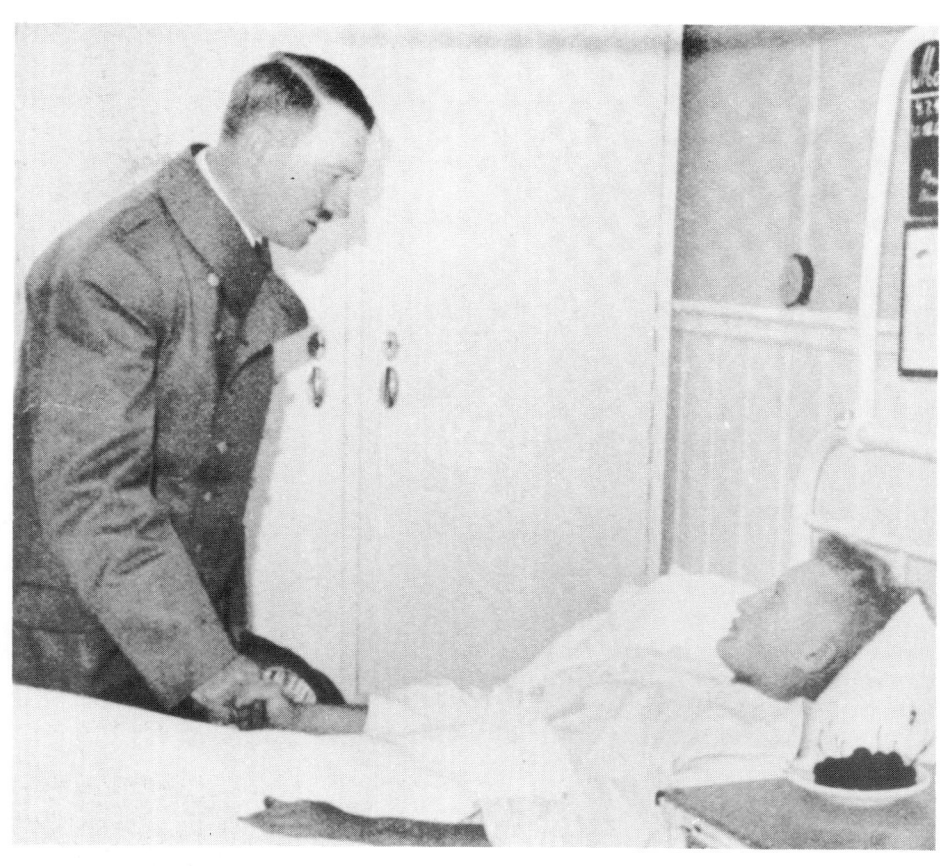

In the early days of the Second World War pains were taken to portray the Führer as a caring and compassionate leader. But when the tide of war turned against Germany he made progressively fewer public appearances, blaming everyone but himself for the disasters on every hand.   TM

well led, and that the campaigns in which they were expected to fight were planned to the last detail.

So in manpower, equipment, mobility, experience and morale, Germany's armed forces held all the cards at the outbreak of the Second World War: little wonder that Hitler's early campaigns were crowned with such spectacular success. How he came to squander the resources which he had done so much to create, and the manner in which he led his country to ruin and destruction is, of course, another story, and one which, appropriately told, would not be out of place in a Greek theatre or on Wagner's stage at Bayreuth.

NOTES

1. *The Memoirs of Field Marshal The Viscount Montgomery of Alamein, K.G.*, London: Collins, 1958.
2. Ibid.
3. General Sir Edward Spears *Assignment to Catastrophe* London: The Reprint Society, 1956.
4. Norman Longmate *How We Lived Then*. London, Arrow Books 1973.
5. 'Little did the foolish boys who passed the resolution,' wrote Winston Churchill in *The Gathering Storm*, 'dream that they were destined quite soon to conquer or fall gloriously in the ensuing war, and prove themselves the finest generation ever bred in Britain. Less excuse can be found for their elders, who had no chance of self-redemption in action.'
6. It has to be admitted, however, that when Churchill finished the draft of his speech, he showed it to his wife and said, with a twinkle in his eye, 'of course, I could have done it the other way round'. Perhaps we should allow the record to stand as the tribute one Prime Minister paid to another, and let history be the final judge.
7. W. S. Churchill *The Second World War: The Gathering Storm* London: Cassell & Co Ltd 1948.
8. Ibid.
9. Francois Fonveille-Alquier *France and the Phoney War* (trans. Edward Ashcroft) London, Tom Stacey 1973. 'But', says the author, 'he thought exactly the opposite and politicians ought to have known this . . . he deliberately couched his praise in such an exaggerated manner that no one could fail to perceive the wink to those who understood, a wink which signified "I don't believe a word of this."'
10. William L. Schirer: *The Rise and Fall of the Third Reich*. London, Secker & Warburg 1960.
11. Ibid.
12. Alan Bullock: *Hitler: A Study in Tyranny* London, Odhams 1952.

Chapter 7

Phase Two
THE CLASH

Blitzkrieg on Poland

With the collapse of the Tsarist Empire in 1917 and the defeat of the German and Austro-Hungarian Empires a year later, the Polish people rose up after the First World War to taste freedom for the first time in more than one hundred years. Not since the partitions of 1772, 1793 and 1795, when Prussia, Austria and Russia systematically, and by degrees, devoured the whole of the Polish kingdom, had these gallant and fiercely patriotic people had a homeland of their own. During the long and bitter years of foreign domination they kept alive their traditions, their culture, their language and, above all, their Catholicism. Now, with all three of their oppressors enfeebled at the same time, they seized

German troops assembled in their concentration area take a meal while waiting for the signal to launch the attack on Poland. IWM

Seen here on pre-war manoeuvres, the gallant Polish cavalry was no match for German panzers. TM

their chance, declared their independence and chose one of their great heroes, the concert pianist Paderewski, to lead them as their first Prime Minister. Among the flags of Europe flew the Polish eagle once again.

It was in this heady atmosphere that the Poles then embarked upon a wild military adventure, driving deep into Russian territory in order 'once more to water their horses in the Dneiper', as H. A. L. Fisher puts it.[1] Weakened and disorganised as they were, the Bolsheviks were in no mood to allow Kiev and the Ukraine to fall into the hands of their upstart neighbours. So they launched a powerful counter-attack and rolled them back hundreds of miles, bringing Russian guns well within range of Warsaw. But just as the proud new republic seemed likely to fall to the Bolsheviks a group of French officers, led by General Weygand, hurried to the assistance of the Polish army. With the veteran General Pilsudski at their head they won a decisive victory against the Russians, who were forced to sue for peace.

German resentment

Not surprisingly, Germany regarded the loss of her important eastern territories, which included the land corridor to East Prussia, the strategic German-speaking port of Danzig and most of Silesia, also German-speaking, as a national humiliation. Hitler skilfully exploited this resentment and put the restoration of the lost areas high on his list of priorities. In doing so, he not only furthered the policy of *lebensraum*, but gave shape to his long-term plan to take revenge on the Poles for regaining their independence largely, as he saw it, at Germany's expense.

With Austria and Czechoslovakia safely in the bag he lost no time in turning his diplomatic offensive, a now familiar mixture of bluff and bluster, threats and intimidation, propaganda and cajolery, on to his Polish neighbours. They, in turn, true to their gallant, not to say quixotic, national character, made it quite clear that they were not prepared to make any concessions and that they would fight alone and unaided if Germany were to attack them.

The Poles knew that they were not, in fact, completely alone. France had guaranteed their territorial integrity as early as 1921 and, in response to the changing mood in Britain, Neville Chamberlain told the House of Commons on 31 March 1939 that Britain and France were ready to 'lend the Polish government all support in their power' if its sovereignty and integrity were threatened. This news was greeted with great acclamation in Warsaw and throughout the whole of the country. Little did the Poles or their allies know that, just six days earlier, the German dictator had issued instructions to the OKW to start preparing for a solution to the Polish 'problem' by military means.

Fall Weiss

On 3 April 1939, three days after Chamberlain's declaration, Hitler issued his annual military directive (*Weisungen*) via the OKW. Part II of this document contains details of *Fall Weiss* (Case White), the code-name for the plan of campaign against Poland. Similar directives issued in previous years had dealt with such matters as the 'Anschluss' with Austria, the occupation of Memel in the event of a Polish invasion of Lithuania, and the occupation of Czechoslovakia under the code-name *Fall Grun* (Case Green). From August 1939 onwards the Führer's directives were numbered in sequence and the series continued until No. 51, issued in November 1943. Thereafter his orders to the various theatres took the form of specific instructions on specific topics. In the introduction to his book on these remarkable documents Hugh Trevor-Roper explains that Hitler saw, as a most important part of his 'historic mission', the need personally to . . . 'lay down general programmes, to expound future events and to dictate "political testaments". Such utterances, he felt, even if his successors did not follow them, would at least ensure that history would judge him aright.'[2]

The *Fall Weiss* directive, drafted by Hitler himself, makes it clear that although he had always wanted to maintain

A column of Pz Kpfw IIs, *led by a* Pz Kpfw I, *halts briefly on its forward advance. To the right can be seen an* Sd Kfz 251/6 mittlerer Kpfw Ausf A. *The dead horse and overturned cart at the roadside tell their own grim story.* TM

A German motorized artillery column makes its way forward from the captured town of Gevorovo. The guns, probably 7.5cm le Feldkanone 18, *are being drawn by* Bussing-NAG BN9 (Zgkw 5t) *half-track vehicles.* IWM

113

The few armoured vehicles the Poles possessed looked almost like toys compared with the formidable German equipment. Here a small column of 'Ursus' armoured cars passes through a village near Warsaw on 12 September 1939, heading for the front line and almost certain destruction.
TM

friendly relations with Poland, the problem on Germany's eastern border was now so serious that it might well have to be solved by force of arms. Preparations were therefore to be made by 1 September 1939 to 'smash the Polish armed forces and to create in the East a situation corresponding with the needs of Germany's defence'.

The reluctant ally
From April to July 1939 Hitler kept up his remorseless pressure on Poland by diplomatic and other means. On 28 April he abrogated the non-aggression pact and sent agitators into Danzig to stir up trouble. On 22 May, after assuring the Italians that there would be no war for several years, he signed the 'Pact of Steel' with Benito Mussolini. This secured Germany's southern flank, but in other respects the Italian connection was to prove a considerable embarrassment to the German leader both at a later stage of the pre-war crisis, and during the war itself. When, later, he told Mussolini that 26 August was the date set for the invasion of Poland and asked him to mobilise the Italian armed forces in accordance with the terms of their treaty, he received the reply that powers of mobilisation were vested in the King of Italy who refused to sign the necessary authorisations. Mussolini went on to say that it might be possible to review the situation if Germany were to supply certain strategic raw materials essential to any Italian war effort, and blandly presented a formidable shopping list.

Hitler was furious. Not only was he being shamelessly blackmailed by his one ally, but he also knew that the Italian authorities would make their position discreetly known to the British and the French, which would have the effect of strengthening their resolve to stand by guarantees to Poland. The Führer was so rattled by these developments that he decided to postpone the German attack by five days in the desperate hope that Britain would once again make a last-ditch plea for a peaceful settlement. That would give him the chance of bamboozling Chamberlain once more and of achieving his objectives by diplomatic means. But no such call came.

The Soviet-German Pact
What did come was news from Moscow of the greatest single diplomatic triumph of Hitler's turbulent career, a coup that

sealed the fate of Poland and made the Second World War inevitable. After weeks of secret negotiation the Soviet foreign minister, Molotov, let it be known that Stalin was ready to sign a non-aggression pact. In the long, murky annals of dealings between sovereign states, there are recorded few transactions more disreputable or more profoundly cynical than this August 1939 agreement between Nazi Germany and the Soviet Union. As Winston Churchill later observed in *The Gathering Storm*, 'only totalitarian despotism in both countries could have faced the odium of so unnatural an act. It is a question of whether Hitler or Stalin loathed it most. Both were aware that it could only be a temporary expedient. The antagonisms between the two empires and systems were mortal . . . The fact that such an agreement could be made marks the culminating failure of British and French foreign policy and diplomacy over several years.'

But in the short term the Pact, signed by Molotov and his German counterpart Ribbentrop, served both dictators well enough. It gave Hitler a crucial guarantee that he would not become involved in an armed conflict with the Soviet Union before the German war machine was ready to attack. And under various secret protocols Stalin gained a great deal more. Not only was he given *carte blanche* to absorb the three Baltic states of Latvia, Lithuania and Estonia, and to attack Finland at a time of his choice, but he was also able to occupy at virtually no cost vast tracts of rich agricultural land at the expense of the overwhelmed and defeated Poles.

Britain acted with uncharacteristic speed as soon as news of the Pact fell on the ears of a stunned world. The Foreign Office issued a written guarantee promising Poland aid from both Britain and France in the event of a German attack. Not even at this late hour was the Führer convinced that the pledge would be honoured, but he took care to ensure that any responsibility for opening hostilities on the western front would be laid at the feet of Britain and France. Furthermore, even if the Allies kept faith, they were prevented by distance and geography from military intervention in Poland on any significant scale. It would always be possible, Hitler reckoned, to arrive at a face-saving peace formula after his seizure of Poland had become a successful *fait accompli*.

The Poles, on the other hand, relied on France to attack in the West as soon as Hitler moved against them, and on that assumption they deployed their armed forces along the full length of their borders with Germany and East Prussia. With the benefit of hindsight we now know that if the French army had moved in strength they would have quickly achieved a breakthrough, and Hitler would have been forced to withdraw substantial forces from Poland to

---

The Supreme Commander of the Armed Forces

OKW/WFA Nr 170/39g. K. Chefs. Li
MOST SECRET
Senior Commanders only
By hand of Officer only

Berlin
31st August 1939

8 copies
COPY No. . . .

Directive No. 1 for the Conduct of the War

1. Now that the political possibilities of disposing by peaceful means of a situation on the Eastern Frontier which is intolerable for Germany has exhausted, I have determined on a solution by force.
2. The attack on Poland is to be carried out in accordance with the preparation made for 'Fall Weiss', with the alterations which result, where the Army is concerned, from the fact that it has in the meantime almost completed its dispositions. Allotment of tasks and the operational targets remain unchanged. The date of attack – 1 September, 1939. Time of attack – 4.45 (*inserted in red pencil*). This timing also applies to operations at Gydnia, the bay of Danzig and the Dirschau bridge.
3. In the West it is important that the responsibility for the opening of hostilities should rest unequivocally with England and France. Minor frontier violations will be dealt with locally for the time being. The neutrality of Holland, Belgium, Luxemburg and Switzerland, which we have assured, is to be strictly observed. The Western frontier will not be crossed by land without my explicit orders. This also applies to all acts of war at sea. Defensive measures by the Luftwaffe are to be restricted to repulsing firmly any enemy air attacks on the frontiers of the Reich. Care must be taken to respect the frontiers of neutral countries as far as possible, when countering single aircraft or small units. Only when large numbers of French or British bombers are employed against German territory across neutral territory, will the Air Force be allowed to fly counter-attacks over the same neutral soil. It is especially important to keep the OKW informed of every infringement of neutral territory by our Western enemies.
4. Should England and France open hostilities against Germany then it will be the duty of the Armed Forces operating in the West, while conserving their strength as much as possible, to maintain conditions for the successful conclusion of operations against Poland. The order to commence offensive operations is reserved absolutely to me.

The Army will hold the West Wall and should take steps to secure it from being outflanked in the north, by any violation of Belgian or Dutch borders by the Western powers. Should the French invade Luxembourg, permission is given to blow the frontier bridges.

The Navy will operate against merchant shipping, with England as the focal point. Certain zones may be declared danger areas in order to increase the effectiveness of such measures. The OKM will report on these areas and will submit the text of a public declaration in this matter, which is to be drawn up in collaboration with the Foreign Office and submitted to me for approval via the OKW. The Baltic Sea is to be secured against enemy incursions. OKM will decide if it is necessary to mine the entrances to the Baltic for this purpose.

The Air Force is primarily to prevent French or English air forces attacking German land forces or German territory. In operations against England it is the task of the Luftwaffe to harrass England's import trade at sea, her armaments industry and the transport of troops to France. Any favourable opportunity to attack enemy naval concentrations, especially battleships and aircraft carriers, must be taken. Any decision to attack London rests with me. Attacks against the English homeland should be prepared, bearing in mind that partial success with insufficient forces is to be avoided at all costs.

signed: **ADOLF HITLER**

(*translated from the original in Part II of the Nuremberg Documents*)

> **Proposed Organisation of German Armed Forces for the attack on Poland**
>
> ARMY GROUP NORTH
> **Third Army** consisting of 8 infantry divisions, a panzer brigade and a cavalry brigade.
> **Fourth Army** consisting of 4 infantry divisions, 2 motorised infantry divisions and one panzer division*.
> **Army Group Reserve** consisting of 2 infantry divisions.
>
> TOTAL Army Group North: 14 standard infantry divisions, 2 motorised infantry divisions, 1 panzer division*, a panzer brigade and a cavalry brigade, plus army group, army and corps troops.
>
> *a second panzer division was assigned to Army Group North just before the invasion was launched.
>
> ARMY GROUP SOUTH
> **Eighth Army** with 4 infantry divisions.
> **Tenth Army** with 6 infantry divisions, 2 motorised infantry divisions, 2 panzer divisions and 3 light divisions.
> **Fourteenth Army** with 5 infantry divisions, 1 light division and 2 panzer divisions.
> **Army Group Reserve** consisting of 3 mountain and 6 infantry divisions.
>
> TOTAL Army Group South: 21 standard infantry divisions, 4 panzer divisions, 2 motorised divisions, 4 light divisions and 3 light divisions, plus army group, army and corps troops.

protect his western front. But he took a gamble that neither France nor Britain would launch an attack. They may do a lot of talking, he told his generals, but they would not fight.

The Führer's nod towards Posterity

Throughout the frenzy of diplomatic activity during those last crucial days of August 1939 German demands remained unchanged: the return of Danzig; a road link between Germany and East Prussia and a plebiscite to settle the future of the Polish corridor, and the cession of all former German territories with majority German populations. Hitler knew perfectly well, of course, that the Poles would not concede any of these claims. But the diplomatic smokescreen gave him the cover he needed to put the finishing touches to his military preparations. They were by now almost complete: only one piece of the jigsaw remained to be placed in position. And that was an excuse for war, a *casus belli*, an incident that would justify his attack upon Poland in the eyes of posterity.

In 1935 at Gleiwitz, among the mines and the slag heaps of Upper Silesia, the Germans had built a radio transmitter to beam anti-Polish propaganda across the border. This was the site chosen for a bogus raid by a 'Polish' patrol which would put the radio station out of action for a short time. Shots would be exchanged, and the body of a man in Polish uniform – probably a Jew or other common criminal – would be left as evidence of the attack. This was to be the act of provocation deemed necessary for the history books of the future. The plan, code-named 'Operation Himmler', was put into effect on 31 August 1939: later that same day, in Berlin, Hitler signed his first war Directive.

Those who seek a symbol to represent the futility of war need look no further than the Gleiwitz radio mast under which the Second World War truly began. It stands to this day on its hill overlooking the same dreary stretch of industrial landscape. Little has changed during the past 50 years, except the name. Gleiwitz has become Glewice. By an ironic twist of history, the town that once belonged to Hitler's Third Reich is now part of the People's Republic of Poland.

The Opening Moves

Acting on the *Fall Weiss* directive of 3 April 1939 the OKH mobilised about 50 divisions to take part in the Polish campaign. They included four (later, six) panzer divisions, four motorised divisions, four light and three mountain divisions. This left only eleven active divisions to guard the western front, where French forces ten times that number were gathered behind the supposed safety of the Maginot line. General Walter von Brauchitsch was appointed Commander-in-Chief and put in full command of operations, although Hitler visited the front from time to time.

Two Army Groups made up the attack force as can be seen from the organisational table alongside. In the north was Fedor von Bock. Under his command was Kuchler's Third Army in East Prussia and Kluge's Fourth Army in Pomerania, threatening Danzig and the Polish corridor. In the south region von Rundstedt had command of three armies. Reichenau's Tenth Army stood poised on the German border for the main thrust on Warsaw. Covering the left flank was Blaskowitz with his Eighth Army and to the south stood List's Fourteenth Army ready to capture the important industrial area west of Cracow. In support of these land armies were two Air Fleets, led by Kesselring and Lohr, who had about 1,600 aircraft under their command.

The Impossible Task

The German strategic plan could hardly have been more straightforward. It was simply to encircle their opponents in a gigantic pincer movement closing at Warsaw, and then systematically and without quarter to destroy all Polish forces within their grasp. Poland, on the other hand, intended to hold back an invading force until Britain and France could intervene. But it was an impossible task. They faced hostile frontiers on all sides. To the west stood mainland Germany, with East Prussia to the north, Nazi-held Czechoslovakia to the south and, at their backs, the old enemy Russia. Reaching to these frontiers were vast open plains, while the Polish heartland was interlaced with river barriers.

In the build-up to their assault, the Germans made effective use of the existing road and rail infrastructure to move the two Army Groups into their concentration areas. Most of the force was transported by rail, but the new autobahns also played their part in getting men and equipment unobtrusively to their forward positions. Although the telephone and telegraph systems were nominally under the civilian control of the postal authorities, special traffic nets were set aside for military use and these were substantially augmented as the build-up progressed. Strict radio silence was observed in the concentration areas as such, but ordinary garrison traffic was maintained to put Polish military intelligence off the scent.

To move one-and-a-half million men into forward positions without attracting undue attention was a formidable achievement in itself, but an even greater triumph for German organisation was the transportation of huge quantities of equipment, ammunition and supplies. Nothing on this scale had ever been attempted before. Motorised war can only be waged with unfailing supplies of petrol, all of which had first to be transported to the forward zone and then carried behind the rapidly advancing motorised columns. Unlike food and forage which, as every soldier knows, can be won from the land if supplies run short, ammunition and fuel have to be carried into battle if the momentum of an advance is to be sustained. The new concept of *blitzkrieg* demanded constant advance, day after day. The supplies simply had to keep up; the logistical problems had to be solved. And solved they were, for despite all the turmoil of activity involving men and the materials of war, the Germans achieved complete tactical surprise. Polish reservists were still being called to their units when the first panzers rolled over their frontiers.

Order of the Day from the OKH[3]

The hour of trial has come. When all other means have been exhausted weapons must decide. We enter the fight knowing the justice of our cause and with a clear goal: the permanent security of the German people and German living space free from foreign trespass and presumptions to power.

The new National Socialist Army, as bearers of the proud traditions of the old army, will justify the trust bestowed upon it. Under the command of the Führer let us fight and be victorious.

We rely on the determination and the unity of the German people. We know the strength and energy of the German defensive readiness. We believe in the Führer.

Forward, with God, for Germany!

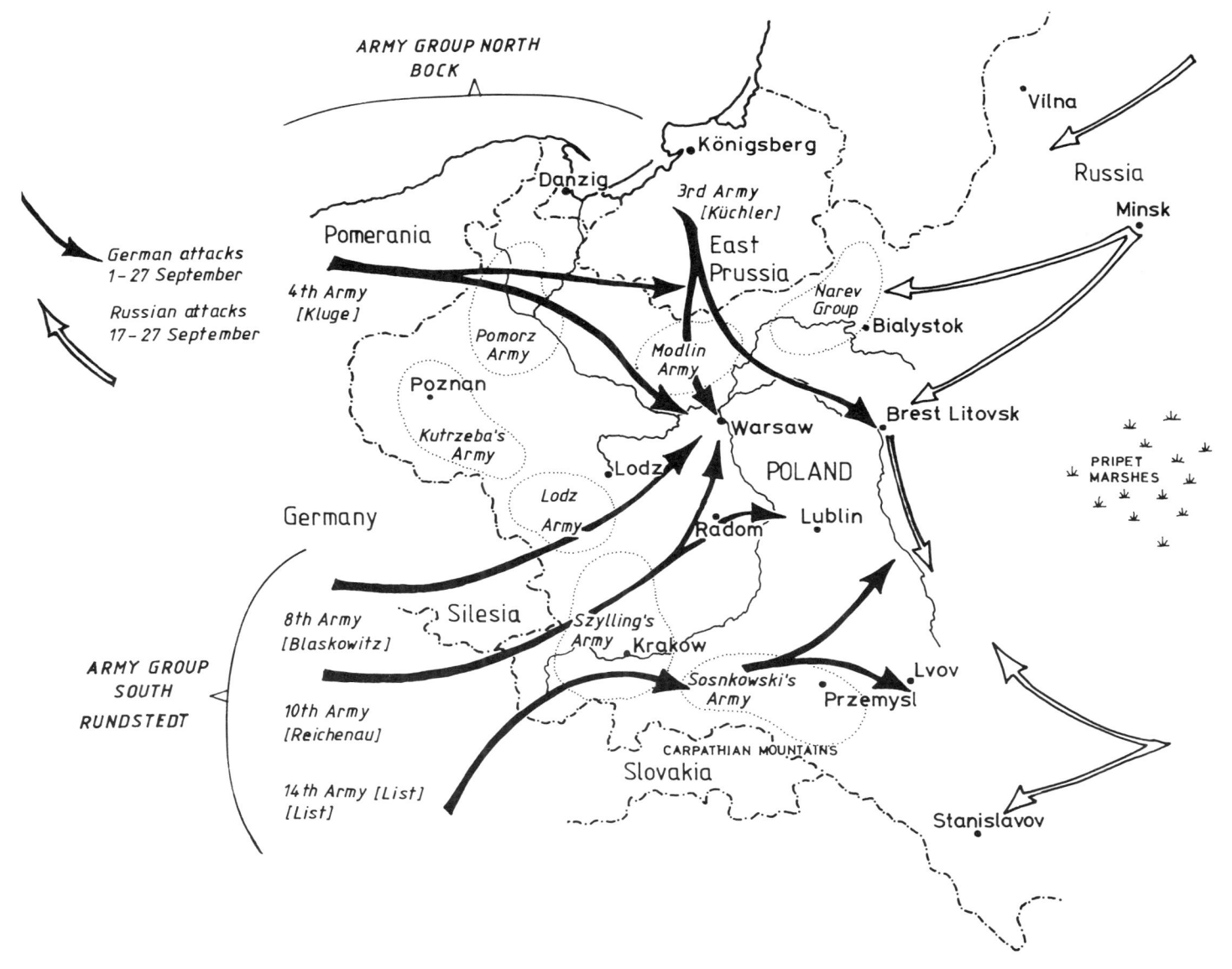

A useful German weapon in close engagements was the Stielgranate 24 *stick grenade, which weighed just under 1½lbs and had a 4½ second delay fuse.* TM

The OKW timetable

On 14 July 1939 the OKW issued a detailed timetable which hinged upon 23 August ('Y' Day) as the date on which the Führer would give orders for the final forward movement to be made in readiness for the attack. With the build-up complete, Hitler chose 26 August as the date for the actual invasion to begin but, as we now know, the British and French guarantees made him hesitate at a very late stage – so late, in fact, that some minor units of the attack force had already crossed the border and hastily had to be recalled. During the brief respite that followed the 10th Panzer Division, formed in Prague early in April and still incomplete, moved into the Fourth Army area. So they, too, were available for the attack, although mostly held in reserve, when it was finally launched on 1 September.

At 4.45am the two German Army Groups moved forward from their concentration areas exactly as planned. In

German infantrymen, using MG34s, take up their firing positions behind an overturned lorry on the outskirts of Warsaw. TM

Hitler watches his Wehrmacht in action as the Polish capital is bombarded into submission. TM

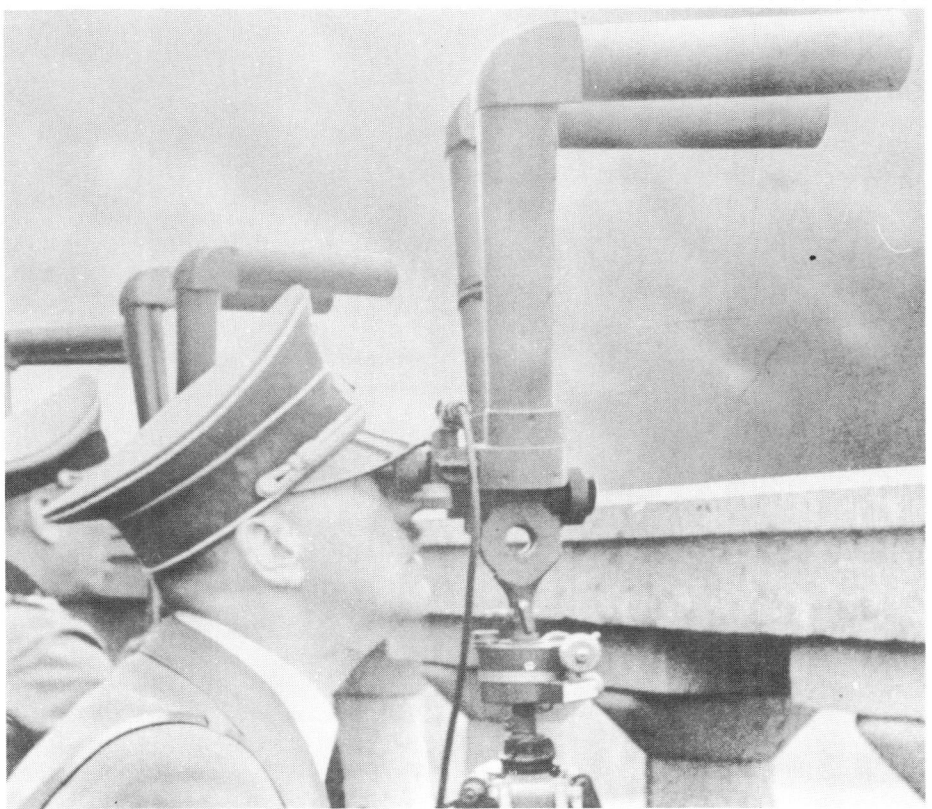

the air, 2,000 Luftwaffe planes launched a massive assault on bases throughout Poland and at 6am bombs were dropped on Warsaw, causing extensive damage and heavy civilian casualties. Although most of Poland's air force was destroyed within two days, her brave airmen accounted for more than 500 enemy aircraft, damaged or destroyed, despite the heavy odds against them and their own largely obsolete planes and equipment. In the Baltic, the German battleship *Schleswig-Holstein* opened fire on the Westerplatte fortress in Danzig harbour at first light. Within a matter of hours Poland's token navy was overcome by the OKM, but not before three destroyers and two submarines had, with great daring, made good their escape across the North Sea to England.

Events moved with equal rapidity on the ground. In the north, Guderian's XIXth Corps gave a convincing demonstration of blitzkrieg in action. After piercing Polish defences, his force raced on ahead of the main advance, covering some 400 miles in 28 days. As Albert Nofi points out in his book *The War Against Hitler*, 'not a bad performance for a motorized outfit by 1939 standards – in fact, the longest motor march in wartime up to 1940.' However, Nofi goes on to say that Guderian's actions provided the only example of true blitzkrieg tactics in the whole of the Polish campaign. The rest of the German armour, although remarkably successful, was handled with far more caution.

Even if the Poles had known in advance where the main enemy thrusts were to be made it is unlikely that their soldiers, for all their dash and courage, could have altered the course of the main battle. Dangerously over-stretched along most of their country's borders, they were out-numbered almost two to one, virtually without armour or motorised transport. They were completely unversed in modern warfare and had little understanding of the power of the armoured fighting vehicle. Stories of valiant charges by horse cavalry against swarms of tanks and armoured vehicles have doubtless gained in the telling over the last 50 years or so, but the fact remains that the 19th century finally met the 20th in that fateful opening clash of arms in the Second World War, with the inevitable result.

119

German tanks batter their way through the suburbs during the final onslaught on Warsaw. TM

Five days after the attack began Poland's frontiers no longer existed. Within a week, Reichenau's Tenth Army had pushed forward to within 40 miles of Warsaw from the south, while Kuchler with his Third Army was only 25 miles away to the north. The pincers were about to close. But in its endeavours to keep up with the main advance the German Eighth Army over-reached itself, and presented the beleaguered Poles with an opportunity to counter-attack. It was a chance they seized with both hands. On 9 September the Polish infantry, regrouped as the 'Poznan' Army, went over to the offensive on the River Bzura and succeeded in pushing the German forces back. This valiant rearguard action disrupted the main German advance. Surrounded on all sides, the Poles stood firm against assaults of ever-increasing ferocity until their positions were finally over-run ten days later.

Meanwhile, reports reached German Army headquarters that enemy units were breaking out of the Warsaw trap and heading south-east towards the relative safety of the short stretch of country bordering on Romania. It was therefore decided on 11 September to embark upon an outer pincer manoeuvre embracing most of the rest of the country. The city of Lemberg in the south-east was the immediate objective set for the Fourteenth Army, which was then to turn north to meet the Third Army sweeping down through Brest-Litovsk and beyond. Such was the speed of their advance, that these two armies met on 17 September, sealing off the last loophole of escape.

The end in sight

It was at this point that the Russians, who had watched the speed and success of the German campaign with considerable awe, decided that the time had come to make their own move. In a well-planned and well co-ordinated attack they crossed the border at several points to be greeted, in some instances, by Polish soldiers and civilians who mistakenly believed that they had come to give last-minute help in the struggle against the Nazi invaders. Disillusion quickly followed. All those wearing Polish army uniform were arrested on the spot, as were civilian officials and others already marked down by Communist sympathisers as 'enemies of the working class'.

The end was now in sight. The battered city of Warsaw capitulated on 27 September. The following day a Soviet-German treaty of demarcation was signed, both armies having taken up their previously agreed positions without incident. In the city of Brest-Litovsk, the German and the Russian military authorities went so far as to organise a joint parade to celebrate their victory. By the end of the first week of October 1939, all organised military resistance in Poland ceased.

During the course of the campaign the Germans took about 700,000 prisoners. Nearly 100,000 Poles escaped through Hungary, Romania and Lithuania, many of them making their way to the West to carry on the fight against the Nazis. But 70,000 Poles were killed (by the Germans: losses against the Russians are not known) and 133,000 wounded. German casualty figures tell their own story: 13,000 killed and 30,000 wounded.

There was no formal surrender. Deserted, as it seemed to them, by their western allies and stabbed in the back by their Russian foes, the Poles fought on until they could fight no more. There are few tributes more fitting that can be paid to a gallant race and to a gallant nation.

Lessons of Victory

Their war in Poland gave the Germans some very useful, hard experience of actual conditions in a blitzkrieg attack which they were not slow to put to good effect. One of the most valuable lessons was that the Pzkpfw I and II light tanks

German troops, each one equipped with the standard 7.92mm Karabiner 98k rifle, break into a house during a lull in the heavy street fighting. TM

were of very little use as fighting vehicles. They were too small, under-gunned and under-armoured, not strong enough and lacked the staying power to survive on a modern battlefield. The obvious conclusion was drawn that Panzer units should be equipped with more Pzkpfws III and IV, and that the lighter vehicles should be used only for reconnaissance and similar duties. The number of tanks lost was not inconsiderable, representing more than 10% of the total force of 2,000

German Tank Losses 1-30 September 1939	
Mk I	89
Mk II	83
Mk III	26
Mk IV	19
Total	217

at the outset of the campaign. However, some of them were reparable and taken back on strength.

Another useful source of making good the losses sustained in the campaign were the tanks that fell into German hands when Czechoslovakia was occupied. It was also decided to strengthen the *leichte* divisions by the addition of a three-battalion panzer regiment, and to redesignate them as the 6th, 7th, 8th and 9th Panzer Divisions.

Guderian singled out the Pzkpfw IV as a highly effective weapon. It was found in practice that both the armour protection and the firepower could be significantly increased without loss of performance in the field, with the result that this fighting vehicle was kept in production throughout the whole of the war — convincing testimony as to the excellence of its original design. By contrast, some of the Mk I and Mk II chassis were put into use as platforms for self-propelled anti-tank guns. Guderian also recommended for panzer units some basic tactical and organisational changes. For example, battalion and regimental HQs should be placed further forward to make them more effective in directing battle operations. It followed that they should be more mobile, better equipped with radio communications and restricted only to a few armoured command vehicles.

There were plenty of other lessons outside the panzer formations to be learned from the Polish campaign. It was found that the MG 34 was subject to frequent stoppages in field use. As a consequence, research on a new machine gun, the MG 42, was brought forward as a matter of urgency. On the other hand, it was found that the policy of developing many different forms of artillery had paid off in practice: sustained fire from many different weapons had been primarily responsible for wearing down the

121

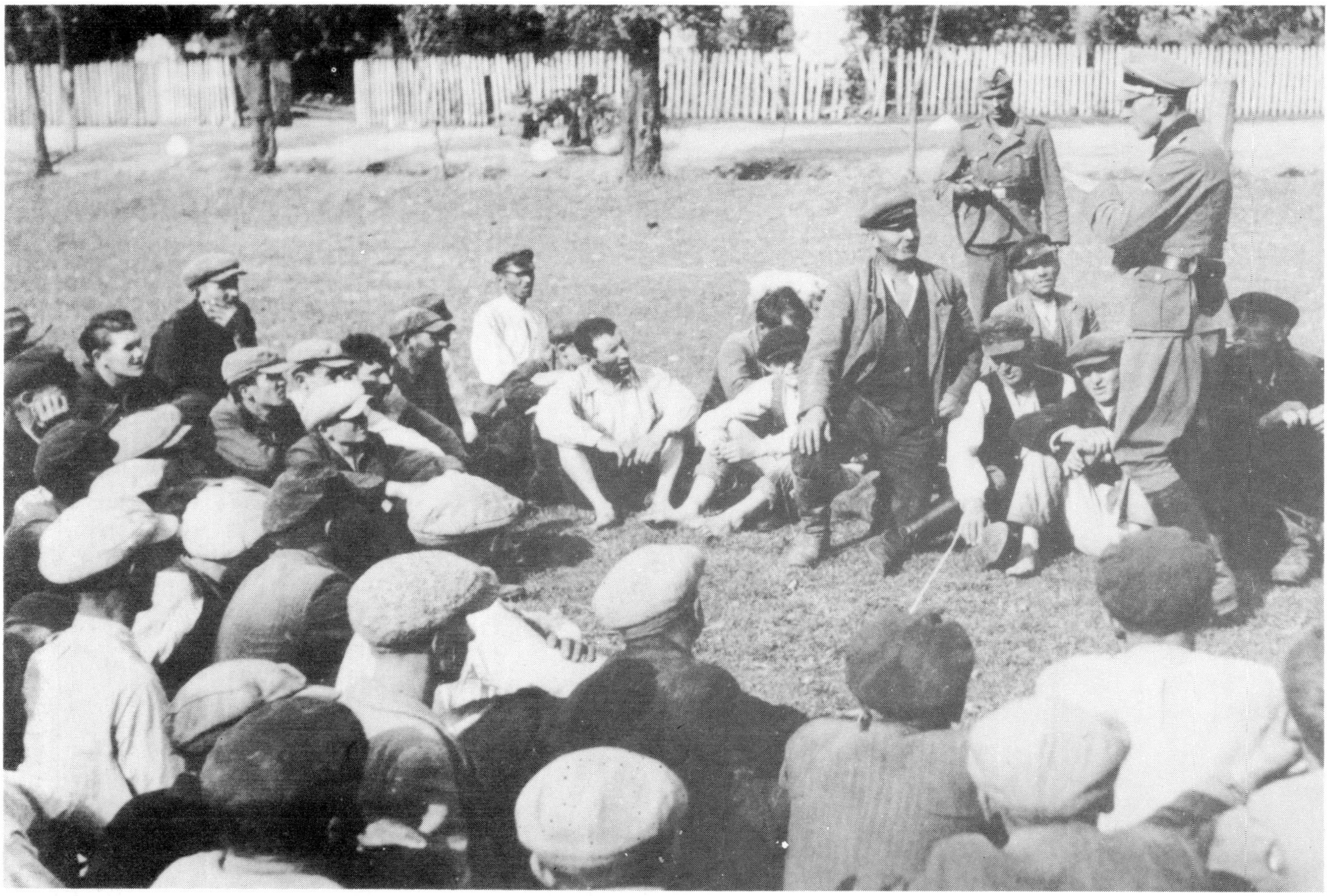

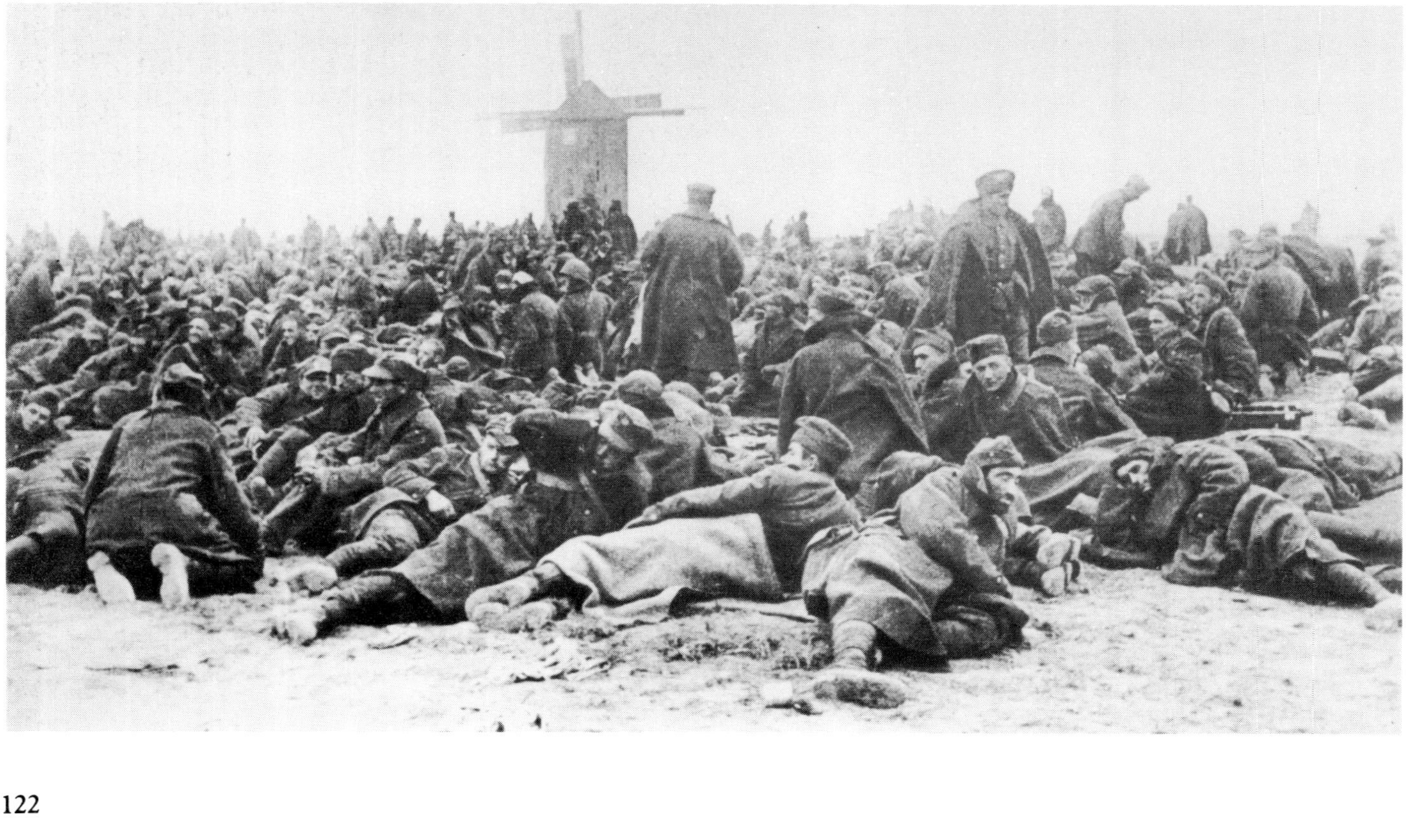

In an area untouched by the fighting a German officer interrogates Polish villagers. IWM

Meanwhile, Polish prisoners bewildered by the speed of the German advance await their fate. IWM

Dividing the spoils. A Russian military representative arrives by a BA 20(V) armoured car to discuss local demarcation details with his German opposite number in Brest-Litovsk. TM

stalwart defenders of Warsaw. In particular, the 88mm AA gun, with its high penetrative power, had proved itself of great value in attacks against bunkers and other fortifications.

Infantry attacks were criticized as being on the whole too cautious, although it was conceded that on many occasions infantry units had to wait while artillery was brought up to support them. General Bock expressed the view that the old adage, 'The infantry must wait for the artillery', should be turned on its head to read 'The artillery may not delay the infantry'. It was recommended that some artillery batteries should be permanently and directly attached to infantry units so that close support would always be available in an attack or forward movement. Looking to another aspect of infantry

'Danzig Greets Its Führer!' proclaims the banner as the Nazi dictator makes his triumphant entry into the city on 19 September 1939. IWM

warfare, the Germans, who were well versed in the movement of troops by night, were impressed by the skill and determination shown by Polish fighting men in actual night attacks, and came to the conclusion that they had something to learn from their opponents when assessing the tactical value and potential of actions of this kind.

The Luftwaffe had shown its power as a weapon of attack, and had clearly demonstrated how battle fronts could be isolated by the bombing of bridges and railway lines, and by the disruption of road traffic. Dive-bombing had also proved of great value in support of advancing armoured columns, and henceforward became an integral part of all blitzkrieg attacks. On the debit side, however, was the unfortunate fact that Luftwaffe pilots had bombed their own forward formations on a number of occasions.

The Propaganda Bonus
The German campaign in Poland demonstrated to the world at large that the Wehrmacht was a formidable and effective fighting machine, the like of which had not been seen before. Nazi propaganda exploited their military triumph to the full, skilfully creating a myth of invincibility that persisted throughout the early part of the Second World War. This undoubtedly had its effect on Allied morale.

The picture presented showed a highly efficient, fully mobile fighting force with massive tank and aircraft support available at all times. The reality, though impressive enough, was rather different. No mention was made of the fact that large numbers of horses were needed to tow the guns and supply waggons, or that most infantrymen in the German army still had to march into battle.

However, none of the skills of the Propaganda Ministry were required to discredit the western Allies. The world was astonished by their failure to bring any kind of meaningful pressure to bear on Nazi Germany during the Polish campaign. And as soon as it had been successfully concluded, the opportunity for military counter-action was lost for good. With Russia as an unlikely ally in the east, Hitler knew he could move most of the German army to face his enemies in the west.

British military circles calculated that no more than 15 to 30 divisions would be needed to garrison Poland, and that most of these could be of fairly inferior quality. Hitler was therefore free to transfer most of his crack troops, now baptised by fire and flushed with victory, to the western front. This gave him an immediate numerical advantage over the combined Allied force of about four to three, without taking into account the large number of reservists still available.

The startling success of his attack on Poland confirmed the Führer's belief, if confirmation were needed, that his strategic skills were far greater than those of his generals and that he had no need of military advice. Accordingly he set work to plan the destruction of French army and the BEF without further delay. Only one of the harshest winters of the century and a barrage of objections, couched in the strongest terms, from the OKH, made him change his mind. With the greatest possible reluctance he allowed himself to be persuaded that the onslaught in the west should be postponed until the spring of 1940.

This unwelcome delay allowed a further intervening act in the drama to unfold.

NOTES

1. H. A. L. Fisher *A History of Europe* London: Edward Arnold & Co. 1936.
2. H. R. Trevor-Roper *Hitler's War Directives* London: Sidgwick & Jackson 1964.
3. J. Pielkalkiewiez *Tank War 1939-1945* London: Blandford Press 1986.

After the Poles surrendered Warsaw the Germans staged a victory parade at which Hitler took the salute. Many of these victorious soldiers were soon on their way to the Western front to face the French army and the British Expeditionary Force. TM

Chapter 8

The Phoney War

When the Germans failed to respond to the British ultimatum to withdraw their troops from Poland by not later than 11am on 3 September 1939 the tired and melancholy voice of Chamberlain was heard, in a broadcast to the world, declaring that 'this country is at war with Germany.' France declared war followed six hours later, before their own separate ultimatum had expired: such was the lack of co-ordination between the western allies in the management of their joint affairs. Other declarations of war from the British dominions and French colonial empire followed. Eire, on the other hand, determined not to jeopardize her hard-won independence, reaffirmed her neutrality.

Other actions at sea followed. Meanwhile, the RAF dropped leaflets to 'rouse the Germans to a higher morality', in Churchill's delicious phrase. And on 7 September General Gamelin, who had earlier promised that he would 'not begin the war with a Battle of Verdun', felt obliged to honour the French pledge to Poland. He therefore gave orders that nine divisions should be moved forward into the Saarland.

'French Army Pouring Over The German Border!' screamed the London *Daily Mail*, but as soon as troops had occupied a handful of villages, penetrating to a distance of about five miles along a sixteen-mile front, the French High Command called a halt to the proceedings. There the *poilus* remained, with strict orders not to advance further or even to provoke the enemy into taking counter-action. Nothing more happened until Poland collapsed, at which point the French pulled back their forces to the Maginot Line. By 4 October the with-

The French President, M. Albert Lebrun, with the C-in-C of the British Expeditionary Force, General the Viscount Gort, VC, KCB, CBE, DSO, MVO, MC, during his visit to the British sector on 9 February 1940. TM

drawal was successfully accomplished. 'It was simply a token invasion,' one French general is reported to have said. 'We do not wish to fight on their territory. We did not ask for this war. Now that the Polish question is liquidated we have gone back to our lines. What else did you expect?'[1] One can, without difficulty, see the shrug of Gallic shoulders.

While the rest of the world looked on in disbelief at the Allies' failure to respond, the Germans themselves could hardly believe their good fortune. Giving evidence after the war at the Nuremberg trials, Marshal Keitel said: "Our astonishment was great to find only minor skirmishes undertaken between the Siegfried and Maginot lines. We did not understand why France did not seize this unique opportunity, and this confirmed us in the idea that the Western Powers did not desire war against us."

So, after all the high drama in Poland, an uncanny calm settled over the free nations of Europe. Like mesmerized rabbits his frightened neighbours awaited the Nazi dictator's next move. Where will the blow fall? And when? Will it be our turn next?

Churchill's assessment

In a private letter of 15 September 1939 to the British Prime Minister, Winston Churchill, who had by then been appointed First Lord of the Admiralty, doubted that Germany would attempt any offensive in the West 'at this late season'. He went on to venture an opinion that Hitler would be wise to press on through Poland and Hungary to the Black Sea to sustain the momentum of his overwhelming military success, and to secure his 'feeding-grounds' for the coming winter.

Chamberlain, for his part, asserted that the main lesson of the Polish campaign was the power of an Air Force when it had complete mastery of the skies to 'paralyse the operations of land forces'. It followed that Royal Air Force should be immediately and significantly strengthened, even if it meant diverting resources away from the other Services. Taking such shots in the dark, Chamberlain's aim was spot on target whereas Churchill's was rather wide of the mark.

There was a remarkable reluctance on the part of the Allies to commit what resources they had at their disposal. When, for example, it was suggested to Kingsley Martin, Britain's Air Minister, that incendiary bombs should be dropped in the Black Forest region, where it was known that considerable quantities of supplies and ammunition were stored, he is said to have replied, "Are you not aware that it is *private* property? You'll be asking me to drop bombs on Essen next!"[2]

Churchill himself, by no means lacking in ruthlessness, thought that the RAF 'should not take the initiative in bombing, except in the immediate zone where the French armies are operating, where we must of course help.' He considered that Britain should conduct the war with a degree of humanity and that 'we should follow and not precede the Germans in the process, no doubt inevitable, of deepening severity and violence.' The French were also most anxious that the RAF should not carry out air attacks on German targets because they feared that the inevitable retaliation would be at the expense of their own unprotected towns, cities and war factories, and not those of mainland Britain.

Hitler and his generals

General Keitel and the three Commanders-in-Chief were aghast when Hitler told them, on 27 September, that

Just like their fathers before them in 1914, many British infantrymen were moved by rail from ports of disembarkation to their forward positions in railway cattle-trucks.

IWM

he proposed to attack in the west without delay. After reviewing his victorious troops in Warsaw he returned to Berlin. Nine days later, on 6 October, he made a speech in the Reichstag in which he suggested that a conference with the western allies should now take place to reach a 'solution before millions of men are first uselessly sent to their death.' He offered no concessions, however, and there can be little doubt that his main motive was to get German public opinion behind him once more by throwing the blame on Britain and France for continuing the war.

What is quite certain is that he did not allow thoughts of a possible peace settlement to hold up his military planning. Only three days after the Reichstag speech he issued Directive No. 6 in which he made it quite clear that the war aim was 'a final military settlement with the West.' To achieve this objective the German Army was to sweep through Holland, Belgium and Luxembourg, destroying all opposing forces before they could form 'a coherent defensive front'. Most of the active units in Poland were to be refitted and moved across Germany as quickly as possible: the attack on the West 'cannot take place too early'.

The generals did not share Hitler's enthusiasm for battle. Many of them believed that Britain and France could be manoeuvred into a compromise peace settlement, and that Germany's immediate objectives could be won without further bloodshed. Some went so far as to consider the possibility of removing Hitler from the scene but, as on previous occasions, nothing came of such conspiratorial ideas.

While not one of the generals dared to defy Hitler openly, they did work together in presenting him with a set of compelling reasons why he should not press forward with his plan. There were many problems involved in re-equipping the German Army and moving it to the West; the risks of getting bogged down in a winter campaign were unacceptable; the strength of the French army and the BEF had not been sufficiently taken into account; the main supply depots in western Germany were not yet ready as most of the available war material had been earmarked for the Polish campaign – these and many other difficulties, real and imaginary, were put to the Führer in attempts to make him change his mind.

Hitler listened to these arguments with growing impatience for he knew, better than his military advisers, that the last thing Germany could afford was a long and protracted war. Time was not on his side, but he kept everyone on tenterhooks until 5 November, when Brauchitsch was summoned for a private interview in the Reich Chancellery. The General repeated all the familiar objections, but when he threw doubt on the morale and performance of German infantry during the Polish campaign Hitler flew into a violent rage and declared that the offensive in the West would be launched, as planned, on 12 November. Then he stormed out of the meeting, leaving Brauchitsch in a state of nervous collapse.

Five days before the attack was due an unfavourable weather report brought about a postponement. A new date was set, but that, too, had to be postponed for the same reason. To complicate matters still further, and to Hitler's growing fury and frustration, various alternative plans were produced which for one reason or another were either rejected completely or amended. These processes continued until the New Year, by which time the whole of western Europe was in the grip of one of the harshest winters in living memory. Even Hitler was finally persuaded that no useful purpose would be served by attempting large-scale military operations in such conditions and, with great reluctance, he agreed to put off the attack in the west until the Spring. So in the end it was the weather that thwarted Hitler as well as his generals. But that did not prevent him blaming them entirely for the delay, or censuring them for their caution, defeatism and lack of enterprise.

The BEF in France

In the warm September days of 1939, when the British Expeditionary Force took up their positions in Northern France, there was no hint of the rigorous winter to follow. The advance party sailed from Portsmouth the day after Britain declared war, and on 9 September the first troop-carrying convoys left Southampton and the Bristol Channel ports.

By 27 September 1939 the Royal Navy with shipping of the Mercantile Marine under their control had moved to France, without the loss of a single life, the following men and materials:

152,031 Army personnel
  9,392 Royal Air Force personnel
 21,424 Army vehicles
  2,470 Royal Air Force vehicles
 36,000 tons of ammunition
 25,000 tons of motor spirit
 60,000 tons of frozen meat

in addition to other stores, equipment and supplies. Thereafter the build-up of British forces and of equipment stores and supplies continued steadily.

Very tight security was imposed on these movements, to the disgust of at least one professional soldier, who wrote in his battalion history:

> Nothing could have been further removed from the traditional departure of troops for overseas . . . than the furtive slinking away to war of one of the most famous of His Majesty's infantry divisions, as this element of the 5th Infantry Brigade cast off and slid into the Channel from Southampton . . . Cannot something better this be achieved in these days of total warfare in the way of a send-off for the armies of Britain dispatched to fight their country's cause?[3]

Once they landed safely in France many of these British soldiers were given a welcome much less restrained. The *History of the Duke of Wellington's Regiment*, for example, records the progress of the 1st Battalion in these terms:

> The transport had an interesting journey across France from Brest to Wailly, near Arras, where they met the remainder of the Battalion. It took the form of a triumphant entry, as in each village and town the inhabitants lined the streets, and threw fruit, flowers and chocolate into the vehicles as they passed.[4]

The consolidation of the British Expeditionary Force continued apace and many of the units were soon engaged in the preparation of defensive position, especially along the so-called 'Gort Line',

On arrival, their first task was usuallly the preparation of defence works. Digging-in was a tedious and laborious business, especially after the fine Autumn weather in 1939 gave way to one of the worst winters in living memory. IWM

Cold comfort in a French barn for soldiers of the BEF on a mid-December evening – but at least someone's remembered to bring the dartboard! IWM

which was – in theory at least – an improvised extension of the Maginot Line. And so British soldiers found themselves digging trenches in the fields of Northern France, just as their fathers had done before them, in conditions which steadily deteriorated as the winter weather set in. The following extract from the war history of the 2nd Battalion of the Dorsetshire Regiment (1939-1942) tells its own story:

> There was a shortage of everything in the forward divisions – clothing, equipment and amenities. When the day's digging was finished at about 4.30 in the evening the troops, soaked through, were marched back to their billets and sat down to the evening meal . . . Facilities for drying clothes were practically non-existent, but the health of the Battalion remained remarkably good. The village itself, apart from a couple of cafés, could provide no source of entertainment for the men . . . Units made their own entertainments.[4]

The history goes on to explain that the most popular form of evening amusement for the men was writing letters home, an activity not at all popular with their officers whose duty it was to censor the letters before they were sealed and posted.

> On the amenities side, the smokes situation improved rapidly, and before long the NAAFI/EF15 opened up a good supply depot in Orchies. Bathing presented difficulties, but these were not insuperable: very soon the basement of the Rumegies Brewery was converted, with the help of the Pioneers and the Sappers and a most Heath-Robinson water-heating machine, into a servicable bath-house.

The attitude of the men of the BEF during that boring, uncomfortable and rugged winter, when scarcely a shot was fired in anger, is summed up in this way:

> Despite the efforts of the Press at home to paint a very much worse picture of the conditions than they actually were, a matter which caused dissatisfaction among the soldiers, who like to do their own grumbling in their own way, the Battalion settled down happily enough in their first winter of the war.[4]

When they were not working on defences or engaged in other front-line duties the men of the BEF had to undergo vigorous training programmes in the use of new weapons and the employment of new tactics, as well as field exercises involving road movement and air co-operation. All this activity helped to sustain morale, in sharp contrast with the situation found in many units of the French Army, as reported to Winston Churchill by Gen Sir Edward Spears:

> Behind one part of the Maginot Line troops who should have been training were employed in digging field works to increase the depth. On other fronts nothing was happening at all. An immense boredom enveloped the armies where little training was taking place and the men were saturated by the ceaseless anti-war, anti-British propaganda of the Germans. Then, my French friends said, officers' wives found their way to nearby towns, where their husbands joined them. NCOs followed suit, and the men, knowing what was afoot, but unable to do likewise, became seriously disaffected.[5]

Allied Defence Plans

The Allied High Command considered three possible plans of defence in the event of a German attack through the Low Countries. The first of these, known as the 'Albert Canal Plan', envisaged the movement of French forces along the Albert Canal and its line of fortifications, to a point as far east as possible. The 'Escaut Plan', on the other hand, simply involved moving forward to the River Escaut (Scheldt/Schelde) to cover Audenarde, Gand and Anvers. The 'Dyle Plan' represented a compromise between the other two, by which a defensive front was to be established along the River Dyle to protect Brussels.

Naturally enough, the Belgians favoured the 'Albert Canal Plan' because it protected almost the whole of their country. However, the French General Staff rejected the plan out of hand because they thought it was far too risky. The 'Escaut Plan' was turned down for precisely opposite reasons: it presupposed the surrender of Brussels and made

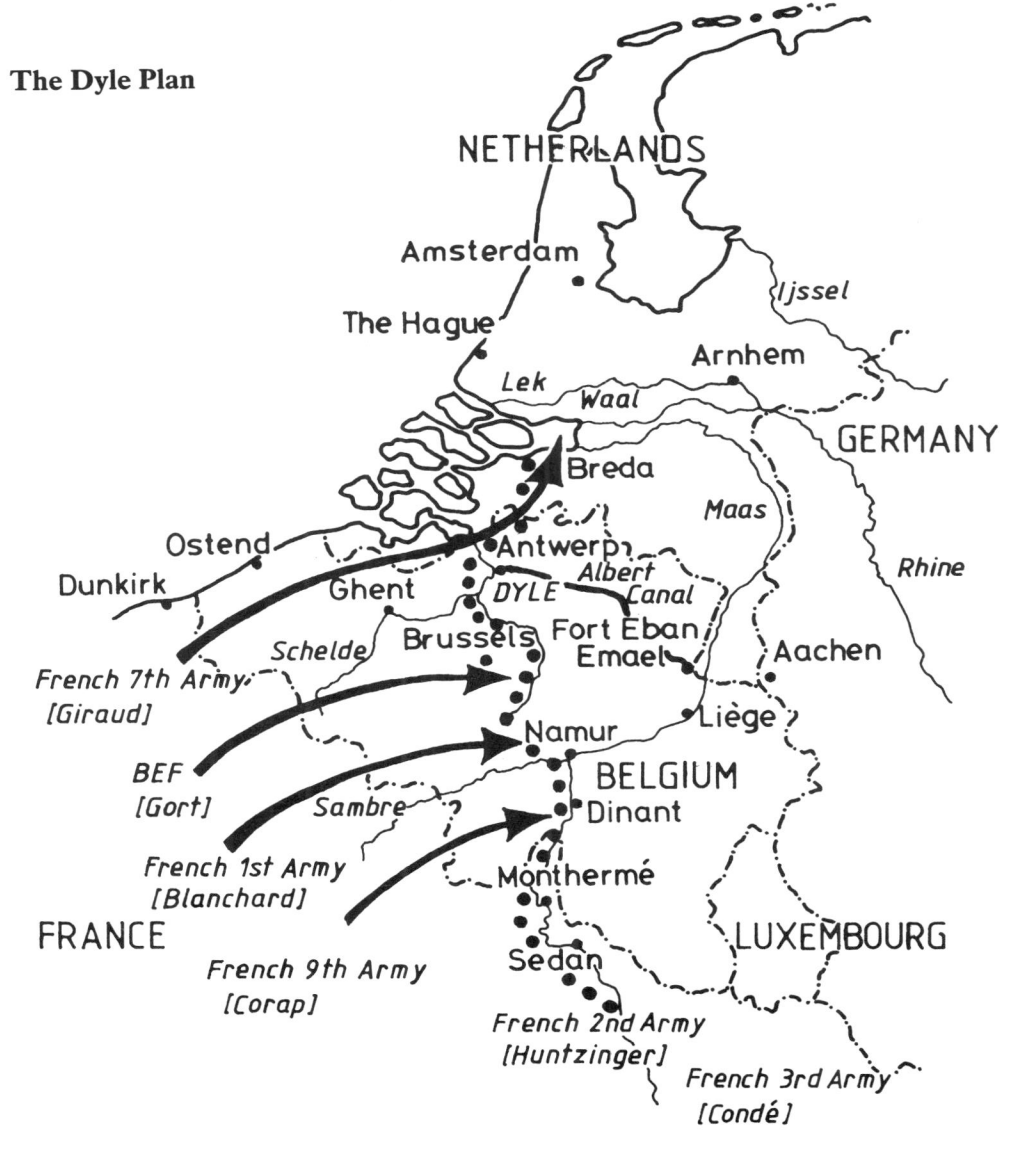

The Dyle Plan

• • •   *The Dyle Line - approx location*

The French C-in-C, Gen Georges, with Lord Gort, Gen Lloyd, Brig Findley and other officers, during a tour of inspection of the BEF. IWM

no provision for a possible link with Holland and the Dutch defence forces.

Gen Gamelin favoured the compromise plan, although his colleague, Gen Georges was not so keen. 'This is happy-go-lucky', he is said to have noted in the margin of his copy. 'If the enemy masks Belgium, he can manoeuvre elsewhere. So do not let us pour our resources into this business. Let us stop dreaming.' Prophetic words that went unheeded by the rest of the Allied High Command, who endorsed the Dyle Plan and made such preparations as they could. An important *caveat*, because while Holland and Belgium remained neutral all such plans were no more than theories, incapable of being put into practice. No Allied force could move into Belgium until it was invited to do so by the Belgian government.

This was not the only constraint under which the Allies had to work during the period of the Phoney War. Another, and far more serious, was the cumbersome system of command and control under which, as is to be seen, each of the three

---

ALLIED COMMAND STRUCTURE

North East Front HQ (Gen Georges) at *La-Ferté-sous-Jarre* was responsible for the 1st ARMY GROUP, commanded by Gen Billotte

Supreme Commander French Land Forces HQ (Gen Gamelin) at *Vincennes* was responsible for the 2nd ARMY GROUP, commanded by Gen Pretelat

GHQ Land Forces (Gen Doumenc) was responsible for the 3rd ARMY GROUP, commanded by Gen Besson

1st ARMY GROUP
Dunkirk to Bailleul
7th Army (Giraud) 9 divisions, including 1st DLM (174 tanks)
Bailleul to Maulde
BEF (Gort) 9 divisions
Maulde to Longuyon
1st Army (Blanchard) 12 divisions with 2nd and 3rd DLM (348 tanks)
9th Army (Corap – later Giraud) 9 divisions, including 1st and 4th DLC
2nd Army (Huntziger) 9 divisions, including 2nd and 5th DLC

2nd ARMY GROUP
Maginot Line
35 divisions (Pretelat)

3rd ARMY GROUP
Maginot Line
14 divisions (Besson)

RESERVE
18 divisions, including three armoured divisions, with a fourth awaiting formation

Army Groups stationed along the entire length of the Western Front had its own separate headquarters.

Behind the Westwall

The codename for Hitler's attack against the West, outlined in his Directive No. 6, was *Fall Gelb* (Case Yellow). The original plan prepared by OKH to achieve the Supreme Commander's objectives was drawn up on conventional lines, and in many ways reflected the opening moves of the *Schlieffen* plan of 1914.[6] The aim was to reach the Channel coast by means of an attack through Belgium and Luxembourg, with the exposed southern flank strongly protected. In Phase I, a pincer movement with Liége as the fulcrum would engulf Brussels and central Belgium. The main force, consisting of 37 divisions under Army Group B, would remain to the north, while Army Group A, with 27 divisions, would cover the southern flank. In Phase 2 the attack continued in a westerly direction towards Ghent and Bruges, and on to the Channel coast. Holland would be occupied by a small force consisting of not more than three divisions. No assault was to be made on the Maginot Line.

The plan was not well received either by the senior generals or by Hitler himself. He declared that he would much rather see the main effort concentrated south of Liége in order to achieve a break-through to the west. After a series of high-powered meetings a revised plan was produced late in October 1939. The introduction contained these words:

> All available forces will be committed with the intention of bringing to battle on north France and Belgian soil as many sections of the French Army, and its allies, as possible. This will create favourable conditions for the further conduct of the war against England and France on land and in the air.[7]

Apart from a limited operation in the Maastricht area, no incursion upon Dutch soil was planned. The main thrust, in accordance with the Führer's wishes,

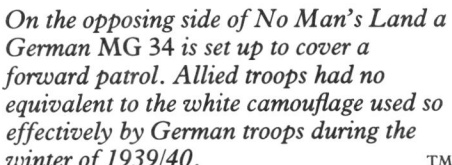

On the opposing side of No Man's Land a German MG 34 is set up to cover a forward patrol. Allied troops had no equivalent to the white camouflage used so effectively by German troops during the winter of 1939/40. TM

Hitler explains the plan to Hess, Keitel and Martin Bormann.

A German patrol edges forward, armed with stick grenades and an MG34. ™

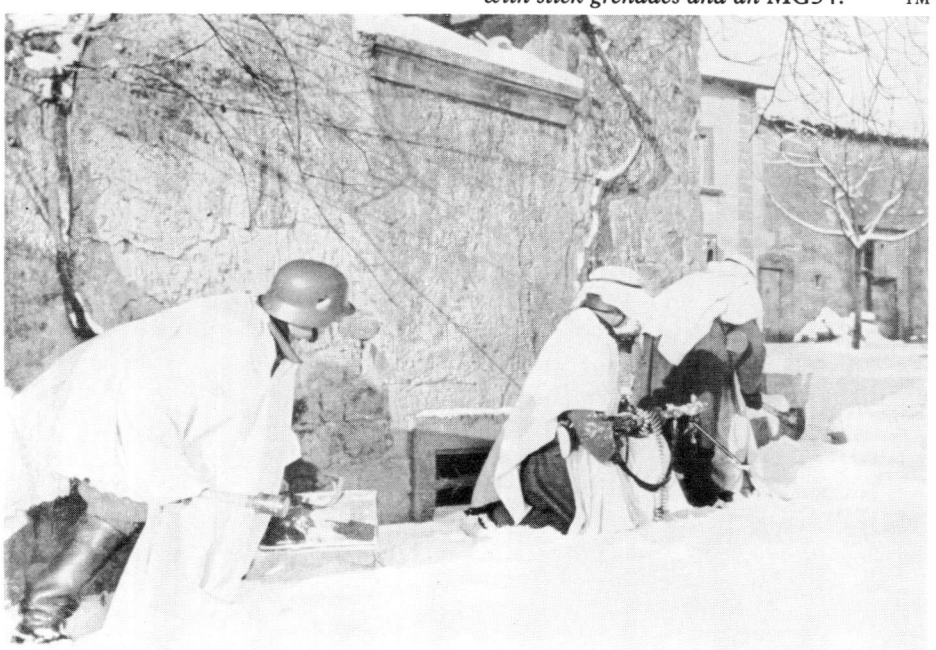

International Boundaries — · — · —
Army Group Boundaries · · · · · · · ·
Army Boundaries · · · · · · · ·
Maginot Line · x · x · x · x · x
Numbers Show Armies eg: 4
Intended Advance Route ⬅
Armoured and Motorised ⬅ Forces

was to be made north and south of Liége by Army Group B, now increased to 42 divisions, before pressing on to the west. Army Group A, now 23 divisions, would attack through the Ardennes, cross the Meuse and then carry on to Rheims and Amiens, protecting the flank of Army Group B as they did so, while the task alloted to Army Group C, with 20 divisions, was to tie down the enemy in the Maginot Line. A reserve of 10 divisions brought the total number required to 95.

Hitler liked this new plan no more than the first. It also received a cool reception from the generals, who considered that failure to invade Holland would allow the Allies to operate from Dutch air bases, at the same time denying their use to the Luftwaffe. This objection was dealt with in a revised version issued by the OKH in January 1940, setting out details of operations to be carried against Holland at the same time as the main attack. But other objections remained, of which the most serious was that the plan was too limited in its strategic aims.

FALL GELB

Army Detachment North
3 Divisions

Army Group B
37 Divisions including
8 Armoured
2 Motorised

OKH Reserve
9 Divisions including
1 Armoured
1 Motorised

Army Group A
27 Divisions including
1 Armoured
2 Motorised

Army Group C
25 Divisions

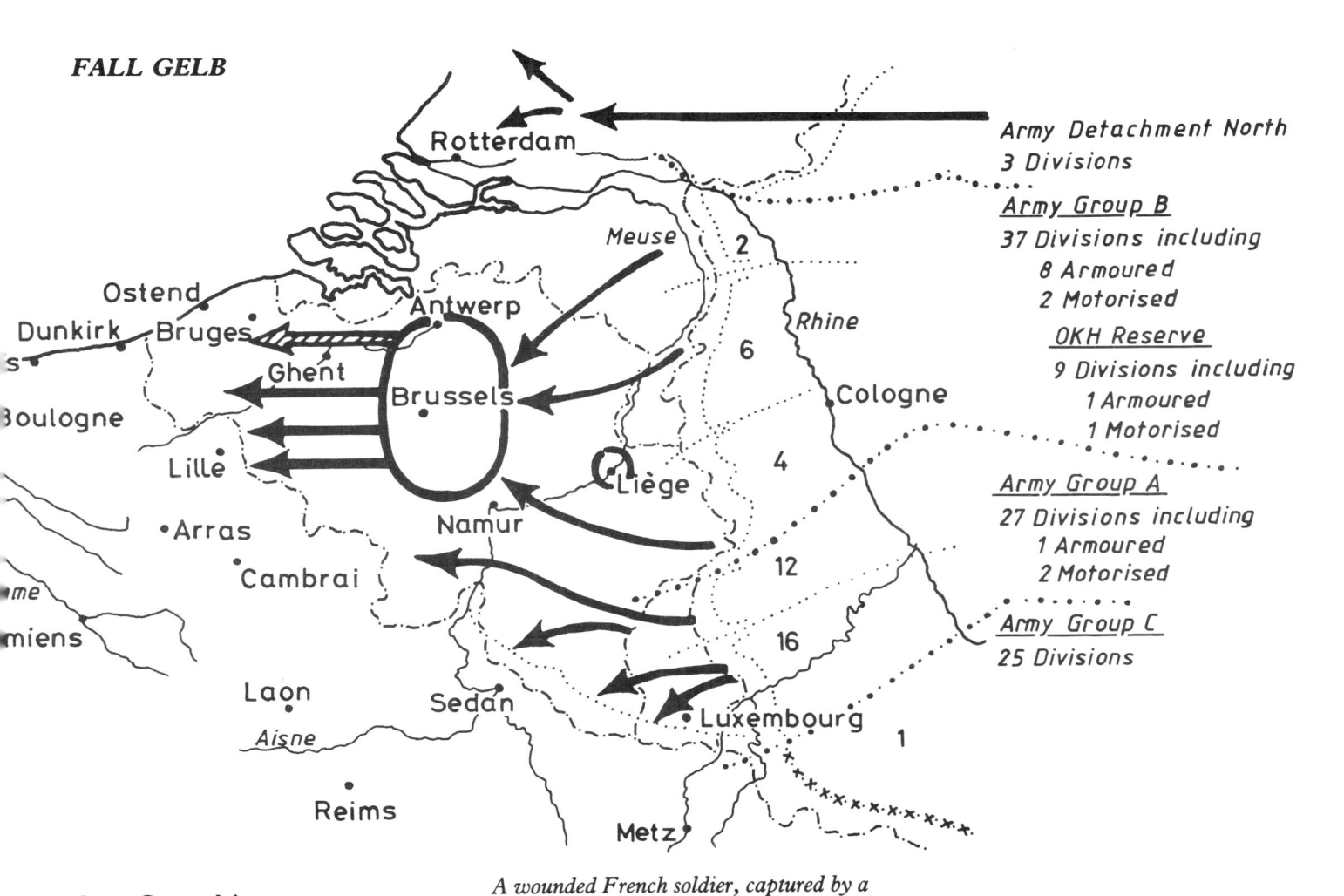

A wounded French soldier, captured by a German patrol, is brought in for questioning.

Army Group A intervenes

Leading the criticism was the Commander of Army Group A, Gen von Rundstedt, and his Chief of Staff, Gen von Manstein. They were strongly supported by a number of panzer commanders including Guderian, who had fought with such distinction in Poland. They put their heads together to devise yet another plan – a far more daring operation in which the main attack was to be made in the Ardennes, precisely the region through which the French were confident no major assault could be launched. Allied defence plans were based on that assumption: so what better place could there be for a surprise attack by a heavily adrmoured Army Group? After dealing with scant opposition, the panzer forces would be able to cross the Meuse and then make for the Channel coast below the mouth of the Somme, completely cutting off all French and British forces drawn into Belgium to meet the conventional attack the Allies had every reason to expect.

FALL GELB
The Final Plan

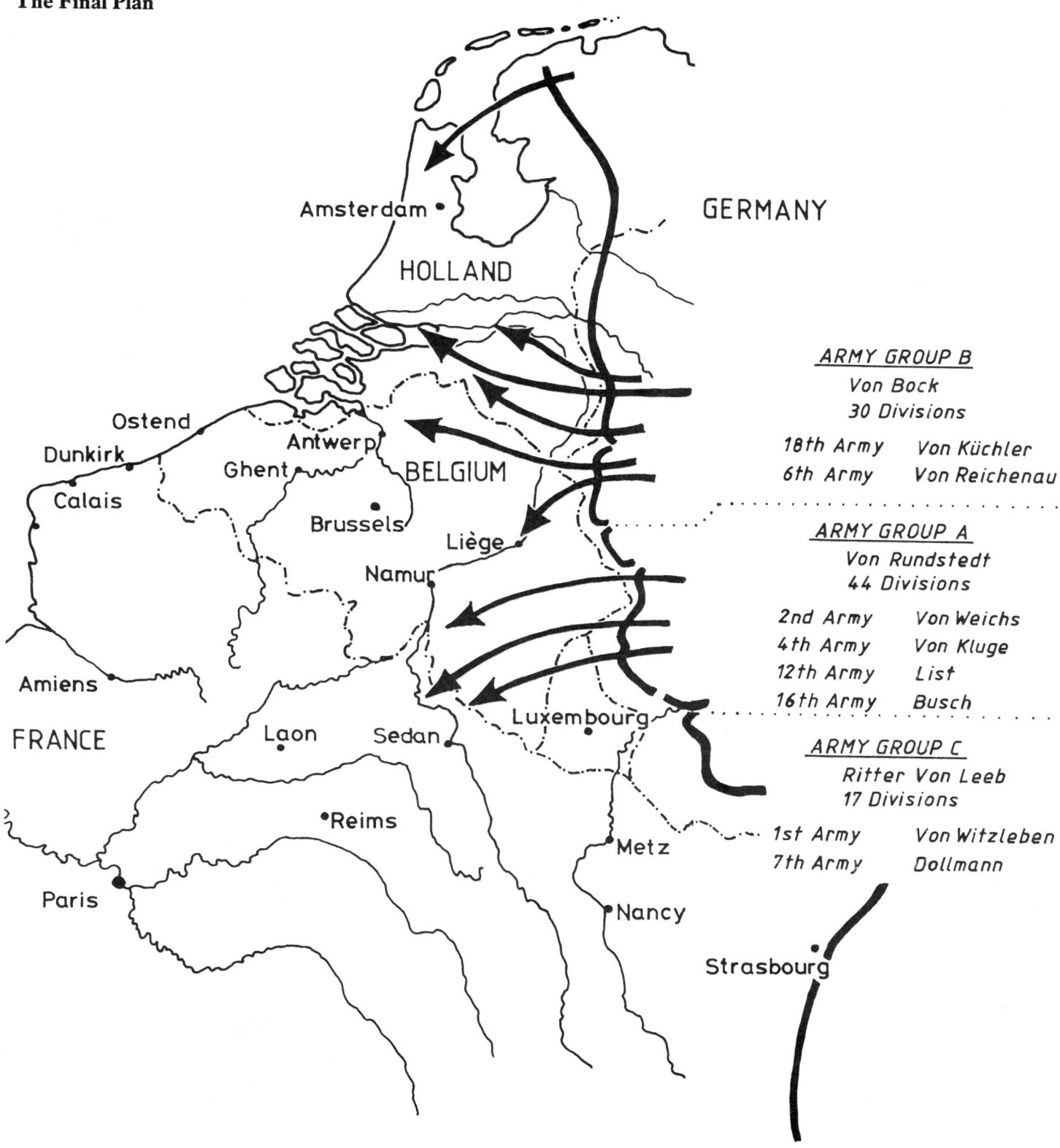

ARMY GROUP B
Von Bock
30 Divisions

| 18th Army | Von Küchler |
| 6th Army | Von Reichenau |

ARMY GROUP A
Von Rundstedt
44 Divisions

2nd Army	Von Weichs
4th Army	Von Kluge
12th Army	List
16th Army	Busch

ARMY GROUP C
Ritter Von Leeb
17 Divisions

| 1st Army | Von Witzleben |
| 7th Army | Dollmann |

The OKH, now fully immersed in the detailed planning of the revised second plan, did not respond with any enthusiasm to this audacious idea. But chance now took a hand in the affair, and played two joker cards. The first of these was a very unusual breach of military security by two Luftwaffe officers one of whom, Major Reinberger, carried in his briefcase top secret papers relating to the revised *Fall Gelb* operation. Flying close to the Belgian border they were obliged to make a forced landing in bad weather conditions. They came down near Mechelen in Belgium, not realising that they had strayed into neutral territory, where they were promptly placed under arrest. In desperation Reinberger tried to burn the papers but was only partly successful in his attempt. The Belgian authorities lost no time in passing on the details to the Allied High Command. On hearing this news, Gen Jodl noted in his diary: 'If the enemy is in possession of all the files the situation is catastrophic.'[8]

However, even if information of this kind is taken at its face value and not treated as a plant, it is one thing to know about hostile intentions, and quite another to do anything about them. Furthermore, the plans as they stood confirmed the Allies' belief that the main weight of the attack was to fall in the north, so to that extent German interests were very well served by the affair and their anxieties about an apparently serious breach of security turned out to be ill-founded.

The second joker card was the onset of winter. The postponement of the attack on the Western Front gave the OKH the opportunity of testing the revised plan in a series of map excercises, which revealed further serious flaws. It also gave them an opportunity to think about the 'reckless' proposal from Army Group A, and the more they thought about it the more they came to see its merits.

It was at this time that Hitler's chief adjutant, Col Schmundt, during a tour of the western front, visited von Rundstedt's Army Group HQ and had a long talk with von Manstein, who was only too eager to sell the new proposals to a member of the Führer's inner circle. On his return to Berlin Schmundt immediately briefed Hitler, who showed keen interest in the idea. On 17 February 1940 von Manstein,[9] accompanied by some recently-appointed Corps commanders, was given the opportunity of presenting the

The crew of this Hotchkiss HS 35 *cavalry tank make the most of natural camouflage as they take a breather deep in the wood near the front line. Note the definitely non-issue shirt worn by the tank driver, not to mention his pet white rabbit on the turret!* TM

The original caption to this German photograph showing a 3.7cm anti-tank gun being moved into position from the Rhine fortifications mentions a 'gun battle which raged all day' with French artillery along the Maginot Line. However, it is difficult to understand what use a light anti-tank gun would have been in an engagement of that kind. A propaganda shot that misfired, possibly? TM

137

Army Group A Proposal in detail to his Supreme Commander, who promptly called von Brauchitsch and Halder to the Chancellory for an emergency meeting the following day. He then proceeded to outline the new plan as though it were his own idea. Hitler found the generals surprisingly receptive, and agreement on all the main points was quickly reached. As Alistair Horne puts it: 'With a new spring in their step, they returned to Zossen to draft an entirely new directive. A bouyant mood of fresh confidence replaced earlier doubts.' The future course of events in the West was no longer a matter of chance: the pattern had at last been decided.

The Norwegian Gambit

The enforced delay in the West gave Hitler time to consider an entirely different project which had been put to him in October 1939 by Admiral Raeder, the C-in-C of the German navy. He was anxious to get hold of bases in Norway to extend the attack on Britain's merchant shipping and sea routes. Hitler showed no interest in the idea at first, but subsequent developments in the Baltic forced him to turn is attention to the region.

Of these the most significant was the Russian attack on Finland in November 1939, in which the Red Army at first suffered a series of humiliating reverses. The courage of the Finns won the admiration of the Allies, and there was even some talk of British and French troops being sent, via Norway, to help in their fight against the invaders. It was a madcap idea, of course, but the Germans took it seriously. For them, the prospect of an Allied right of passage across Norwegian territory, or worse still, an Allied occupation of the country, was not to be contemplated, for their whole war economy depended upon the vital iron ore link with Sweden.

By February 1940 these dangers had receded as the regrouped Russian forces mounted a massive and final assault on their Finnish neighbours. But an audacious operation was carried out by the Royal Navy in neutral Norwegian waters, in which British prisoners were rescued from the German merchantman *Altmark*, infuriated Hitler. On 21 February 1940 he ordered Gen Falkenhorst to prepare plans for the invasion of Norway. Meanwhile, Raeder continued to press his

A Pz Kpfw I moving forward in Denmark after German forces crossed the border on 9 April 1940. The entire country fell to the invaders in a single day without a shot being fired. TM

Finnish troops and civilians inspect a pair of Russian light tanks captured in the early stages of the Soviet attack on their country. They are T37 amphibious light tanks, based upon the British Vickers Carden-Lloyd design. TM

German soldiers disembark in Oslo harbour. Although the southern part of Norway was quickly occupied, stiff resistance in the north won enough time for an Allied expedition to be mounted to assist Norwegian forces. TM

German tanks and infantry on the move during the Norwegian campaign in April 1940. After a gruelling six weeks' struggle German armed might prevailed, and one more proud and independent country came under the Nazi hammer. IWM

case, stressing the importance of forestalling any Anglo-French expedition to occupy the strategic Norwegian coastline. He also produced a traitor, Vidkun Quisling, one of the very few members of the Nazi party in Norway, who assured anyone prepared to listen that sympathy for the German cause was widespread among his countrymen, and that he was ready to form a puppet government under German occupation.

Invasion preparations were ignored by Denmark and Norway, and on 5 April Chamberlain made his fatuous remark that 'Hitler had missed the bus.' In fact, at that time German supply ships were already at sea, ready to support the brilliant combined operation launched by the Germans four days later. Naval landings were made at Oslo, Kristiansand, Stavanger, Bergen and Oslo, where one of two parachute drops were made, with a naval bombardment added for good measure. Complete surprise was achieved. Denmark capitulated at once, but stiff Norwegian resistance enabled an Allied expeditionary force to be assembled and sent to Trondheim in the north.

This operation can only be described as a shambles. The British contingent was separated from all its artillery, tanks and most of its stores in an 'embarkation/disembarkation/re-embarkation' muddle at the departure port of Rosyth in Scotland, and did not land in Norway until 15 April. The French performance was no better. Their token force reached Norway four days later, but it was discovered that the ship carrying all their weapons, equipment and supplies was too large to enter the habour chosen for the landing.

The Royal Navy took a heavy toll of enemy shipping, but in the course of six weeks' fierce fighting the German army gained the upper hand on land, and an Allied evacuation was ordered on 8 June. King Haakon and many members of the Norwegian government narrowly escaped to England on board *HMS Devonshire*. Meanwhile, in Oslo, Quisling enjoyed the fruits of his treachery – but not for long.

The Balance of Power
The final moves in the Norwegian campaign were, of course, completely overshadowed by momentous events on the western front, where the long-awaited blow finally fell on 10 May. When, in the

light of our present knowledge, comparisons are made between the relative strengths of the German and Allied armies on the eve of the battle, it is difficult to escape the conclusion that a smokescreen of misinformation has been deliberately created at an early stage, especially, it has to be said, by the French, in an attempt to explain away ignominious defeat.

This has been done mainly by representing the German forces as being much larger than they actually were. It is true that they had more aircraft and anti-aircraft artillery, and that their tanks were grouped in a much more concentrated and effective way than those of the Allies. It is true that the German Army held the initiative, that they could choose when and where to strike. It is also true that their troops were full of confidence, physically fit and eager to fight. But in terms of numbers, were they really the overwhelming force so many sources would have had us believe?

Now, fifty years after the event, the facts can be set out and readers left to draw their own conclusions.

Forces on the Western Front: May 1940

	French	British	Total (Allies)	Belgian	Dutch	Total (All)	German	Total
DIVISIONS								
Infantry	73+22res	13(a)	108	18	8	134	81+42res	123
Lt. Mech	3	–	3	–	–	3	–	–
Motorised	2	–	2	–	–	2	3	3
Armoured	0+ 3res	1(b)	4	–	–	4	10	10
Totals	78+25res	14	117	18	8	143	94+42res	136
[Troops in '000s]	2,200	394	2,594	650	400	3,644	2,400	2,400
WEAPONS								
AFVs	3,100(c)	400	3,500	few	few	3,500+	2,574(d)	2,574
Art'y guns	11,200	2,800	14,000	few	few	15,000+	7,700	7,700
AA guns	1,500	500	2,000	few	few	2,500+	9,000	9,000
AIRCRAFT								
All types	1,350	630(e)	1,980	180	120+	2,280+	2,750	2,750

Notes:
a) includes 52 (Lowland) Division, landed in France after 10 May
b) includes 1st Armoured Division, landed in France after 10 May
c) some 900 of these Armoured Fighting Vehicles were not in the battle area
d) this figure is taken from a letter dated 7 November 1944 written by the Inspector General of Armoured Troops to the Führer's Military Adjutant, in which the total is broken down as follows:
   523 Pz Kpfw I   955 Pz Kpfw II   349 Pz Kpfw III   278 Pz Kpfw IV
   106 Pz Kpfw 35t   228 Pz Kpfw 38t   96 Pz Kpfw I Befels   39 Pz Kpfw III Befels
                                       (Command)
e) includes RAF units based in England but operating over the Continent

NOTES

1. A Horne *To Lose A Battle* London: Macmillan (1969).
2. Gen Sir Edward Spears *Assignment to Catastrophe* London: The Reprint Society Ltd (1956).
3. Lt Col O. G. W. White *Straight on for Tokyo: The War History of the 2nd Battalion, the Dorsetshire Regiment 1939-1948* Aldershot: Gale & Polden (1948).
4. Brig C. N. Barclay (ed) *History of the Duke of Wellington's Regiment 1919-1952* London: Wm. Clowes & Son (1953).
5. As Note 2.
6. Graf Schlieffen, Chief of the German General Staff from 1890 to 1905, developed a plan by which French armies were to be quickly enveloped and destroyed. The mass of available German forces were to be concentrated on the right wing and then perform an enormous wheel, pivoting on the fortified area of Metz-Thionville, to sweep through Belgium and northern France. Then, continuing the arc, they would gradually wheel eastwards to force the French back towards the Moselle, where their armies could be smashed against an 'anvil' formed by the Lorraine fortresses and the Swiss frontier.
7. M. Cooper *The German Army 1933-1945* London: Macdonald & James (1978).
8. As Note 1.
9. Hitler and Rundstedt, as well as Manstein, have been credited with devising the final, audacious *Fall Gelb* plan of attack, but it is very clear from Manstein's autobiography *Lost Victories* that he considered himself to be its chief architect. 'After all,' he wrote, the ideas behind the plan were mine . . . it was I who drafted all the memoranda to OKH by which we sought to have the operation planned on the only lines conducive, in our opinion, to its decisive success in the West.'

Chapter 9

The Hammer Blow Falls

The story of the first five hectic days of battle that followed the German onslaught in the West on 10 May 1940 concerns three distinct, but closely connected, operations:

1. The airborne assault and subsequent over-running of Holland to protect the northern flank of the German armies advancing into Belgium, Luxembourg and France;
2. the air and land attacks on Belgium with the objective of drawing the Allied armies forward to their Dyle Line positions, and *away from* the planned main German thrust, namely –
3. the advance through the Ardennes and Luxembourg by strong armoured and mechanized forces to siege bridgeheads across the Meuse in the Sedan area.

The second of these operations has been compared to the flourish of a matador's cloak, concealing the deadly thrust of the sword beneath. With a large number of troops engaged in all three attacks there was a great deal of movement and fighting along the entire length of the Dutch, Belgian and Luxembourg borders from the North Sea to the Ardennes. Even to the south of Luxembourg, along the Maginot Line, a semblance of pressure was maintained to keep the Allies guessing. Thus the Germans held the initiative all along the line and were able to dictate the tempo of the battle.

In late April and early May German troops were secretly moved into position on the Western Front. At the same time, rigorous training and the full-scale re-equipment of units back from Poland kept officers and men at full stretch. While all this was going on inside Germany the Allies paid little heed. They were more concerned with other matters, especially the growing threat to the beleagured Norwegian expedition. An imminent attack on France or on the neutral Low Countries was not expected and, in any event, the British and French commanders relied upon the 'Dyle' defence plan to contain such an attack if it should take place. So far as land operations on the European continent were concerned the Allied governments appeared content to allow the Phoney War to continue indefinitely.

Zero Hour

At 0535 hours on the morning of Friday, 10 May 1940, the Germans launched the *Fall Gelb* assault. First into action were two special forces, one making its attack by land and the other by air. The first of these was a unique organization known as 'Brandenburg', taking its name from

Their mission accomplished, the heroes of task force Granite *return to their Battalion HQ at Maastricht on 11 May 1940.*

Hans Teske

141

German paratroops make their drop over Holland from a Junkers 52.

the depot at Brandenburg/Havel. This was an elite and highly trained force of commandos who had already proved their worth in Poland. The other special force consisted of paratroops from Goering's Luftwaffe.

Although these special groups were few in number compared with the rest of the attacking armies, their rôles were considered so crucial that the timing of the whole operation hinged upon their actions. These included the capture of the Belgian fortress of Eben Emael in front of the German 6th Army, and air attacks and paratroop landings on Dutch airfields and bridges ahead of the 18th Army. While these preliminary actions were taking place, the Luftwaffe bombed Belgian airfields and other selected targets.

Brandenburg operations
The Brandenburg commandos had to attack three main groups of targets: bridges over the Meuse (known in Flemish as the Maas) at Massyk and at Gennep, and four more over the Juliana Canal at Berg, Uromon, Obicht and Stein. They also had the job of capturing and holding key positions along the Luxembourg frontier and Siegfried Line. To achieve these objectives they employed ingenuity and skill mixed with a great deal of bluff. Each man was fluent in the appropriate language of the country in which each operation was mounted, and every one of the force was highly trained in silent movement and the silent kill. If the need arose they were quite prepared to disguise themselves in enemy uniforms – a practice which, contrary to popular belief, is permitted under the rules of war provided that such uniforms are discarded before the order is given to open fire.

On the night of 9 May, small groups of Brandenburgers wearing Dutch military police uniforms slipped across the frontier and went into hiding until the time came for action. At Gennep, south of Nijmegen, they waited anxiously under cover, near a railway bridge, for several hours until the two German troop trains appeared. At which point they had to take over the bridge very quickly, before it could be blown up by Dutch sentries, to enable the trains to cross over and press on into Holland. They did this by posing as Dutch policeman escorting German saboteurs, getting close enough to the sentries and overpowering them before an alarm could be raised. The detonating mechanism in the centre span of the bridge was disconnected by soldiers who leapt out of the train as it passed over the bridge.

Paratroop operations
Like the commandos, the paratroops also had three main groups of targets of which the first were strategically vital bridges for Moerdijk, crossing the Meuse, at Dordrecht, over the Waal and at Lek, in front of Rotterdam. Their second task was nothing less than the occupation of The Hague to destroy the Government and the military high command and, if possible, to take prisoner members of the Dutch royal family. And lastly, the paras were ordered to capture the seemingly impregnable fortress at Eben Emael, and three nearby bridges over the Albert Canal.

Gen Kurt Student, commander of the German airborne forces, made his dispositions. The three bridges over waterways which formed a series of defensive walls around the heart of the country, sometimes called rather optimistically 'Fortress Holland', had to be captured intact and held until they were reached by the main invasion force. *Fallschirmjaeger Regiment I* was given this important task, and roughly one battalion was allotted to each of the three targets.

Fallschirmjaeger Regiment 2 had the spectacular job of landing on The Hague in support of the 22nd Infantry (Air Landing) Division, a force of 760 paratroopers and 1,900 air landing troops placed under Gen Student's command especially for this operation.

The Eben Emael fortress was to be destroyed by the Assault Force *Koch*, named after its commander. Their targets also included the three Albert Canal bridges at Veldwezelt, Vroenhoeven and Canhe.

It was the fortress attack that fired the imagination of friend and foe alike. Meticulously planned, carefully rehearsed and carried out with great bravery and élan, it was an operation vital to the success of *Fell Gelb*.

Task Force *Granite*
Eben Emael occupied a key position in the defence of the city of Liège, and thus of Belgium as whole. It stood on the direct attack route of Reichenau's 6th Army in

THE ASSAULT ON THE WEST

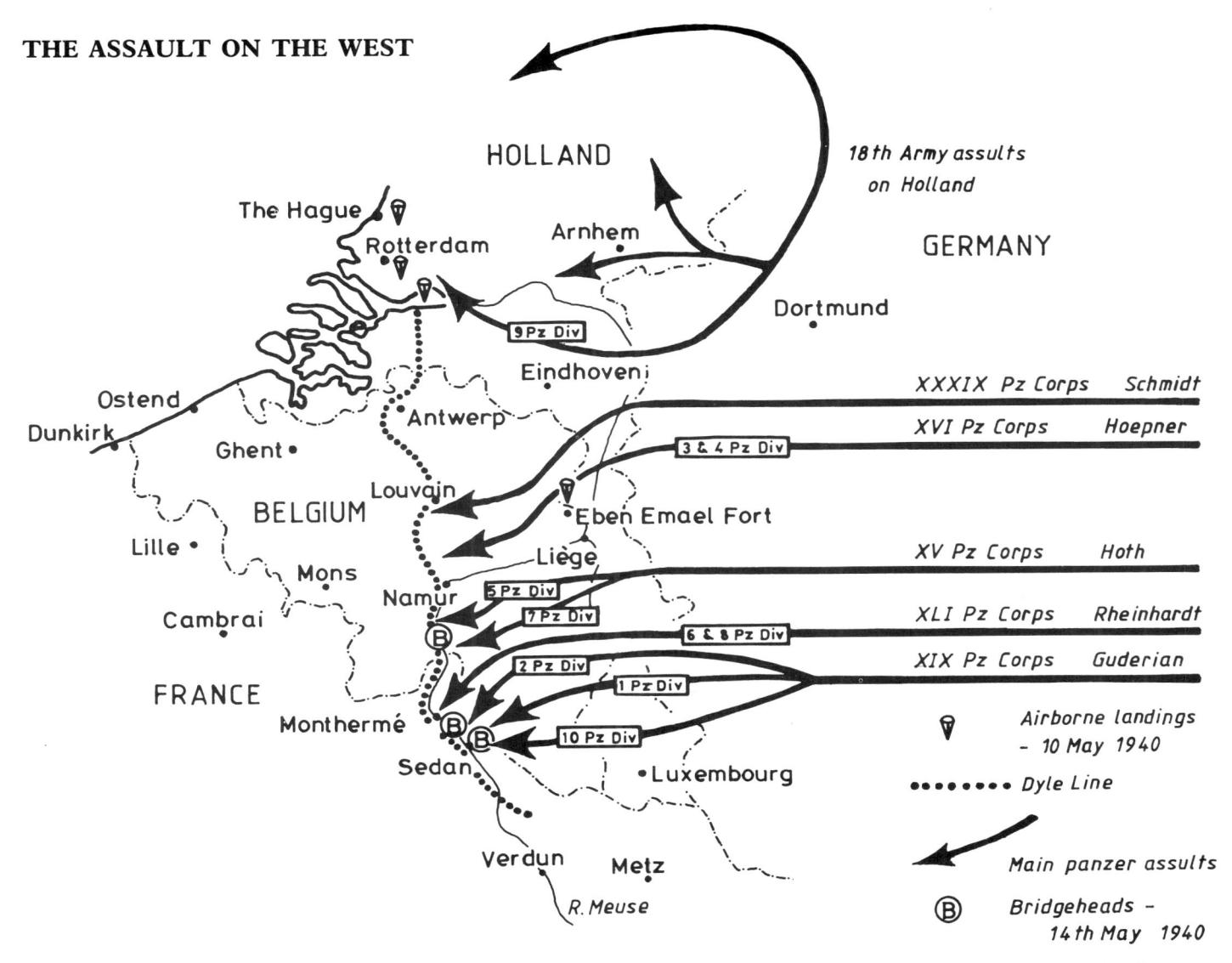

Gen von Bock's Army Group B. It was a modern, well-built fortress of steel and concrete, with artillery emplacements for long-range bombardment and machine-gun nests for close-in protection. Each of the emplacements, including the main fortress itself, was protected by deep minefields, barbed wire and entanglements and anti-tank ditches, some filled with water. The garrison, which consisted of about 1,400 officers and men, were well-trained and confident of withstanding any assault mounted against them. Little did they know that their enemy, using exact models of the fortress, had been rehearsing an attack for weeks.

The plan was that an assault force, codenamed *Granite* and consisting of 85 men commanded by Oberleutnant Witzig, were to be carried in eleven gliders and landed directly on the main roof of the fort. The rest of Koch's men, less than 500 in all, were split into three groups. They were also to be carried by glider to each of the three bridges. All these vital objectives were to be captured and held until the arrival of reinforcements.

Before dawn on 10 May 1940, at about 0430 hours, the task force became airborne, towed by Junkers 52 aircraft climbing to a height of 7,000ft before releasing their gliders while still over German soil. They began the silent descent onto the sleeping targets below. But already there had been a mishap because two of the gliders, one carrying Witzig, were released too soon, either by human error or as a result tow-ropes breaking under the strain. Although this seriously reduced the size of *Granite*, there was no question of abandoning the attack, which now came under the command of the next senior officer, Hauptfeldwebel Wenzel.

As planned, the gliders, each with barbed wire wrapped round its fuselage to bring it more quickly to a stop in the confined area, landed on top of the fortress. Within seconds the paras disembarked and raced towards their targets, putting to good effect all the rigorous training of recent weeks. Amid the chaos the men in the green smocks knew exactly what they had to do.

The Belgian garrison was, on the whole, slow to react. One alert sentry gave the alarm as the gliders approached, but the fire from his AA machine gun post did not herald the storm of shells and bullets the attackers expected. By the time the rest of the garrison was roused it was already too late. With crisp

already too late. With crisp efficiency the paras carried out their allotted tasks, destroying the gun emplacements with the 2½ tons of special explosive they had brought with them, shattering the armoured observation domes with specially-shaped charges, placing other charges down the barrels of the artillery guns and killing their crews with a deadly combination of machine-gun fire and flamethrower attack. Within an hour of landing the task force had successfully carried out the first part of its mission. The objective had been achieved; the main gun turrets had been destroyed. Provided Wenzel and his small band of paratroops could hang on to the fruits of their victory, the great fortress of Eban Emael would play no further part in the battle.

The attack on the three bridges over the Albert Canal was not nearly so successful. The Belgians had managed to destroy all of them before they fell into enemy hands, and prevented any advance by the main German force with well-placed artillery fire. The congestion on all roads leading to the border as the ground forces struggled to press forward was severe, and for a time the whole attack appeared to be in jeopardy.

The victors of Eban Emael had no idea that all this was going on behind them or that their promised relief force was so bogged down. But at this point their morale was lifted by the sudden arrival on the scene of Oberleutnant Witzig, who had used his considerable force of personality to persuade the Luftwaffe that he needed another glider and a Ju 52 to tow it. Accordingly, he and his men landed in the area at about 0830 hours, and his first action was to spread a large German flag on the roof of the fortress as a signal to the Luftwaffe. For the rest of the day the small force grimly held their ground, and shortly after night fell they were joined by men from the second missing glider, who fought their way across Belgian territory to join their comrades.

At dawn the following day leading

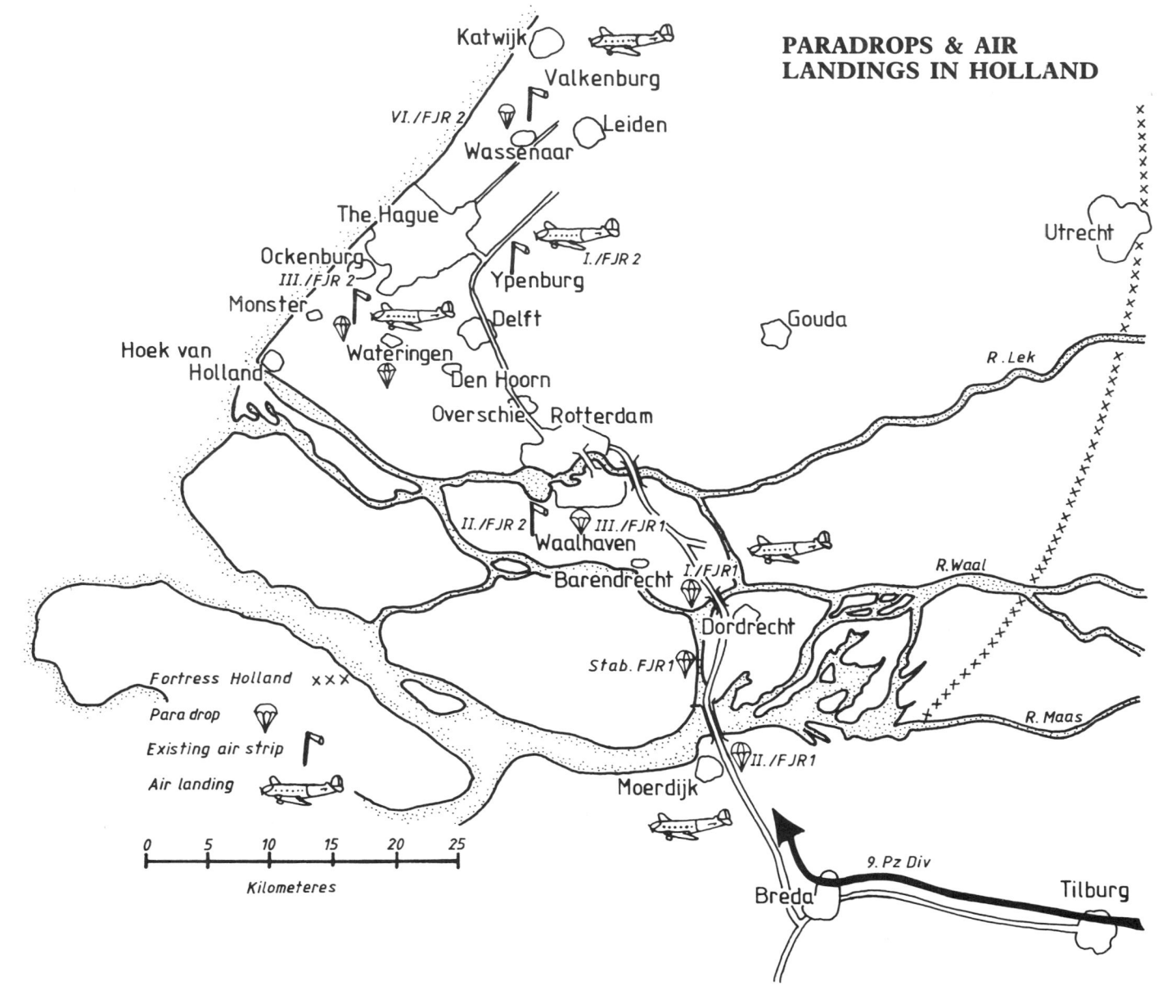

PARADROPS & AIR LANDINGS IN HOLLAND

elements of the 51st Engineer Battalion crossed the Albert Canal, but not without heavy casualties, and achieved the link-up with the para force at about 0700 hours. Four hours later, under a white flag, the commander of the Belgian garrison formally surrendered to the German Army. Despite the mishaps and the initial failure of the attack on the bridges, Koch's operation was crowned with remarkable success. Not only had he gained his main objective but he had done so with only 6 killed and 20 wounded from his original strength of 85 men.

The taking of 'Fortress Holland'
Reconnaissance had revealed three places near The Hague as possible landing sites for the 22nd Air Landing Division commanded by Maj Gen Graf von Sponeck. These were the Ypenburg and Valkenburg airfields to the south and north of the city, and what appeared to be a large sports field to the west, near Ockenburg. Sponeck's plan was to divide *FJgR 2* into three initial assault groups to secure these sites, and to hold them so that all follow-up landings could be made safely. Then, when his force was fully up to strength, he proposed to mount a three-pronged attack on the capital.

At 0300 hours it was dark when the aircraft took off. 'We sat close together,' the history of the *Fallschirmjaeger Regiment 2* records, 'packed full with everything we needed, all our kit plus a webbing chute weighing 8kg alone. It was a heavy load. Two to three hours we sat in the Ju52. The order "get ready to jump" came as a relief.'

The main attack was preceded by a heavy bombing strike, by some 175 aircraft of the Luftwaffe, in order to soften up the anti-aircraft defences. Nevertheless, as the paratroops landed they were met by heavy fire, causing confusion and some loss. Many more casualties were inflicted by the Dutch, who defended their positions bravely in the ensuing action, as this further extract reveals:

> As the 41 machines approached the Ypenburg airfield, heavy AA fire caused the formation to split up. The jumping began much too early – 60 men dropped south of Delft, others right on top of the airfield and into the Dutch defensive positions to the east, while others were 3km away to the north and widely scattered. Those who landed close to the airfield came under the withering fire from the Dutch defenders (3 Regt Grenadiers) who were in well-built defensive positions and gave a good account of themselves . . . Our airborne troops eventually managed to occupy the airport buildings, but only half-an-hour remained before the 22nd Division was due to arrive – not enough time to clear the airfield of enemy. As the aircraft came in to land they were met by fire from several enemy machine guns, light flak and some light tanks. Seventeen Ju52s burst into flames, but more kept coming in. Collisions occurred while taxiing, and still more aircraft went up in flames.

Men of the Fallschirmjaeger Regiment 2 *make their way to Rotterdam during the German attack on Holland.* TM

As it was now quite impossible to land more aircraft, pilots following on had to look for alternative landing places in nearby meadows, and even on the roads between Delft and The Hague. Several Ju52s came down south of Delft, and the men formed a separate battlegroup under the command of their senior officer, who happened to be the divisional doctor. They rejoined the Division three days later. Other smaller groups formed 'hedge-hog' defensive positions in farms around the airfield, but these were blasted to pieces when the Dutch defenders brought up a battery for 6pdr field guns. By nightfall, the last of these positions fell: the attack on Ypenburg had failed.

The pilot of the plane carrying Gen von Sponeck, unable to land at Ypenburg, turned away towards Ockenburg, but as he did so the aircraft was hit and he was obliged to make a forced landing on a nearby beach. Meanwhile, the attack on

The people of Rotterdam seek the comparative safety of open ground as their city burns. IWM

An amateur photographer captures this dramatic scene in Rotterdam's dock area following the Luftwaffe *attack.* IWM

Ockenburg itself was also going badly wrong. Only one paratroop group was dropped into the right place, a small force of 35 men commanded by Lt Genz, who did succeed in keeping the airfield clear of the enemy. However, it was soon discovered that the field was far too small for the number of aircraft involved in the attack, and Dutch artillery engaged the transport planes that did manage to land. Then a flight of three Dutch *Fokkers* carried out a successful bombing raid, scoring direct hits on the runway and damaging more aircraft. This attack put the airfield out of action and prevented any further landings.

Gen von Sponeck managed to join his men before they were surrounded. They now found themselves in an extremely vulnerable position, but later that evening they were joined by another group of 70 paras who, under the command of Oberleutnant von Roon, fought their way through, increasing the total number of the force to 320 men. The Dutch failed to attack, and the following day (12 May) the Germans were able to break out.

The situation was little better at Katwijk. Here the sportsground was found to be unsuitable for air traffic. There was no flak, but the Dutch defenders had plenty of light machine guns which they turned on German paratroops as they landed in a neighbouring field. Those who survived this hostile reception desperately tried to clear neighbouring ground for the transport aircraft behind them, but when the first Ju52 landed it got stuck in the mud and could not be moved.

Further south, the attack was more successful, and the bridges between Moerdijk and Rotterdam had been secured. In order to cut off the city from the North Gen Sponeck was ordered to take up positions near Overshie. Before the Dutch forces realised what was happening, the Germans broke out from Ockenburg and moved towards their new position. In spite of coming under heavy fire at Wateringen they achieved their objectives and so were able to witness at close quarters what the Germans described as 'the unfortunate bombing of Rotterdam'.

Such apologetic phrases cannot excuse this bombing, which was a carefully prepared operation. When Gen Schmidt, Commander of the XXXIX Corps, was planning to attack Rotterdam, he decided to precede it with a bombing raid timed to begin at 1300 hours on 14 May. Accordingly the Dutch were given an ultimatum. They stalled for time and were granted an extension to 1630 hours. However, as the Dutch representative left the meeting-place at about 1320 hours, a formation of Heinkel 111 bombers was seen approaching the city. At about 1330 hours some 50-plus aircraft began bombing the city, causing extensive damage and huge fires. Two hours later Rotterdam surrendered and the Germans occupied the city. Later, Gen Schmidt expressed his personal regrets to the Dutch commander.

At first it was thought that some 30,000 civilians had been killed in this ruthless attack, but in fact the final death toll was just under 1,000. According to the British official history:

> There are two aspects to be considered. Firstly, the legitimate use of air bombardment in support of ground operations. Secondly, the more questionable use of air power to hasten the surrender of the town.

Much has been written about this attack, which probably did more than anything else to hasten the surrender of the Netherlands, but there is little doubt that it was a deliberate act of terror rather than an unfortunate mistake. In an all-out war it forced the Dutch to surrender much earlier than expected. This merciless bombing, like the earlier attacks on Warsaw and the later raids on London and other British cities hardened the hearts of the Allies when they were in a position to attack German cities later in the war. On the other hand, it is highly likely that these German terror tactics did much to hasten the defeat of the Allies in 1940 and avoided a long drawn-out campaign.

The conquest of Holland took just five days. In spite of strong Dutch resistance, together with flooding and demolition, Gen Kuechler's 18th Army advanced at great speed and in three days was threatening 'Fortress Holland'. With the bombing of Rotterdam all resistance collapsed and the Dutch surrendered on 15 May. Two days earlier the Royal Navy had taken Queen Wilhelmina, members of her Government and the Allied Legation Staffs to safety in Britain.

The Germans knew that the Dutch would destroy as many of their canal bridges as they could in order to hold up their attack, so they made certain that their forward units had enough pontoons, rope ladders and other equipment to overcome the many water obstacles they encountered during their advance. TM

Waiting for the enemy, Dutch infantry man a well prepared defensive position in 'Fortress Holland'. But such 1914-1918 tactics were of little use against the formidable German military machine. S-MG

Dutch artillerymen drive a 75mm field gun across fields deliberately flooded to keep out the invader. ANEFO-Amsterdam

Belgian girls present bunches of lilac to British despatch riders moving forward to the Dyle line. IWM

The assault on Belgium

The airborne attacks at Eben Emael and other vital points were accompanied by heavy airstrikes on Belgian air-fields plus a major ground assault by the German 6th Army in the Maastricht-Liège area. The Belgian Air Force's official policy and practice on how to survive air attacks was a mixture of camouflage and constant movement. Anti-aircraft defences were extremely weak, and in the event of an alert all units were under instructions to leave their regular airfields and move to 'assigned combat airfields'. These were usually nothing more than stretches of pasture-land kept drained and free from obstacles. German Intelligence was aware of these orders and had pin-pointed all 'combat airfields'. Also, it is clear that the Belgians were taken completely by surprise, as this extract from an article by Lt Col Michel Terlinden BEM shows:

> On the afternoon of May 9, 1940, authorization was given to grant five-day leaves. This was the first sign of relaxation after the alert of May 7: one of the numerous false alarms the Belgian forces had experienced since August 1939. During the evening hours, however, a state of alert was once more declared, which no one took any more seriously than the previous ones. Why should this be different from all the others?[1]

Terlinden then recounts the experiences of the Fifth Squadron of the Third Regiment, which was equipped with Fairey *Battles* and stationed at Evere near Brussels.

> This squadron, reinforced by a few elements of the Ninth Squadron, left the Brussels base of Evere only a few minutes before the German bombing of this field began ... The squadron's destination was a redeployment field west of Antwerp. As the *Battles* came in for landing, soldiers on the ground lit fires to indicate the wind direction to the circling pilots.

Terlinden describes the abortive attacks on three bridges over the Albert Canal, constantly harassed by enemy fighters and AA fire. The first group of three *Battles* made for the Veldwezelt bridge:

> Approaching the general area, two Luftwaffe fighters sliced across their formation, turning and climbing for the inevitable attack. Their superior speed and heavy armament outclassed the hapless light bombers.

The centre aircraft went down to low level and skimmed along, hedgehopping, trying to draw off the fighters, while his two wing-men flew on towards their target. Terlinden continues:

> Down on the deck the lonely *Battle* jumped fences, trees, houses, barely missing church steeples. But the effort was in vain. The speed of the German fighters left them free to choose the moment and the direction of their attacks. After fifteen minutes of cat-and-mouse tactics one of the fighters swooped in very low for the final burst, aiming for the front cockpit of the *Battle*. The pilot slumped forward, shot in the back. Once more the rear gunner turned to his guns to aim at the German fighter now on his tail. The gunner too was hit – in the hands. The pilot, bleeding heavily, summoned all his strength, chopped the throttle and skidded in for a landing in a farmer's field.

The other two *Battles* managed to reach their target, but unfortunately their bombs hit the roadway, not the bridge. One was then shot down by enemy fighters, but the third managed to get safely back to base.

British carriers cross the French frontier into Belgium. IWM

Pz Kpfw II is held up by a broken-backed bridge in Belgium as a severely damaged village still smoulders from the recent attack. TM

149

British Bren gun carriers, each with a Boys anti-tank gun mounted at the front, move in convoy to the forward zone. TM

A young troop leader of the 13/18th Hussars gives final orders to his tank commanders before moving into position. TM

The second flight made for the Vroenhoven bridge. Though heavily attacked by enemy flak, they reached their target, only to be frustrated by mechanical faults. First, the bomb mechanisms failed to release the bombs, and when they made another attack and actually hit the bridge, they saw to their dismay that the damage done was not enough to hold up the advancing enemy troops.

Further north, the remaining flight, sent to bomb the Briedgen bridge, was unlucky from the start. One aircraft was shot down by friendly AA fire. Another was shot down by enemy AA. Though the third reached the target and the pilot dropped his bombs, it too was hit and had to make a forced landing, with some of its bombs still rigged to its belly. Terlinden concludes:

> The mission was over. Back at base the ground crews patiently waited. The bombing of the three Albert bridges was completed, but the bridges remained. Of the nine air-craft assigned, six were shot down. Of the eighteen crew members, five were dead and six wounded.

Following these heroic but fruitless attacks, both the French Air Force and the British Advanced Striking Force tried to destroy the bridges, but were beaten off with heavy loss. Later, a Belgian officer was killed while blowing up the Briedgen bridge.

Allied reactions

> At General Headquarters in Arras the stillness of a spring night was rudely broken just before daybreak on the morning of the 10th of May, when German aircraft roared over the city and bombed the neighbouring fields.

So starts the British Official History's account of Allied operations in response to the German onslaught. It adds that soon afterwards a message was received from French HQ ordering a full *alerte*. Some thirty minutes later came the order to execute the Dyle Plan. BEF HQ then sent out the following signal:

> Plan D.J.1 today. Zero hour 1300 hours. 12,L may cross before zero. Wireless silence cancelled after crossing frontier. Command Post opens 1300 hours. Air recces may commence forthwith.[2]

The Allied generals surmised that the main German attack would come exactly where they had always anticipated it.

When Hitler heard what was happening he is reported to have said: 'I could have wept for joy; they had fallen into a trap! It had been a clever piece of work to attack Liège. We had to make them believe that we were remaining faithful to the old Schlieffen plan.'[3]

After a morning of hectic preparations, armoured car patrols of the 12th Royal Lancers cossed the frontier into western Belgium at 1300 hours precisely and reached the River Dyle that evening. Their history reports:

> Major Clifton-Browne, commanding the Regiment in Lumsden's absence, was ordered to cross the Belgian frontier, and at 10.20 the Squadrons moved off from Hebuterne... The first British units into Belgium, they reported the first bound clear, were slightly bombed on the second – training in road discipline paying a big dividend – skirted a welcoming Brussels, and by 6pm were in position covering the Dyle line.
> Meanwhile the No. 3 wireless set, the essential link with GHQ, which the War Office had tried to appropriate before the Regiment left England, was sent to GHQ Adv Ops at Wahagnies, and Sgt Crebbin, the resident pigeon specialist, was dispatched to Lille to receive the birds with the squadrons if the wireless should fail to work. The stage was set for action – almost. At five minutes before midnight the cast was completed by the arrival of Lt Col Lumsden, who had only heard the news of the German advance that morning in London.

These first units were quickly followed by the four armoured reconnaissance units which had been allocated to I and II Corps (4/7 DG, 13/18 H, 15/19 H and 5 DG). The light tanks and carriers of these four mechanised cavalry regiments provided a screen in front of the main force of the BEF, now moving up behind them.

The Luftwaffe made no serious attempts to bomb or strafe the Allied forces. There were probably two reasons for this. First, the Germans needed to deal with airfields and other vital targets. Secondly, the RAF Air Component was protecting the Allied forces: they flew over 160 sorties that first day. It is also possible that the Germans refrained from attacking in order to encourage as many Allied troops as possible to advance into Belgium: they could then be cut off when the main attack through the Ardennes crossed the Meuse at Sedan. It

British riflemen take up a position of static defence while German infantry press home their attack. IWM/TM

A German 3.7cm Pak 35/36 L/45 anti-tank gun in action. TM

was Belgian aircraft who suffered most on 10 May, over half their aircraft being destroyed before they could take off.

The Dyle Line
The Dyle Line to which the French and British armies were moving ran from Sedan to Antwerp. For most of its length it was protected by natural anti-tank objects – canals and rivers – except in the area known as the Gembloux gap (between Namur and Wavre) where the Belgians had made some attempt to construct obstacles. The French High Command, anticipating that the main German attack would come between Namur and Antwerp, had concentrated their strongest forces in that area. Most of the units of the First and Seventh Armies were Series A units, which consisted of the highly-trained regular troops. With them were '. . . almost the whole of our resources in motor transport, anti-aircraft groups, regiments of tractor-drawn artillery and battalions of modern tanks. In front of them were the three light armoured divisions, whose armour was the most powerful of the French Army's mobile formations.'[4]

The French High Command had always assumed that the Belgians' defence of their frontier, together with the French and British cavalry screen, would hold up the German forces long enough to prevent them reaching the Dyle line until the Allies had completed their move forward. This did not happen. Thanks to their capture of the Albert Canal bridges and the fortress of Eben Emael, the Germans quickly established a foothold on the western side of the canal and attacked the Belgian 7th Infantry Division defending the canal in that area. The Belgians resisted stoutly but failed to push back the panzer units which had crossed the bridges. Very soon the Germans reached the Tongres area, some miles to the west. The Belgian High Command considered that this rapid enemy advance posed a serious threat to their troops still on the line of the canal and to those manning the fortifications at Liège. Reacting to this German pressure and to the news of the Dutch withdrawals further north, on the evening of 11 May they gave the order to withdraw to the Dyle. The failure to destroy the Albert Canal bridges had undoubtely proved decisive.

The following day, in the Hannut area in front of the Gembloux gap, panzers of Gen Hoepner's XVIth Panzer Corps soundly defeated Gen Prioux's French cavalry corps (comprising 2nd and 3rd DLM) who were acting as a screen for the French 1st Army.

> The enemy was able to call on a powerful air force, whereas Allied air defence was nil. Brave as they were, our units, fighting in small groups, could no longer withstand the onslaught of the German armour.[5]

In this situation, Gen Prioux sent the following signal to his Army Group Commander on the afternoon of 11 May:

> In the absence of fighter forces it is impossible to guarantee that a fierce thrust by the enemy will not speedily reach a point in the position to be covered.[4]

So while the Belgian forces, with their Allied covering screen, were withdrawing eastwards towards the Dyle, the main body of the Allied forces (some 35 of their best divisions, including most of the BEF) was advancing eastwards to reach it. Confusion was inevitable, especially as the Allied troops had problems of recognition. Some of the covering troops, their morale already badly shaken, were inclined to be trigger-happy, and there were unfortunate incidents. The 4th/7th DG, for example, suffered their first casualty of the war, when a tank of the DLM, retiring through B Squadron's position, mistook one of their carriers for a German vehicle and gave it an anti-tank round at point-blank range.

The heavier French armour, in the shape of 1 DCR, suffered a fate as humiliating as that of Gen Prioux's DLMs. The armoured divisions had been kept in reserve for the purpose of reinforcing French forces in Belgium when they moved up to the Dyle Line. 1 DCR was therefore sent forward on 11 May – tanks by rail on special railcars, wheeled vehicles by road. From then on, the tanks and their essential supplies of fuel and ammunition were separated and were not reunited until too late.

The advance guard reached Charleroi on 12 May: two days later the division was placed under 9th Army's command for use around Dinant. By then refugees were blocking all roads, and progress forward was at a snail's place. Leading elements of the division did not reach the Dinant area until 15 May. The German 5th and 7th Panzers made short work of them the same day, and they ceased to be an effective fighting force.

The problem of refugees

Allied planning seems to have made little or no allowance for the problem of military movement on roads blocked by crowds of terrified refugees – no doubt because they had not foreseen that such large numbers would be involved. They had not anticipated that the Nazi blitzkrieg would terrorize the civilian population in the way it did. The history of the 5th Royal Inniskilling Dragoon Guards gives this vivid description of what the Regiment encountered while moving forward:

> Young and old, rich and poor, hale and sick, all were packed in two sweating, heaving columns. Prosperous-looking gentry with Hebraic features, accompanied by obviously expensive ladies, sat anxiously peering out of sleek limousines; peasants and their care-worn wives trudged the 'pavé', children dragging at their hands; townsfolk, clerics, professors, clerks, shopkeepers, country-folk with great panniers on their backs; here and there a sprinkling of bedraggled men in uniform – every type was there, pressed close, a pathetic mass of puzzled, distressed humanity bound together with a common bond of fear. Vehicles of every kind, motors great and small, buses, vans; horse-drawn wagons, carts and traps; push-carts; barrows; perambulators – all piled high with junk, with luggage, pots and pans, chairs, cradles, casks of vegetables and bread, hams, barrels of wine, crates of poultry, pigs (alive and dead), cats and dogs. It was a frightful spectacle.

Covered by a supporting gun crew, German infantrymen make an unopposed river crossing during an early stage of the campaign in the Low Countries. In such a tranquil setting this looks little more than a military exercise, but it was real enough for the men taking part. TM

By helping them to overcome the many water obstacles in their path, the ordinary rubber dinghy played a vital role in maintaining the impetus of the German advance forces. TM

Belgium surrenders
On 12 May the Belgians stopped fighting as an independent force, and King Leopold III formally handed over the conduct of operations to Gen Gamelin. At that time the Belgian Army was making a fighting withdrawal to the Dyle Line, between Antwerp and Louvain, although some of the fortress garrisons in the Liège area stayed and fought on. The last, Pepinster, did not fall until 28 May.

The original plan was for the Allies to reach and occupy the Dyle Line by the 15 May. On 11 May Gen Billotte advanced this date by 24 hours. In fact, some Allied units reached the line by the 13 May, after a series of forced marches, sometimes forty miles at a stretch. Minus their artillery and exhausted on arrival, they were not a moment too soon, as at 1500 hours that day GOC 3 DLM announced that he was withdrawing fast under pressure. As the Cavalry Corps fell back through 1st French Army's outposts they suffered casualties, not only from enemy air attack and tank fire, but also from their own anti-tank mines – they had not been told the location of minefield gaps. Shortly afterwards they were followed by the Germans who, as one French historian commented bitterly: '. . . had no great difficulty in finding the gaps and negotiated them without much loss.'[7]

The Main Attack
Meanwhile, south of Aachen and Liège, the panzers of German Army Group A were advancing towards the Meuse. In the north, on the evening of 12 May, XV Panzer Corps of Gen Kluge's 4th Army closed up to the river between Namur and Dinant, just at the junction point of the French 9th and 2nd Armies (see map). In the centre, Panzer Group Kleist of List's 12th Army had passed through the supposedly 'impassable' Ardennes, and had also closed up to the river, in the area of Sedan and Montherme.

The German tanks moved through the deep wooded valleys in tightly controlled columns. 'The three blocks were positioned one behind the other in a kind of giant phalanx,' explained Gen Blumentritt. 'They stretched back for a hundred miles, the rear rank lying fifty miles to the east of the Rhine.'[8] This enormous mass of armour – about 2400 tanks, comprising three Panzer Corps: Hoth's XVth (5th and 7th Panzer Divs), Reinhardt's XLIst (6th and 8th Panzer Divs) and Guderian's XIXth (1st, 2nd and 10th Panzer Divs) was about to force the crossings of the Meuse and provide the main 'Schwerpunkt' to seal the fate of the Allied armies.

The first panzer division actually to cross the Meuse was Erwin Rommel's 7th 'Ghost' Division to the north of Sedan. The 5th and 7th Panzer Divisions were given as their objective the area between Givet and Namur, and were technically positioned to protect the main crossing in the Sedan area by Guderian's XIX Corps. But the planners had not allowed for Rommel's flair for seizing the initiative and doing the unexpected – characteristics which later helped to create the legend of the 'Desert Fox'.

The Belgians put up a brave defence: they had plenty of field artillery as well as anti-tank guns in concrete strongpoints, and they turned houses into defensive pill-boxes. The action at the river was extremely fierce, and in the midst of it 7th Panzer's engineers were building pontoons to enable the tanks to cross. The 'Rommel' legend was born that day when his men saw their divisional commander up to his waist in water, helping to move heavy baulks of timber, staying with them under heavy fire until the job was done.[9] Of course, the story spread around the division like wildfire.

Belgian counter-attacks were beaten off, and by last light that day the first panzers of the 'Ghost' Division were across the river, with Rommel's eight-wheeled command vehicle on the first pontoon.

Both 5th and 7th Panzer Divisions pressed forward from their bridgehead and made contact with 1 DCR on the afternoon of 15 May. They caught the French tanks while they were being re-fuelled by their echelon – which had at long last caught up with them. The heavy *Char B1-bis* tanks, which had thicker armour and larger guns (75mm) than their attackers, were thus reduced to the status of immobile pill-boxes. By the end of the day, when the French armour withdrew, they had fewer than 50 serviceable tanks left out of 158. This total was quickly reduced to under 20 during the night retreat, as a result of breakdowns and crews abandoning their vehicles. The next day Rommel's panzers finished off the last tanks of 1 DCR in a short action at Avesnes. An entire French armoured division had been lost through poor logistical planning, poor reconnaissance and forethought, sluggish reactions, and above all through ineffective command and control.

Guderian advances
Gen Guderian's XIX Corps crossed the Luxembourg frontier 0530 on 10 May, the Corps Commander being well to the fore with 1st Panzer Division. By that evening the division's advance guard was through the frontier defences, but was held up by demolitions which could not be by-passed in the difficult terrain. However, a breakthrough was achieved the next morning and the advance continued all that day. They crossed the Semois the following morning and by the evening of 12 May they reached the Meuse. Gen von Kleist ordered Guderian to attack across the Meuse at 1600 hours next day and to precede the attack with mass bombing of the defences. But Guderian had already agreed with the Commander of the *Fliegerkorps* supporting XIX Corps, Gen Lorzer, that his

As First Lord of the Admiralty and as Britain's Prime Minister, Winston Churchill made a number of visits to France both before and during the German onslaught.   IWM

aircraft would be better employed supporting the river crossing rather than making a massive preliminary airstrike with no further support thereafter. Time was short, and the only way for Guderian to send the necessary orders to his divisions was to use the orders used during war games held at Coblenz before the launch of *Fall Gelb*. All that was necessary was to change the time of 'H' hour from 1000 to 1600, and so the real orders were issued without any delay. This shortage of time before the assault crossing worked in Guderian's favour, because it made it impossible to send out the order for the airstrike before H hour. Accordingly the *Fliegerkorps* provided the air support Guderian had called for – which, fortunately for him, was completely effective.

2nd Panzer Divison crosses the Meuse
Gen Schroeder's anthology of battle stories gives a graphic account of the crossing of the Meuse on Whit Monday 13 May.

The orders of yesterday correspond widely with the exercises carried out in Koblenz. It is fascinating to see how accurately the happenings of today were planned then. Again, the night was very short. What is going to happen today? Today is a decisive day. We have completed our advance through difficult conditions in the Ardennes. Now it is important for XIX Panzer Corps with its three divisions to achieve a breakthrough, through the extended Maginot Line between Sedan and Donchéry. In the centre, that is at the 'Schwerpunkt', is 1 Pz Div with the Grossdeutschland Infantry Regiment and the attached Sturm Pioneer Bn 43. On the left 10 Pz Div is in action. Both 2nd and 10th Panzer lose their artillery battalions to the centre division. The Corps order defines very clearly the boundaries between divisions. After crossing the Meuse a right turn has to be carried out – westwards.

2 Pz Div will start to cross the Meuse at 1600 hours and capture the high ground

A Pz Kpfw III Ausf B of the 4th Panzer Division forces its way through a burning street at the height of the attack. TM

on the southern bank. Then, without delay, we will cross the Ardennes Canal, including the bar loop towards the west, so as to roll up the Meuse defences with the attack direction being between Saponge and Feuchère ... The 1 (H) 14 Pz is to reconnoitre around Charleville for the division on the right wing ... Strong units of the Luftwaffe will be supporting the attack over the Meuse, bombers and fighter-bombers, protected by fighters. For the section Sedan to Donchéry there will be: 280 × Me 109 90 × Me 110, 180× Ju 87, 360 × He 111 and Do 17, altogether 910 aeroplanes.

... During the morning our Luftwaffe appears. While the morning mists still hang over the Meuse, our aircraft set to work on the southern bank, with bombs of all calibres to knock out French bunkers, infantry and artillery positions. We now know that the opposition was not of the first quality. One could almost feel sorry for the lads over there. Our panzers, riflemen and motor-cycle mounted riflemen advance out of the forests north of the river. Of course the French artillery is not going to miss such a target, but the gunners over there have good reason to look skywards as fresh Luftwaffe squadrons fly in to bomb them.

... At 1600 the great attack across the whole front line is breaking loose. The divisional staff has moved to Bosseval-et-Briancourt. Air activity intensifies. On the opposite of the river things are getting very uncomfortable. Stukas howl through the night sky, diving onto the enemy, while high above them the wings of our fighters are flashing in the sun. It is surprising how quiet the French airforce are ... By now the battle is in full swing. Enemy artillery is hammering 2nd Panzer, firing at Donchéry and the railway embankment to the north. Our panzers fire into the slits of the bunkers. We miss our heavy artillery; however, we are consoled by the fact that 1 Pz Div is moving smartly forwards. At 1900 some of our riflemen have crossed near Donchéry. They reach the southern bank by swimming. Some use inflatable rafts. It is a very tough fight with considerable losses. But the bridgehead is secured ... The result of the evening: we have crossed the Meuse with all three divisions.

Guderian commands from the front

Like Rommel, Guderian crossed the Meuse in the first assault boat at 1st Panzer Division's crossing-place. The motor-rifle regiment had already crossed. As he reached the far bank he was met with a cry of 'Joy-riding in canoes on the Meuse is forbidden!' from Lt Col Balck, CO of the 1st Rifle Regiment. As Guderian recalled in his book *Panzer Leader*, he had used these very words himself in one of the exercises in preparation for the operation, because 'the attitude of some of the younger officers had struck me as rather too light-hearted. I now realised that they had judged the situation correctly.'

The German attack was highly co-ordinated, every element playing its allotted role. The AA gunners, for example, destroyed over 150 French and British aircraft in the bridgehead area, as the Allies strove desperately to stem the German advance. Quoting again from Gen Schroeder's anthology:

During the previous night, in order to secure the crossing points against air attack, many flak batteries have taken up position ... We now have in the area Sedan-Donchéry 81 × 2cm, 54 × 3.7cm and 36 × 8.8cm AA guns. In the air we are protected by some 90 Me 109s. How necessary these precautions are was soon made clear. During the morning British and French aircraft – Battles and Blenheims, as well as Bloch, Amoit and Potez. They concentrate their attacks on the crossing points, ferries and bridges ... These attacks increase during the day. The pilots are very brave, often coming in only 600 to 800 metres up. But they don't realise how strong our concentrated defences are.... With a tremendous screaming, a wall of fire went up, as the flak guns barked their deadly fire into the air. One of the leading machines was shot to pieces, another burst in flames, a third fell about as if drunk. They were forced to jettison

Following the main advance, German infantry patrols carefully searched all damaged buildings for hidden snipers and other remnants of the defending force. TM

their bombs. We see parachutes floating in the sky. Our soldiers stand in groups on the river bank, staring skywards. No one thought of taking cover. The only danger was from crashing aircraft or jettisoned bombs.

The Germans worked all through that night, building tank ferries to get the panzers across. By first light the combined bridgehead made by 1st Rifle Regiment and the *Grossdeutschland Regiment* on their left measured some three miles in width by six miles in depth – a tremendous achievement, and a springboard for greater things to come.

3 DCR destroyed
The Corps Commander of the French XXI Corps, Gen Flavigny, was ordered to contain the German bridgehead at Sedan and then to counter-attack and drive the enemy across the Meuse. To achieve this objective he had 3 DCR, 5 DLM and the 3rd Motorised Division. Unfortunately, the chapter of accidents that resulted in the annihilation of 1 DCR further north was now repeated. Orders took too long to prepare and despatch, no warning order was given, and vehicle replenishment was too slow. Gen Flavigny did not help by changing his orders shortly before H hour, deciding that his units should take up defensive rather than attacking positions. All this took the better part of 14 May, giving Guderian's panzers time to advance from their bridgeheads and start breaking through the surrounding French forces.

On 14 May and again on the 15th, 3 DCR missed the opportunity to attack the flank of the advancing panzers, even though Gen Georges, the North-East Commander, had ordered them to renew their attack as soon as possible on 15 May. This attack never actually took place, and was finally countermanded at 1700 hours that evening. 3 DCR was then reduced to a static defensive role in support of infantry divisions, which of course made no use of its superior mobility and firepower. The GOC of 3 DCR was sacked and thereafter his division was employed, and destroyed, piecemeal. All this happened because no French commander understood how to use tanks except as static support for infantry. French armour stood no chance against the enthusiastic, daring and ever-resourceful panzer commanders.

By 15 May there were signs of complete collapse on the Allied side. In the North, the Netherlands were out of the battle. Bock's Army Group B had reached the Dyle Line much faster than anticipated, and Belgium was being rapidly overrun. In the centre, the main German attack by Army Group A was already across the Meuse and advancing from its bridgeheads ready for its 'gallop to the sea'. In the south, the Maginot Line appeared to be holding but was in danger of being turned at its north-west end by Guderian's panzer divisions.

Allied air losses were heavy, although many German aircraft had also been destroyed. In the first six days of the battle 539 German aircraft were destroyed and

Allied air losses were heavy, although many German aircraft had also been destroyed. In the first six days of the battle 539 German aircraft were destroyed and 137 damaged. At sea, the main [Allied] effort had been rescuing VIPs, moving to safety Dutch gold and diamond reserves, merchant shipping and the like, while a limited amount of demolition had been carried out in Dutch and Belgian ports. One very unusual operation, code-named

A bewildered family flees before the German invaders. TM

'Royal Marine', was also put into operation. This consisted of launching floating mines into the main German rivers, either from their tributaries or by air. This began on 10 May and by 24 May the official history reports:

> 'that some 2300 floating mines had been streamed into the Rhine, Moselle and Meuse ... Although there was some evidence of damage to the enemy river traffic, ... its extent could not be ascertained with accuracy in the circumstances which then existed.'[10]

On 15 May, Paul Reynaud rang Winston Churchill, who had succeeded Neville Chamberlain as Britain's Prime Minister five days earlier, on the very day Hitler launched his assault on the West. Without any preamble Reynaud said, in English, 'We have been defeated.'

Churchill made no reply.

Reynaud said again, 'We are beaten; we have lost the battle.'

Churchill said, 'Surely it cannot have happened so soon?' But Reynaud replied, 'The front is broken near Sedan; they are pouring through in great numbers with tanks and armoured cars.'

Churchill did his best to reassure the French Prime Minister, but to no avail. Time and again during the course of this fateful telephone conversation he returned to his opening statement: 'We are defeated; we have lost the battle.'[11]

NOTES

1. This and the subsequent extracts are quoted from an article published in *Air Combat Magazine*.
2. Major L. F. Ellis *The War in France and Flanders 1939-40* London: HMSO, 1953.
3. J. Toland *Adolf Hitler* New York: Doubleday & Co. 1976.
4. J. Benoit-Mechin *Sixty Days That Shook The West* London: Jonathan Cape 1963.
5. Ibid.
6. Ibid.
7. Ibid.
8. Ibid.
9. This story is told in Desmond Young's biography of Rommel, but does not appear in *The Rommel Diaries* edited by Liddell Hart, where it says that Rommel stopped the engineers building 6ton pontoons and ordered them to build 12ton pontoons instead.
10. As note 2).
11. The actual verbatim quotes are taken from Churchill's own account of this conversation as given in *Their Finest Hour* London: Cassell & Co. Ltd. 1951.

Chapter 10

Advance to the Sea

Such was the power of the German onslaught on the Low Countries that within less than a week Lord Gort came to the conclusion that the Dyle Line was no longer defensible, and could not be used as a position from which to launch a counter-attack. In a despatch to London he said that the French 1st Army on his right flank was unlikely to recover lost territory 'despite the support I have given them in the air and on the ground', and that a further withdrawal was likely to be forced upon them 'by events in the south'. He acknowledged that there had been no serious attack on Belgian positions to his left. Nevertheless, the Belgian Army would have to pull back when the BEF retreated, to avoid being cut off. This, in turn, would bring about the almost certain loss of Brussels and Antwerp.[1]

Very early in the morning of 16 May, Gort sent a representative to General Billotte, the officer responsible for co-ordinating the movements of the British, French and Belgian forces. He wanted to know at once the 'policy and timing' of any proposed withdrawal. Back came the reply that a general withdrawal to the Escaut position was to begin that same night. The fate of Belgium was thus sealed.

While von Bock's Army Group B were enjoying these spectacular successes in the north, Guderian lost no time in enlarging the vital bridgehead won by Army Group A at Sedan. By the evening of 15 May a gap over 60 miles wide had been torn in the defences, and every attempt to stem the tide was brushed aside by the rapidly advancing German force. Orders from French commanders were slow to reach their formations because radio equipment was inadequate: even when orders did get through, the response was often dilatory and half-hearted. It seemed that the generals and their soldiers in the field had already lost the will to fight.

It was not the strength of the opposition in battle that concerned Guderian and his colleagues but the cautious attitude of the German High Command, who were now determined to slow down the speed of the headlong advance across northern France. This caution came right from the top, from Hitler himself, as we see from this extract from a report of a meeting held at noon on 17 May written by Gen Franz Halder, Chief of the General Staff:

> Apparently little mutual understanding. The Führer insists that the main threat is from the south. (I see no threat at all at present!) For that reason the infantry divisions should be moved up at the earliest to protect the south flank. The armoured divisions should, in themselves, be sufficient to extend the breakthrough in a north-westerly direction.

To Guderian's fury, von Rundstedt shared Hitler's view of the situation and, to be fair, it was a view by no means without justification. Behind Guderian's spearhead formations there had opened up a large and ever-increasing gap, because the following infantry simply could not keep up with the speed of his advance. If the French were to attack from the Verdun area to the south, they could completely separate the panzers from their supporting columns. It seemed inconceivable to Hitler that they would miss the opportunity of delivering so obvious a counter-thrust, and he therefore fully supported von Rundstedt's order to von Kleist that his Panzer Group was not to cross the River Oise before 18 May.

Guderian's reaction was entirely predictable and in character. As he wrote in his autobiography:[2]

> I neither would nor could agree to these orders, which involved the sacrifice of the element of surprise we had gained and of the whole of the initial success we had achieved . . . the conversation (with von Kleist) became very heated and we repeated our various arguments several times.

He goes on to claim that von Kleist did agree that the advance should be maintained for a further 24 hours in order to clear sufficient space in the bridgehead for the infantry troops following on in the rear. After this encounter Guderian hurried back to his forward troops to urge them on to even greater efforts, and in

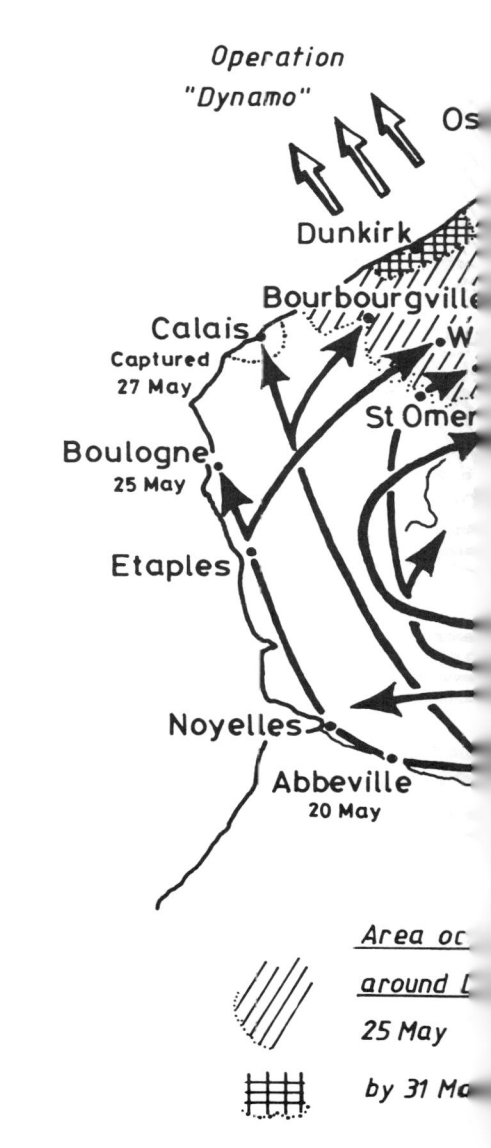

160

the market-place of Montcornet he met the Commander of the 6th Panzer Division from Rheinhardt's XLI Panzer Corps. Together they reached a private agreement that the two corps would continue their advance until they ran out of petrol. Guderian did not believe that Hitler, who had approved of Manstein's plan and had accepted his own proposals for exploiting the breakthrough, could now be frightened 'by his own temerity and would order our advance to be stopped at once.'

As he later admitted, he could not have been more wrong. On the very next day, 17 May, he was ordered to report in person to Gen von Kleist on the XIX Corps' airstrip. There he was given a severe tongue-lashing by his commander, who accused him of disobeying orders. As soon as von Kleist paused for breath, Guderian asked to be relieved of his command. Further exchanges followed involving von Rundstedt and Colonel-General List, who was sent as a peacemaker. Eventually Guderian was told that he would not be permitted to give up his command and that he was, in future, strictly to obey orders. However, he would be permitted to undertake a 'reconnaissance in force' – but his HQ must remain where it could be 'easily reached'. Honour thus satisfied, Guderian returned to the front and the panzers started to roll forward once more.

De Gaulle attacks

If Hitler had realised how far French army commanders had failed to understand the role of the tank in modern warfare, even after the lesson of the Polish campaign, he would have dismissed all fears of a French counter-attack. As it was, only one French officer of any consequence grasped the importance of keeping armoured formations together and not dispersing them as infantry support units. His name was Charles de Gaulle. Although he had never seen tanks in action, having been taken prisoner in 1916 before they made their first appearance on the Western Front, he published in 1934 a small book on the subject, *Vers l'Armée de métier* (Towards a Professional Army). This made an eloquent case for a standing professional army and for the development of strong armoured brigades.

Like his British counterparts he was ignored, and official disapproval went to

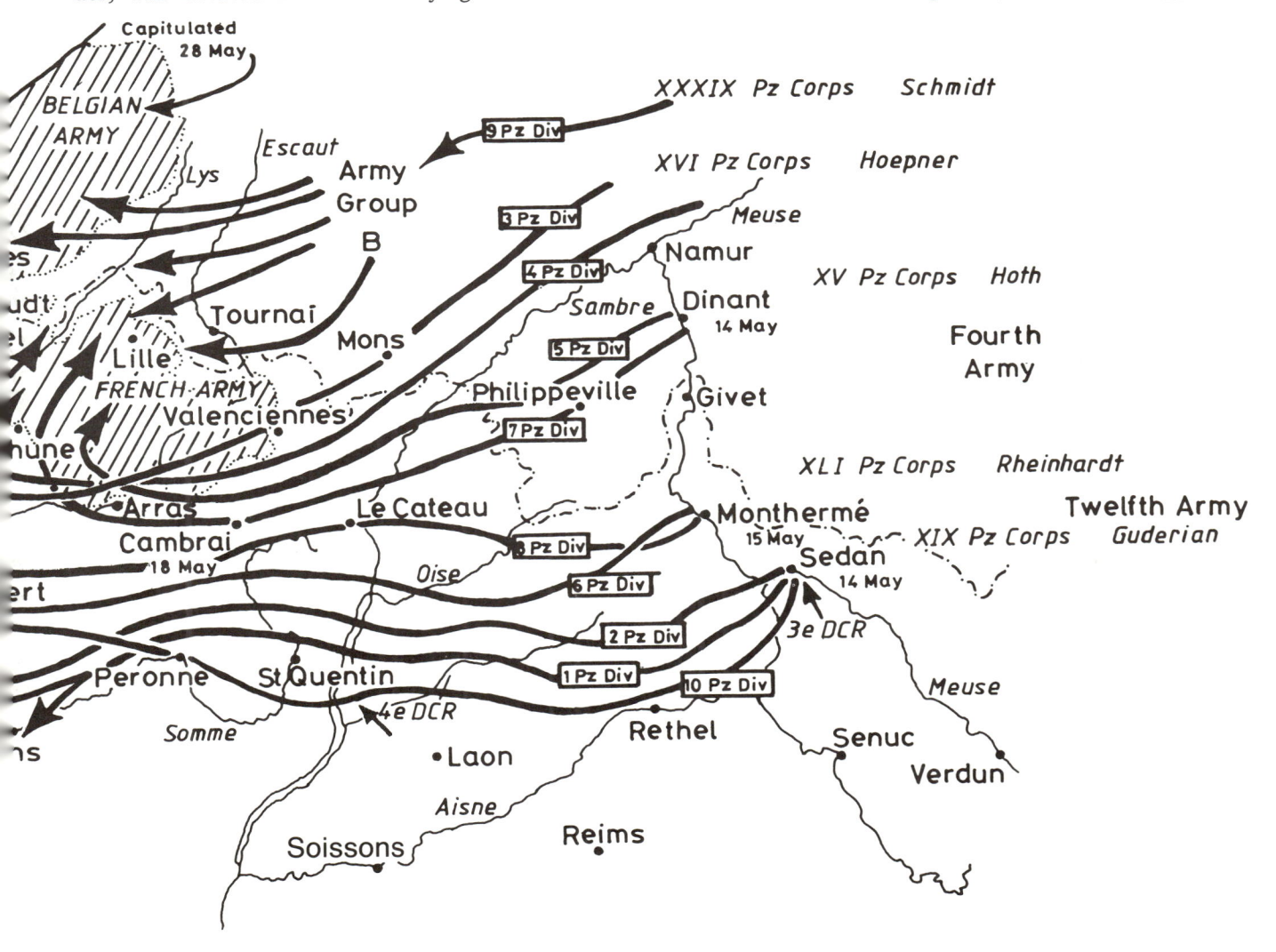

Hotchkiss H39s make their way through a ruined town centre in northern France, 25 May 1940. TM

the extent of removing his name from the 1936 promotion list. In 1940, he was still only a colonel, but on 11 May he was given command of the embryo 4th DCR. 'There de Gaulle!', said Gen Georges, sending him on his way, 'For you, who have for so long held the ideas the enemy is now putting into practice, here is your chance to act.'[3]

De Gaulle decided that the best point at which to cut German supply lines was at Montcornet, a town standing at the centre of an important road network, where Guderian had met his fellow Panzer commander a few days earlier. 4 DCR's assembly point was about 20 miles to the south-west, and although de Gaulle's division was incomplete, not properly trained and short of equipment and weapons, it went into the attack at first light on 17 May. Advancing up the road from Laon to Montcornet his forces overran German reconnaissance and other 'soft-skinned' vehicles, and destroyed everything that 'had no time to flee', as he later recalled.

At that time Montcornet housed the headquarters of the 1st Panzer Division, and its streets were filled with German supply columns and other vulnerable targets. There was little armoured support, but the Germans quickly organised an *ad hoc* defence which halted the French attack. Short of fuel and ammunition, de Gaulle was obliged to withdraw. In later years, when he was the symbol of French resistance and commander of the Free French forces, he was inclined to embroider the story of this action. In fact, it achieved little and Guderian's XIX Panzer continued their advance to the Oise unhindered.

Having fallen back to Laon, de Gaulle's Division was then ordered on 19 May to cross the Serre at Crecy-sur-Serre and to attack Guderian's lines of communication. But the Germans had mined the bridges and had brought up anti-tank guns. By 0900 hrs the advancing French column was halted by the Panzerwaffe and their Stukas. Next day the Division withdrew across the River Aisne, suffering fairly severe losses. Guderian recalled this incident in 'Panzer Leader', commenting that 'the danger from the flank was slight'. However, he noted that some of de Gaulle's tanks penetrated to within a few miles of his advance HQ, and frankly admitted that he 'passed a few uncomfortable hours until at last the threatening visitors moved off in another direction.'

By nightfall on 19 May Guderian's 'reconnaissance' forces reached the line Cambrai-Peronne-Ham. The following day they made their longest advance, from the Canal du Nord to the sea at Abbeville, an amazing 56-plus miles in a single day. Rheinhardt's XLI Corps on the right flank advanced almost as far. In effect, German Panzer forces had cut France in two. Allied forces in the north were now completely isolated.

Counter-attack at Arras

The German advance also continued on the right flank of this penetration, but in places the fighting was much harder, because it was here that the best Allied troops were to be found. Hoth's XV Panzer Corps had to fight through French border defences which had been well prepared the previous winter. Rommel's 'Ghost' Division succeeded in pushing forward, but their advance was on a very narrow salient some thirty miles deep but only two miles wide – 'like a finger pointing into the heart of France'.[4]

The infantry following the panzers met with very heavy fighting as they mopped up strong Allied resistance. Rommel's daring was well rewarded – his division took more than 10,000 prisoners and destroyed many Allied tanks, guns and other equipment, for the loss of only 35 killed and 59 wounded. But even Rommel did not have everything his own way. On 21 May, in the Arras area, 7th Panzer were counter-attacked by British armour and suffered not only their first major reverse of the campaign, but also a reverse that was to have the most far-reaching consequences.

Leading elements of 7th Panzer Division (25th Panzer Regiment) had arrived in the outskirts of Arras by early evening on 20 May. Reconnaissance reported stiff resistance in the town and in the villages to the south. Determined to maintain pressure, Rommel gave orders for an attack to the south-west of Arras next day. He set H hour for 1400 hours in order to give his troops time for badly-needed rest and reorganisation.

On the British side, the BEF had completed its withdrawal from the Dyle Line by 20 May. Lord Gort despatched the 5th and 50th Divisions to protect his right flank and to hold Arras. These two formations were called 'Frankforce' after its commander, Maj Gen Franklyn, the GOC 5 Division. The Allied master plan was for the French to attack northwards towards Cambrai, while the British were to move towards Arras and then attack southwards, cutting off the menacing enemy penetration.

Troops allocated for the operation were drawn from the 50th Infantry Division (TA), mainly Brigadier Churchill's 151 Infantry Brigade (6, 8 & 9 DLI), supported by 1st Army Tank Brigade (4th & 7th RTR), containing the only heavy tanks (Matilda Mk Is & IIs) in the BEF. All were battle-weary; the infantry had marched for ten days in sweltering heat, while the tanks had driven some 120 miles on their tracks in the past five days. More than a quarter had been lost through breakdowns. The infantry had not worked with tanks before and so there were no effective infantry-tank communications.

Brigadier Churchill gave out his orders at 0945 hours on 21 May. The attack was to be in two phases. Phase I was to clear the area as far as the River Cojeul, some five miles south-east of Arras; and Phase 2 was to clear as far as the River Sensée, a few miles further on. The objective of this counter-attack was to capture the

Matilda Mk II *tanks of 7th RTR burn after the battle of Arras, 21-22 May 1940.*
TM

163

A German mechanized column on the move. TM

high ground between these two rivers and so hold up the German advance, providing a breathing-space for the BEF. Churchill divided his small force into two mixed columns, each consisting of a tank battalion, an infantry battalion, a field battery, an anti-tank battery and a machine-gun company. 7th RTR led the right-hand column with 8 DLI. The left-hand column consisted of 4th RTR and 6 DLI. In reserve was 9 DLI plus what remained of 4 RNF (MG bn). The two columns were about three miles apart and were ordered to advance southwards, just to the east of Arras, and then turn southwards to capture their objective. There was very little time to prepare, and some tanks had to leave their leaguer areas even before they had been given their detailed orders. Maps of the area were desperately short. However, the high morale and training of the two RTR battalions made up for some of these deficiencies.

The Left-hand Column (4 RTR & 6 DLI)

By 1345 hours the left-hand column was in action between Dainville and Arras. A sizeable party of enemy infantry in lorries was attacked by machine guns of 4th RTR's Matilda Mk Is. As they pushed on, the column was heavily shelled by a battery of field artillery firing over open sights. The Germans quickly discovered that the Matilda's thick armour could not be penetrated by their standard 37mm anti-tank gun, and so they frequently used field artillery as anti-tank guns. The 4th fanned out, but they came under more artillery fire from 105mm guns to the south, around Mercatel. Their CO (Lt-Col Fitzmaurice) was killed by a direct hit from a 105mm shell. To knock out these guns, A Squadron was ordered to advance to their flank. WO III 'Jock' Armit's troop was detailed for this job and moved forward, supported by Squadron HQ. On crossing a crest they ran into six German anti-tank guns at point-blank range. What followed, Armit describe in his own words (*see panel on this page*).[5]

The Right-hand Column (7 RTR & 8 DLI)

Almost from the start everything went wrong with this column. The recce forces got separated, the scout cars racing ahead while the motor cycle patrols stayed in reserve. The main task force (7 RTR) soon found itself well ahead of the infantry. To make matters worse, the enemy were encountered even before the column reached the start-line. They were dealt with rapidly, but then the leading tanks turned SE instead of SW and became entangled with the rear of the left-hand column. The CO and Adjutant of 7 RTR were both killed, but in spite of all this the column pushed on to Wailly, where it came to a halt. The place was packed

---

Warrant Officer 'Jock' Armit remembers . . .

My .50 machine gun was brought into action, and I got two of them before they realised I was on them – the range was approximately 200 yards. The other guns started on me now and one hit the gun housing. This caused the recoil slot-pin of my gun to snap and shook the gun back in the turret, jamming me between the shoulder piece and the back of the turret. I forced the gun back and pressed the triggers of my two smoke mortars, but they did not fire. I found out later that they had been shot straight off. During this time, which was only the space of a minute, they hit my tank about ten times, but none of the hits did any real damage. I quickly made up my mind that the best way out was to back over the crest until I could get my gun cleared, so I gave my driver the order and we slowly zig-zagged back a distance of about 100 yards. I got my gun going again and, thirsting for revenge, I returned to the attack. They must have thought I was finished, for I caught the guns limbered up, moving to another position, and revenge was sweet.

with Rommel's guns and vehicles. Writing afterwards, in a successful recommendation for a well-deserved DCM for Sgt B Doyle, Lt-Col John King, who was at the time commanding B Squadron of 7 RTR, described the action that followed:

> Early in the action I and Sgt Doyle's section (4 Matilda Mk IIs) became heavily engaged with a German anti-tank battery. All four of the enemy guns and two Matildas were put out of action, leaving just Sgt Doyle and myself. Behind this German battery small parties of Germans with machine guns, who had been maintaining an intense fire on the tanks, rose from cover and retired as we reached their positions. There must have been about 150 men in all and they were practically all knocked out by the MGs of the two Matildas.
>
> The two tanks then went to the assistance of the five Matilda Mk Is, which were armed only with machine gun and were in difficulties with four German tanks armed with cannon. Sgt Doyle and I knocked out these four German tanks and left them burning, killing those of the crews who attempted to escape. A little later we ran up against another four-gun German battery and put all those guns out of action, Sgt Doyle, under intense fire, going straight for one gun and running over it. Both tanks now had fires in their forward tool-boxes, and had to repeatedly open the top covers to avoid suffocation by fumes. While taking a breather myself, I saw Sgt Doyle doing the same thing with smoke pouring out of his top cover. I also noticed that his 2-pounder gun was pointing at me, that is, to his left, and surmised that his turret had been jammed by hits on the turret ring, as had my own. Shortly after this engagement, on reaching the crest of rising ground, I came on a German 88mm AA gun about 20 yards from the track on which I was moving. He depressed onto me, but before he could fire I was able to run between two high banks, which bordered the track here, for about 200 yards.
>
> My turret was jammed with the gun pointing right rear and the 88mm gun was on the left of the track. As we moved out of cover my driver swung the tank and brought the gun onto the target. Almost simultaneously, Sgt Doyle, who had appeared on the crest behind, quickly grasped the situation, swung his tank and opened fire. He scattered the crew with his machine guns and then shelled the gun with his 2-pounder, thus relieving what was, for me, a critical situation. I halted and opened my top cover, and my tank then flared up inside and we had to get out. Sgt Doyle moved up and showed me his right hand which was minus the two centre fingers, these having been shot away on one of the occasions when he had opened his top cover to get air. His tank was still emitting smoke and he told me his driver couldn't stick the heat and fumes much longer. He also told me his turret had been jammed in the action with the second anti-tank battery and all his periscopes were shattered. I gave him my map and told him to carry on to the rallying point as quickly as he could, and off he went. I met him again two days later as a prisoner in Cambrai. I consider he behaved in a very gallant manner, and showed exceptional devotion to duty throughout the afternoon's battle.[6]

This 'small battle fought by the British around Arras,' as Winston Churchill called it, succeeded in knocking out many German tanks and guns, and for a brief time caused Rommel some anxiety. Total German losses were 90 killed, 120 wounded, 400 taken prisoner, and 30 tanks destroyed. It is not surprising that Rommel was given an exaggerated impression of the size of the British force,

Enterprising British Tommies solve at least one of the problems of retreat. IWM

which was reflected in his divisional battle report:

> Between 1530 hours and 1900 hours, heavy fighting took place against hundreds of enemy tanks and following infantry. Our anti-tank gun is not effective against the heavy British tanks, even at close range. The enemy broke through the defensive line formed by our anti-tank guns, which were put out of action or over-run and most of their crews killed.

The Germans rallied quickly and restored the situation by late evening on 21 May, but the important effect of this British counter-attack was to demonstrate to the higher German HQs, including the Führer's, that their leading panzer divisions were vulnerable. It sowed the seeds of doubt in the minds of many senior commanders. Writing after the war, von Rundstedt commented:

> A critical moment came just as my forces reached the Channel. It was caused by a British counter-stroke southwards from Arras on 21 May. For a short time it was feared that the panzer divisions would be cut off before the infantry divisions could come up to support them. None of the French counter-attacks carried the threat of this one.[7]

Two days before the battle at Arras Gen Weygand was appointed Supreme Commander Allied Forces in place of Gen Gamelin, and on 22 May the Allied Supreme War Council approved the 'Weygand Plan' to stop and then to defeat the German armies. This called for concerted attacks towards Bapaume from the areas of Arras and the Somme, striking the flanks of the panzer divisions. But it was already too late. The general inadequacy of the French forces available and the breakdown of communications between them doomed the Weygand Plan to failure, and it was abandoned on 24 May.

By then the German 'big squeeze' had begun. The French 1st Army, the Belgian Army and the BEF were all being pushed into a northern coastal pocket with Dunkirk to their rear. The Channel ports of Boulogne and Calais were also coming under attack. Weygand then ordered the Allied forces to establish a bridgehead covering a wide area around Dunkirk. 'This bridgehead,' he ordered, 'will be held without any thought of retreat.'

The 'Halt Order'

It was at this point that a direct personal intervention by Hitler came to the rescue

Every available vehicle was commandeered by Allied forces retreating on Dunkirk and then abandoned in the street. TM

of the beleaguered Allied forces. Von Rundstedt's advancing panzer divisions received orders direct from Hitler's HQ to halt and not to cross the Aa channel. This stopped Guderian from sending his 1st Panzer Division to attack Dunkirk, and he says he was left 'utterly speechless' by the Führer's unexplained change of mind. No reasons were given in the order, which merely instructed the panzer divisions to hold the line of the canal, rest and recuperate, adding that 'Dunkirk is to be left to the Luftwaffe. Should the capture of Calais prove difficult, this port too is to be left to the Luftwaffe.'[8]

There is little doubt that this order saved the BEF. Why was it given?

At least three possible explanations have been offered. The first is that Goering, jealous of the success of the Panzer Divisions and of the glory accorded to the Panzerwaffe, persuaded Hitler to leave the destruction of the trapped Allied forces to the Luftwaffe. Second is the even less likely suggestion that Hitler, having brought France to her knees, hoped that the British might be persuaded to make peace and that the necessary goodwill would be created by allowing the BEF to escape. This rather fanciful notion is certainly not supported by his War Directive of 13 May 1940, which makes it clear that 'the next object of our operations is to annihilate the French, English and Belgian forces.' The third possibility is that after the Arras counter-attack Hitler feared a series of similar assaults on his widely-dispersed panzer units. Time was needed for them to reorganise and recuperate, and it was considered that vulnerable armoured forces should not be further endangered.

The distinguished military historian, Sir Basil Liddell Hart, had no doubts about the reasons for the 'Halt Order'. In his history of the Royal Tank Regiment he concluded:

> It may well be asked whether two battalions have ever had such a tremendous effect on history as the 4th and 7th RTR achieved at Arras. Their effect in saving the British Army from being cut off from its escape port provides ample justification for the view that if two well-equipped armoured divisions had been available the Battle of France might also have been saved.[9]

The defence of Calais
By 23 May the port of Calais was isolated. Two days earlier its garrison had been reinforced from England by 30th Infantry Brigade commanded by Brigadier Nicholson, supported by 3rd RTR. These forces had been sent to honour Churchill's promise that 'Calais should be fought to the death.' Lord Gort had intended to use the tanks (a cruiser regiment) on the canal line, but it was already too late, and instead they were employed in defensive roles in and around the port. 30th Brigade was violently and repeatedly attacked by tanks and infantry supported by hordes of Stukas. Every inch of every street was fought for, amid the rubble of bombed and battered buildings. Brigadier Nicholson refused all offers of surrender, and he and his brigade fought to the last. One small group of defenders after another was surrounded and overwhelmed, and the fighting did not cease until the evening of 26 May. The Official History records:

> ... they gained the distinction of having fought to the end, at a high cost of life and liberty, because this was required of them. They helped make it possible for the BEF to reach Dunkirk and by their disciplined courage and stout-hearted endurance they enriched the history of the British Army.

The capture of Boulogne
Further down the coast Boulogne was also surrounded, and there was a similar fight to the end. The 20th Guards Brigade under Brigadier Fox-Pitt, was sent from England on 22 May to strengthen the mainly non-combatant British Military Pioneer Corps who worked the port.

Carrying a flag of truce, the crew of a German staff car accepts the surrender of a group of Belgian soldiers. TM

facing page
From the comparative safety of a rescue ship men of the BEF watch as their comrades make their way from the shore to the ship's side. Men were up to their necks in water, but many still carried their rifles.
TM

The Germans lost no time in turning the Dunkirk evacuation into a propaganda weapon aimed at dividing the Allies. In this striking poster, brutal British officers are shown preventing the embarkation of wounded French soldiers who have covered their retreat to the beaches. TM

The Guards were almost immediately in action against German tanks. They were supported by fire from British naval destroyers, which had great success against enemy gun sites and machine-gun nests. Meanwhile non-combatants and wounded men were being evacuated. The Guards fought heroically until orders came to evacuate the port completely on the evening of 25 May. The last ship to leave Boulogne was the destroyer *Vimiera*, which sailed in the early hours of 24 May, dangerously overloaded with some 1400 men. Remnants of British and French units continued fighting a little longer, until they ran out of ammunition and realised that no more ships could come to their rescue. The Germans reported Boulogne captured on 25 May.

The chronicles of most fighting nations are full of accounts of actions such as these, in which gallant defenders fight on to the last bullet or the last man against overwhelming odds. With the benefit of fifty years' hindsight it may be asked whether these heroic stands at Calais and Boulogne served any useful military purpose. Churchill entertained no such doubts: he was quite clear that the three days gained by the defence of Calais enabled the Gravelines waterline to be held, and the evacuation at Dunkirk to proceed. Of course, his is not a disinterested view: by this stage of the war he was himself a major protagonist. But even with the same hindsight there seems no good reason to challenge his assessment.

Belgium surrenders

Late on 26 May Hitler's 'Halt Order' was rescinded and the panzers allowed to roll forward once more. That same day King Leopold warned the Allies that his armies were crumbling in the face of renewed German thrusts and that they would soon be forced to capitulate. Also that day Lord Gort decided on his own responsibility to use the BEF to fill the gap left by the Belgians. In agreement with the French commander he gave orders for a withdrawal behind the River Lys: the Allied line was now little more than a semi-circle around Dunkirk.

At 1700hrs the following day King Leopold asked the Germans for a cessation of hostilities. Hitler replied with a demand for unconditional surrender. This was agreed later that evening, and came into force at 0400hrs on 28 May. Under the terms of the surrender the Belgian soldiers were allowed to keep their arms, and the castle at Laeken was put at the disposal of the King as a residence for himself, his family, military retinue and staff.[10]

Night attack on Armentières

As the Allied forces withdrew behind the River Lys they were pursued by Panzer Regiment 35 of 4th Panzer Division, who were ordered to outflank them in the south-west by occupying the Lille-Armentières road. This operation is described in their official history *So Lebten und Starben Sie*:

> It is already a very dark night. We still roll forwards. French motorised transport is joining our marching column, not realising it is us. We allow them to travel with

us, but let them know later who we are – and they are astounded! To the right and left of the road lie abandoned wagons, guns, etc. It is midnight when we pass through Boutillerie. In Touquet we meet an enemy column with artillery. They want to break out northwards, so we get into a fight. The enemy defend themselves, firing with heavy guns, aiming directly at us. Houses are burning. To the right, left and behind us, French 'fairy lights' glow in the night sky. We are deep inside enemy territory and on the cross-roads in front of us are substantial enemy units all trying to withdraw.

Our ammunition is in short supply, therefore the decision is made to postpone the attack until the early morning. We ask permission to pull forward our artillery and ammunition transport. The ammo arrives, but no artillery. The division has to wait and, at 0645 the following morning, we reach Armentières. Enemy transport is coming out of the town, loaded with Frenchmen. They think we are English and are very pleased that we are at last coming to help them. Yes, we will help them all right! After we explain the truth they are very disappointed. Hundreds of them march back into captivity – possibly 2,000 men. Sometime around 1200 the rest of the Division arrives. Oblt Berger is decorated by Gen Hoepner with the Iron Cross First Class. On 29th May we are pulled back approx 5 kms to rest. The number of our battle-ready tanks had already increased to 130, thanks to the excellent performance of our Workshop Company. The losses of the Regiment are 25 dead and 77 wounded, so in barely three weeks a quarter of our fighting strength has been lost.

Dunkirk

By 30 May most of the BEF and some French troops were within the Dunkirk perimeter. The panzers had been withdrawn and the destruction of the Allied forces was left to the Luftwaffe. British units included the 13th/118th Hussars who had moved back from the Ypres-Poperinghe-Stavele area. Their CO, Lt Col Stirling reported to Gen Alexander (whom Lord Gort had put in command of the defence of Dunkirk), while the troops dug holes in the sand and tried to get some sleep. The Regimental History records:

> Eye-witnesses in the Regiment were unanimous in asserting that the discipline and morale of the British was high. The organisation for control was good. The parties patrolling the beaches marched up and down as if on the barrack square, and

Two of the little ships, loaded to the gunwales, make another perilous crossing to Dover before returning to pick up more survivors.   RN Museum

gave a feeling of confidence and military good order. Although very weary and exhausted, the men showed no signs of fear, and retained their cheerfulness and sense of humour.

Orders to proceed independently to Dunkirk had also been received by 4th/7th Dragoon Guards. Their armoured squadron encountered four lanes of traffic on the Poperinghe-Dunkirk road, where there was complete chaos:

> . . . everyone was running around and pointing revolvers at each other and shouting. The vast army in retreat was something that none of us can forget and never wish to see again. There were about four French vehicles (many of them horse-drawn) to one British. Fifty yards without a stop was good going. All our drivers were deadbeat and fell asleep every time the column halted. Some of the people ahead had abandoned their vehicles and were legging it to the boats, with the result that enormous queues built up behind deserted lorries . . . With the prospect of some really heavy bombing in view at daylight, Major Williams, now in the lead, took to the fields and led us over quite a nice line of country with some stiffish fences, eventually arriving on the canal crossings N of Dunkirk with most of the squadron intact.[11]

The task of 4th/7th DG within the bridgehead area was to provide a rearguard for the troops struggling down to the beaches, so they spent the next two days patrolling and observing, while roads were mined and bridges blown. Their History records:

> Although enemy air activity had increased and the RAF seemed to have vanished, there were only minor encounters with German advanced elements, during which time one sergeant was wounded and one trooper killed. Much time was spent in the grim task of shooting wounded French horses which lay about roadsides and ditches, having been deserted by their artillery and transport owners. The whole area resembled a vast dump, with wrecked or abandoned lorries, trucks, tanks, guns and motor-cycles. In one spot a battery of 75mm guns lay with their muzzles blown open in fantastic flower shapes. At 1100hrs on June 1st, the Squadron handed over to some French infantry at a blown bridge and, acting as rearguard to a column of Green Howards, arrived at the outskirts of Dunkirk where they destroyed their last tanks and carriers, and then marched to the Mole on the beach. Here amid the seething crowds of troops they discovered A Squadron of the 5th Dragoon Guards and happily took shelter with them under their wrecked vehicles, which had been driven thus far. At first light next day the shelling and bombing was resumed, causing many casualties among the congested mass.

The RAF at Dunkirk

Although the men of the 4th/7th DG could not see the RAF over the Dunkirk beaches, they were in fact there. 'Hour after hour,' wrote Churchill in *The Second World War: Their Finest Hour*, 'they bit into the German fighter and bomber squadrons, taking a heavy toll, scattering them and driving them away.' On 28 May RAF Fighter Command was instructed to '. . . ensure the protection of the Dunkirk beaches (three miles on either side) from first light to darkness by continuous fighter patrols in strength.' Air operations to protect troops being evacuated took many forms. Reconnaissance alone required thirty sorties a day, not including fighter escorts. Every day some fifty Blenheim bombers attacked the enemy forces closing in on Dunkirk, and every night a similar number of heavy bombers concentrated on the road approaches to the beaches, while others attacked enemy communications in depth. All these operations were not seen by the men being bombed and strafed on the beaches, but when it was witnessed it was quickly appreciated. A typical air support operation is quoted in the RAF History – the bombing of Nieuport on 31 May on behalf of the 12th Infantry Brigade, where the effect 'was instantaneous and decisive – all movement of enemy reserves was stopped; many of the forward German troops turned and fled, suffering severely from the fire of our machine guns . . .'

By this time RAF operations were controlled from the UK, the AOC of the Air Component having transferred his HQ from France on 22 May. In May and June 1940 the RAF exacted a high toll on the enemy at the cost of 959 aircraft lost. The spirit of the pilots and ground crew may be judged from a letter written to his mother by Flt Lt R. D. G. Wright, which is quoted in the RAF History:

> If anyone says anything to you in the future about the inefficiency of the RAF – I believe the BEF troops were booing the RAF in Dover the other day – tell them from me we only wish we could do more. But without aircraft we can do no more than we have done – that is, our best, and that's fifty times better than the German best, though they are fighting under the most advantageous conditions. I know of no RAF pilot who has refused combat yet – and that sometimes means combat with odds of more than fifty to one.[12]

Operation 'Dynamo'

As soon as it seemed likely that the BEF would have to be evacuated by sea, the War Cabinet agreed on 20 May 'that as a precautionary measure the Admiralty should assemble a large number of small vessels in readiness to proceed to ports and inlets on the French coast.' (Winston Churchill, *Their Finest Hour*) This was the origin of 'Operation Dynamo', control of which was placed in the hands of Admiral Ramsay, commanding at Dover. During the following days an immense fleet of small ships of all kinds was assembled – motor launches, fishing craft, yachts, lighters, barges, pleasure boats, tugs, trawlers, any vessel that could be used to rescue the men on the beaches. These were, of course, in addition to ships of the Royal Navy. As Churchill put it, 'everyone who had a boat of any kind, steam or sail, put out for Dunkirk.' From 26 May a great tide of small vessels took badly-needed food, water and ammunition to the waiting troops, and ferried men back to waiting larger ships – under ceaseless enemy bombing. Altogether some 860 Allied vessels (nearly 700 British) rescued over 338,000 men between 29 May and 4 June, when Dunkirk fell to the Germans. The commander of the BEF, Lord Gort, left as ordered on 1 June, after handing over to Gen Alexander the task of completing the evacuation. The Official despatches reported:

> By midnight on 2nd/3rd June, all the remaining British troops had been embarked. Major General Alexander, with the Senior Naval Officer (Capt W. G. Tennant, RN) made a tour of the beaches and harbour in a motor boat and on being satisfied that no British troops were left on shore, they themselves left for England.

Winston Churchill was in sombre mood when he addressed the House of Commons on 4 June 1940. 'We must be careful,' he declared, 'not to assign to this deliverance the attributes of a victory. Wars are not won by evacuations.' He added that there was a victory inside this delivery – the victory gained by the RAF against the much stronger Luftwaffe. This alone gave reason for confidence in ultimate victory, even though Britain now stood alone. Though 'large tracts of Europe and many old and famous states have fallen or may fall into the grip of the Gestapo and all the odious apparatus of Nazi rule, we shall not flag or fail. We shall go on to the end . . . we shall defend our island, whatever the cost may be. We shall fight on the beaches, we shall fight on the landing-grounds, we shall fight in the fields and in the streets, we shall fight in the hills; we shall never surrender.'

NOTES
1. Lord Gort's Despatches *London Gazette (Supplement), 10 October 1941*.
2. Guderian, Gen H. *Panzer Leader* London: Michael Joseph, 1952.
3. Horne, A. *To Lose a Battle* London: Macmillan, 1969.
4. Young, Desmond *Rommel*.
5. From *A Short History of the RTR* published privately in 1980.
6. From *Recommendations for the Award of a Distinguished Service Medal to Sergeant B. Doyle, 'B' Company, 7th Bn Royal Tank Regiment* Tank Museum Library.
7. As note 2.
8. As note 2.
9. Liddell Hart, B. *The Tanks. Vol 23* London: Cassell, 1959.
10. Robins, Yves *The First Days of the Belgian Invasion*, published in *Armies & Weapons*.
11. Brereton, J. H. *History of the 4th/7th Royal Dragoon Guards* published by The Regiment in 1982.
12. Richards, D. *Royal Air Force, 1939-1945, Vol I, The Fight at Odds* London: HMSO, 1953.

Allied troops who failed to reach the rescue ships were rounded up on the quayside and sent to prison camps. TM

Chapter 11

The Battle of France

In his War Directive No 13 dealing with the annihilation of the Allied armies around Dunkirk, Hitler also outlined his intentions for the destruction of the remaining enemy forces in France 'in the shortest possible time'. This final offensive was to be carried out in three phases:

Phase One – starting 5 June, a thrust between the sea and the River Oise, as far as the lower Seine below Paris, to support and secure the right flank of the main attack to follow. This preliminary move was to be made by Bock's Army Group B, with six panzer divisions of which two (XVth Panzer Corps) were to be directly subordinated to Kluge's Fourth Army, and the remainder to operate under the command of Gen Kleist. The Eighteenth Army, still mopping up in the Dunkirk area, was also placed under Bock's command.

A mixed Panzer column crosses the River Somme at Pont Remy during the push to the south. Author's collection

Phase Two – starting 9 June, was to be the main attack, driving south-east on either side of Rheims in order to destroy the major part of the French Army in the Paris-Metz-Belfort triangle, and to isolate the Maginot Line. Von Rundstedt's Army Group A was given this task, with four panzer divisions forming the spearhead of the assault. Gen Heinz Guderian was given command of this new Panzer Group, which comprised XXXIX and XLI Pz Corps.

Phase Three – starting 14 June, there was to be a subsidiary attack, on the left flank of the main thrust, against the Maginot Line at its weakest point. Army Group C was to carry out this operation, aiming towards Nancy-Luneville.

Allied Defences

In the face of a rapidly re-deploying enemy the desperate attempts by Gen Weygand to organize a defence in depth, behind the Somme and the Aisne, met with little success. The *quadrillage* (chequer board) defence system he ordered needed strong mobile reserves to mount a counter-attack, but by that time such reserves were virtually non-existent. Weygand had only 65 divisions left: of these 3 were re-constituted armoured divisions, and 17 were either second-line reserve formations or part of the Maginot Line garrison.

Under the command of the French IX Corps was the 51st Highland Division (TA), which had been unable to join the rest of the BEF at Dunkirk. It consisted of three brigades, commanded by Maj Gen V. M. Fortune, occupying positions on the lower reaches of the River Somme. Other British forces still in France included the much-weakened 1st Armoured Division, and various improvised units drawn from troops who had previously manned lines of communication – 'Beauforce', 'Vicforce' and 'Digforce'. The last of these consisted of reservists serving with the Auxiliary Military Pioneer Corps.

Altogether more than 140,000 British soldiers remained in France after Dunkirk, and their numbers were actually increased as attempts were made to form a new BEF, once again under the command of Lord Gort. For example, on 7 June, the 52nd Lowland Division, with elements of the 1st Canadian Division, were sent to France with Lt Gen Alan Brooke as their Corps Commander. Even if these movements had been known to the ordinary British public at the time, which they were not

> **Order of the Day**[1]
> Officers, NCOs and soldiers of the French Army! The Battle of France has started. The order is to defend our positions without thought of withdrawal. Let the thought of our country, wounded by the invader, inspire in you the unshakeable resolve to stand firm. Hold on to the soil of France, look only forward! The fate of our country, the preservation of its freedoms and the future of our sons depends upon your tenacity. **Weygand**

for obvious reasons of military security, their significance would in any case have been quite lost in the shadow of the momentous drama of Dunkirk evacuation and the preparations for national defence that followed. But the longer view of history requires it to be noted that Britain did not abandon her ally after Dunkirk, and that British soldiers fought and died in the Battle of France.

Blitzkrieg again

At 0400 hrs on 5 June the Germans heralded their renewed attack with a massive air and ground bombardment. There swiftly followed a concentrated assault by some 600-plus tanks along a six-kilometre front. The French fought desperately, but the *Blitzkrieg* was unstoppable. The panzers were everywhere, '. . . making use of the terrain, slipping through gaps . . . giving strong points of the front-line a wide berth, limiting themselves to occasionally detaching one or two sections to explore the outskirts of a village and neutralize it, or lend a hand with the infantry, but never tarrying'.[2] By noon they were six miles ahead of their infantry, and achieving a great deal by their deep penetrations. Rommel was well in the lead, as his tanks advanced towards Rouen, '. . . firing and fighting without pause . . . they forged on through the fields where the corn was already tall. All the enemy detachments hiding in them were destroyed or forced back'. Army Group B took just one day to establish itself south of the Somme and on 9 June it reached the Seine. The shattered French forces could only withdraw in front of this onslaught.

This was the moment when von Rundstedt's Army Group A launched its attack, but Guderian's panzers did not have things all their own way. The French slowed the German advance with several well-directed armoured counterattacks. Guderian recalled a tank battle south of Joinville which lasted two hours before his panzers got the upper hand. While this action was in progress he himself engaged in a duel with a *Char B*, which he tried in vain to destroy with a captured 47mm anti-tank gun: '. . . all the shells I fired at it simply bounced harmlessly off its thick armour. Our 37mm and 20mm guns were equally ineffective . . . As a result we inevitably suffered sadly heavy casualties'.[3] However, French counter-strokes were a case of 'too little, too late'. The Fourth Army, strove to hold the German main attack and to keep in contact with the French Sixth Army in the west, which was also being forced back. But it, too, had to give way, and once more the panzers broke through and rolled on.

A French tank commander surrenders his Char B1 to enemy infantry. TM

A radio-equipped, 8-wheeled heavy armoured car, the Schwerer Panzerspahwagen (Fu) (Sd Kfz 232). *The commander is seen receiving his orders for a reconnaissance operation.* TM

The Italian assault on southern France. Benito Mussolini talks to an artilleryman before the attack, and a jubilant Italian soldier brandishes his national flag from the window of a captured French customs post on the border. Historical Branch, Italian Army

Italy Declares War

On 10 June Italy declared war on France and Britain. Mussolini made his motive very clear:

> I can't just sit back and watch the fight. When the war is over and victory comes I shall be left empty-handed.

However, the Italian invasion army of some 30-plus divisions waited until 21 June before launching its offensive, and even then failed to make much impression on the handful of French Alpine Divisions barring the way. Along the French coast, its progress was equally slow, but eventually the Italians succeeded in taking Menton on 23 June. The French were outnumbered twelve to one in parts of the Alpine front, but they still gave a good account of themselves. As Alistair Horne noted: '. . . on the Côte d'Azur the Italian invasion was held up by a French NCO and seven men'.[4]

Meanwhile, in the centre of France, Guderian's panzers were across the River Aisne and advancing rapidly to the Marne. The French armies in the area were shattered and broken, and as earlier in the north, the roads were jammed with fleeing refugees. On 12 June recce forces from Guderian's 2nd Panzer Division crossed the river at Chalons-sur-Marne. They captured the bridge intact but failed to examine it for demolition charges, and it blew up while German troops were crossing.

The German Army was by no means entirely composed of mechanized forces. Reiter Regiment 2 (later mechanized as Panzer Regiment 24) was a horse cavalry regiment which fought with distinction in the Polish campaign and in the earlier part of the campaign in France. On 16 June they were ordered to cross the Seine at Meulan, not far from Paris, for further operations southwards. This crossing is described in their history, *Unser Regiment*:

> In the early morning the Regiment crosses in two places. As always, in front swims our Regimental Commander with his horse 'Flavy' in the first wave across the river. The rider squadrons are the first ready to proceed on the other side of the river.
>
> On the 15th June in the morning, about 1100, we start to cross over. Light flak as well as heavy machine-gun fire secure our

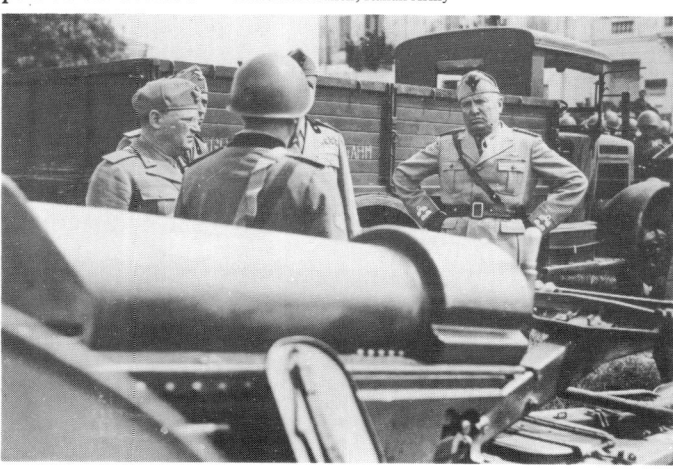

crossing against enemy attacks. Quickly we unsaddle the horses. A landing and swimming troop is formed and the course for the rubber dinghies is selected. As so often practised, all our belongings are packed in our saddle-bags. The calmer horses of the squadron, guided by our swimmers, cross over. It is more difficult with the younger and more inexperienced horses. Slowly they are guided into the water, and the boat crews take over. They must now swim and pull the rubber dinghies, loaded with the saddles. With tremendous patience and calm the crossing is carried out.

Paris Surrenders
A few days earlier, at dusk on 13 June, German forces approached the French capital from three directions. The Military Governor of Paris, Gen Hering, with a newly-formed army, was ordered by Gen Weygand to retreat southwards to join the French armies which were by-passing the city. Reynaud and Weygand had decided that Paris was to be declared an open city, and accordingly a notice was posted on the city walls:

> General Hering, having been called away to command an army, is placing the military government in the hands of General Dentz. Paris is declared an open city. Every step has been taken to ensure in all circumstances the safety and provisioning of the inhabitants.[5]

In fact, nothing whatsoever had been done apart from the declaration itself. The Government and its ministries and staffs had already left, and there was a vast exodus of Parisians by train, car, bicycle, cart and on foot.

The Germans did not waste time. Soon after 0200 hrs on 14 June the French picked up a message calling for the immediate surrender of the capital and indicating that the Germans would send an envoy, under a flag of truce, to the Porte St Denis to discuss terms. All was quickly arranged, and on 15 June the Germans marched into Paris.

By this time the BEF too could do no more. The 51st Highland Division attempted to withdraw to Le Havre, hoping to be evacuated by British ships, but in company with the remainder of the French IX Corps they could only get as far as St Valéry. To release as much transport as possible for troop carrying, they jettisoned most of their non-fighting equipment and reduced their artillery ammunition to 100 rounds for each gun.

Hard on their heels was Rommel's 'Ghost' Division, which seized the high ground to the west, enabling them to cover the port.

That afternoon (10 June) Rommel himself led the 25th Panzer Regiment into the attack, supported by elements of the 6th Schutzen Regiment. The Highlanders fought desperately and kept the enemy out. The 11 June had been chosen as the night to rescue the Division, but fog prevented embarkation.

Rommel sent a handwritten note to Gen Fortune, GOC of the Division, demanding his surrender. This was refused.

Soon after the open city of Paris fell on 14 June 1940, the Germans mounted a huge celebration parade through the main streets. TM

But at 0800 hrs on 12 June, the commander of the French IX Corps, Gen Ihler, surrendered, and Gen Fortune was left with no choice but to follow suit. In any event, as St Valéry was surrounded by German artillery and machine guns, and the beach was under direct fire, it would have been highly dangerous to attempt an evacuation. There would have been many casualties. In the event, 12,000 Allied Troops were taken prisoner, of whom 8,000 were British.

The 52nd Lowland Division and the depleted 1st Armoured Division were more fortunate. Along with elements of the 1st Canadian Division together with Gen Alan Brooke and his staff, they were successfully embarked from Cherbourg on 17 June. However, Rommel and his panzers were only three miles from the port when the last rescue ship sailed. Some 30,630 men were brought home from Cherbourg, and the Royal Navy continued evacuating Allied troops of all nations until 14 August. The number of those rescued after Dunkirk was 191,870, bringing to a total of 558,032 those men who eluded the enemy's attempts to capture or destroy them.[6]

'The Fighting Must Cease'

While the fate of the remaining French armies was being decided on the battlefields, their senior commanders and the politicians were considering surrender. As early as 12 June Gen Weygand asked the Government to seek an armistice. A few days earlier Reynaud, at that time against any thought of capitulation, had invited Gen de Gaulle (who was known for his determination to continue the fight at all costs) to join the Government as Under-Secretary of State for National Defence.

In those fateful last days the flagging French leaders did not lack for British advice and encouragement. Winston Churchill visited Reynaud and his ministers twice in the final weeks – on 11 June and 13 June – and a third visit planned for 17 June was frustrated at the last minute by the fall of Reynaud's Government. On these occasions he attempted, vainly, to persuade them to continue the fight at all costs, if necessary from French North Africa. He urged them not on any account to allow the French fleet to fall into German hands, and this Admiral Darlan solemnly promised. Above all, Churchill declared again and again that no matter what happened to France, Britain would fight on alone.

It was during these visits that de Gaulle got to know the British Prime Minister, and they came to respect, if not like, each other. On a flying visit to London on 9 June, de Gaulle appealed to Churchill to send more RAF squadrons to support the shattered French armies, but in vain. Churchill knew that those few remaining squadrons were Britain's last defence.

The steady refusal of the British to commit more of their forces to the battle

The Faces of Defeat. TM

for France – particularly their remaining fighter squadrons – seems to have indicated to the French Government that they secretly thought the French cause was lost, whatever they might say in public. This view was shared by the French Vice-President, the elderly Marshal Pétain, who had been recalled by Reynaud from Spain (where he was ambassador) in the hope that 'the Hero of Verdun' would revive French morale. When Reynaud resigned on 16 June President Lebrun invited Pétain to form a Government. The new Premier announced almost immediately that the fighting must stop. *'C'est la catastrophe, c'est la débandade,'* he said again and again. Gen Sir Edward Spears, Churchill's representative in France, recalled that Pétain's tone astonished him:

> '. . . I noted that his voice sounded satisfied, almost as if he accepted defeat joyfully. I was so taken aback that I saluted but did not shake hands as I broke away. That was the last time that I ever spoke to Marshal Pétain privately. I never sought another interview; it would have been a pure waste of time.'[7]

Pétain's Broadcast
On forming his Government Pétain instructed his new Foreign Minister to ask the Germans and the Italians for an armistice. His request was sent to Hitler via the Spanish Ambassador in Paris and to Mussolini via the Vatican. The Marshal had reached his decision in the light of the news coming from the front lines, which was all bad. A despairing message from Gen Georges reported that German forces were in Dijon and on the River Saone, while in the centre they were advancing on La Charité and had occupied the forest of Fontainebleau. Everywhere French troops were being surrounded and cut off from their supplies. Masses of refugees jammed every road, making re-supply virtually impossible. Combined with the constant German bombing of roads, bridges and railways this made tactical manoeuvre extremely difficult. Gen Georges ended his message with the words: 'Vital you make decision'.

Soon after midday on 17 June Pétain broadcast to the French people. After saying that President Lebrun had asked him to assume control of the Government, he continued 'it is with a heavy heart that I say we must end the fight. Last night I applied to our adversary to ask if he is prepared to seek with me . . . the means whereby hostilities may cease'. After he had spoken, the same cry was heard all over France: 'It's over! It's over!' Everywhere crowds gathered to cheer and to weep – happy that the nightmare had ended, grief-stricken for the defeat of France, but above all grateful to the old Marshal who had taken on himself the burden of their humiliation.

Not every Frenchman shared Pétain's enthusiasm for negotiating with the

The Face of Defiance. TM

enemy. As soon as the Marshal took office, Gen de Gaulle, fearing arrest, resolved that he could no longer remain in France. He concocted a plan to escape with Gen Spears, for whom a flight in a light aircraft had already been arranged. As they shook hands on departure, Spears suddenly pulled de Gaulle inside and shut the door. The pilot took off at once, and Spears later recalled the astonished look on the face of their chauffeur as they passed the car still parked on the runway. Churchill wrote later that Spears carried with him in that small aircraft 'the honour of France'.

As soon as he arrived in London de Gaulle assumed the leadership of the 'Free French' and made a series of powerful broadcast speeches, appealing to all Frenchmen to continue the fight and castigating the Pétain Government for its shameful surrender. Whatever happened, he declared, '. . . the flame of resistance must not and will not be extinguished'. For his impertinence he was struck off the roll of officers of the French Army. Later, in his memoirs, he recalled how he had felt himself, at the age of forty-nine, to be embarking on an adventure '. . . like a man flung out on a limb by fate'. On a practical note, he called on all French officers and soldiers, engineers and skilled workers at present on British territory to get in touch with him.

The day after the French collapse and Pétain's speech, Churchill also spoke on the future of France:

> However matters may go in France or with the French Government or other French Governments, we in this Island and in the British Empire will never lose our sense of comradeship with the French people . . . What General Weygand called the Battle of France is over. I expect that

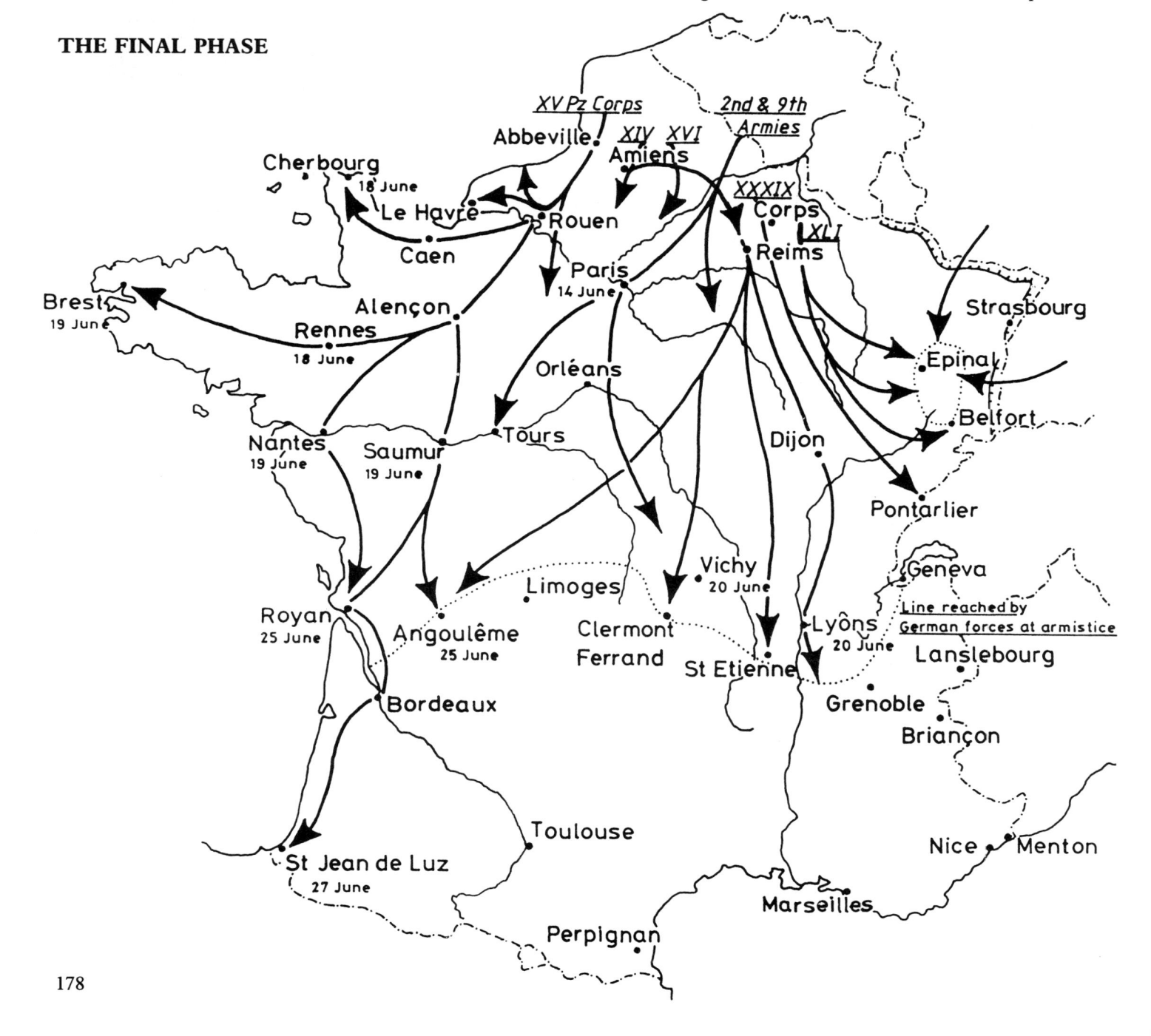

THE FINAL PHASE

the Battle of Britain is about to begin . . . Let us therefore brace ourselves to our duties, and so bear ourselves, that if the British Empire and its Commonwealth last for a thousand years, men will still say: 'This was their finest hour'.

The Panzers Roll On

While the politicians waved their olive branches and talked, von Bock's Army Group B crossed the lower Seine and then fanned out. One column of Hoth's XV Panzer Corps moved westward to Caen and Cherbourg (which they reached on 19 June). Another column drove south-west to Alençon and Rennes, and then turned further west to clear the Brest peninsula (19 June). Yet other panzers advanced to the River Loire, reaching Nantes and Saumur (also on 19 June). Saumur was (and still is) the home of the French Cavalry School (*L'École d'Application de l'Armée Blindée-Cavalrié*) and its students were determined not to give up their School without a fight. They defended a front of 15 miles on the Loire between the bridges of Montsoreau and Gennes. Armed with only training weapons, they fought for two days until their ammunition ran out and the Germans broke through.

Von Rundstedt's Army Group A pressed forward with its advance to the south and south-east, with Panzer Group Guderian leading the way. They reached Briare on 18 June, and Vichy and Lyons two days later. XLI Panzer Corps turned eastward to help trap the remnants of the French 3rd, 5th and 8th Armies against the Maginot Line. Oberst Fabian von Bonin-von-Ostau took part in this operation and gives this vivid account of the capture of Belfort . . .

. . . the last bastion of French defence to be captured by us. Our aim was to bypass Belfort to the west and south, thus encircling it. By the evening of 17 June, first Panzer Divison had swarmed past the town, while 4 Panzer Recce Regiment was already close to Hericourt, 12km south-west of Belfort. The CO . . . issued orders to Capt Graf (Count) Bellegarde, the OC of 3 Company, to advance with the adjutant in a radio vehicle to Belfort and make the fortress surrender, a procedure which had already proved successful on many other occasions. Favoured by darkness and the entanglement of French troops, the Count, who spoke French fluently, managed to get into the fortress. However, the French Commandant rejected any negotiations and arrested Capt Bellegarde and his men.

The following morning our patrol, together with 1st Panzer Division, penetrated the Belfort perimeter. It was easy to overcome the French in the town area, but the fortress and its surrounds were subject to a very aggressive and determined defence.

It was about noon when my armoured reconnaissance vehicle secured the area in front of the railway station, close to the *Hotel de Paris*. All of a sudden, General Guderian, who stood upright despite the heavy enemy fire, knocked on my turret, a stick in his hand, and gave me the order to drive past the fortress between our own lines and those of the enemy, with an artillery officer on board to recce the most vulnerable targets. Under both German and French fire I was driving through that sector like a phantom. Fortunately, we both got back unharmed, the artillery officer having seen all he wanted to see.

Over in the fortress all hell had broken loose. Capt Bellegarde and his men urged the French to give up their pointless resistance, while the rattle of approaching tank tracks and the thunder of artillery both had their effect. A number of French soldiers were close to throwing down arms when a Lieutenant – his name was Müller and he was Alsace-born – appeared, and prevented them doing so by pointing his pistol at the Count. However, as the shelling continued he was forced to hand over the fortress to Count Bellegarde – 12 officers and 1,300 soldiers surrendering.

The Maginot Line is attacked

At a crucial moment during the Army Group A attack on the French side of the Line, Leeb's Army Group C had to cross

Oberst Fabian von Bonin von Ostau, who commanded an Sd Kfz 221 light armoured car during the campaign in France, seen here with his driver. von Ostau

the Rhine and attempt a breakthrough in the Saar area, using Gen von Witzleben's 1st Army. Gen Dollman's reinforced 7th Army was to make a secondary thrust south at Colmar.

On 14 June 1st Army launched its attack between Saaralbe and St Avold. They engaged the French XX Corps as they were in the process of withdrawing from the area in order to shorten the French over-extended front line. The Maginot Line was at its weakest in the area the Germans chose to attack, as it was a 'zone of inundations'. In theory this should have been protected by an impassable water barrier, but these defences were never completed. The German Stukas, artillery and tank gunfire made short work of the inadequate line of casemates in the area. However, the forts on the flanks, although cut off and surrounded, held out for six more days and nights. On 15 June the attack across the Rhine at Colmar began, and four German divisions established crossing points between Marckolsheim and Rheinau. The bunkers were quickly eliminated by air and ground assault, and within two days the Germans were heading for the Vosges with the aim of harrrying the flank of the demoralized French forces.

The Germans were by no means successful all along the Maginot Line. Where the forts were well sited, well constructed, equipped with mutually supporting weapons, and manned with well motivated and properly supplied garrisons, they held out against all enemy attacks. Even the terrible Stuka and its bombs could not break their resistance. A number of such forts held out until the evening of 24 June, when they received a radio message calling for a cease-fire at 0035 hours on 25 June, and to remain in their positions. Even so, one or two forts continued firing until representatives of the French High Command arrived and informed the garrisons that they were now prisoners-of-war.

Hitler Decides the Fate of France
The Führer and his advisers now faced a difficult problem of negotiation. He needed France to be powerless and completely detached from Britain, but at the same time he needed France to remain a sovereign state – otherwise Britain might seize the French colonial empire. In the terms of the armistice the French had to have some free territory left to govern, and so German troops were not allowed to occupy the whole of France. The French Army had to be moved into this

The Vichy puppet regime survived until 11 November 1942, when Hitler decided to occupy the whole of the country. Here, a few glum citizens of Toulouse watch as a German armoured column enters their city.
TM

unoccupied area and demobilized. The French Fleet was to be neutralized and placed under the control of unoccupied France (later 'Vichy France'), in order to prevent it from sailing to British territory for use against the German Navy.

At Compiègne on 21 June the French delegation were handed the Armistice terms, and informed that no discussion was permitted but they could request clarification where they felt it necessary. The basic terms were:

1. Immediate cessation of all hostilities on French soil, including French Protectorates and Mandates, and on the high seas.
2. Occupation of three-fifths of French territory, in which area the German Reich would enjoy all the rights of an occupying power.
3. French prisoners-of-war not to be released immediately. All French tanks, artillery guns, military aircraft and various other types of heavy weapons to be surrendered.
4. All French Forces on land, sea and air to be disarmed and demobilized.
5. All German prisoners-of-war to be released immediately.
6. The costs of German occupation to be paid for by France.

At 2100 hours on 24 June the French High Command was told that hostilities were to cease on all fronts, and that a cease-fire would come into effect at 1235 hrs the following day. Hitler broadcast to the German nation:

> After fighting valiantly for six weeks our troops have brought the war in the West to an end against a courageous enemy. Their heroic deeds will go down in history as the most glorious victory of all time. We give thanks to the Lord for His benevolence.
>
> I order that flags will be displayed throughout the Reich for ten days and bells pealed for seven days.
>
> **Adolf Hitler**

Having dealt so successfully with their arch enemy, the Germans now had time to relax and celebrate their 'most glorious victory of all time'. They could deal at their leisure with the island that stood between them and the road to world domination. Victory had come so quickly – a mere six weeks had passed since the initial *Blitzkrieg* which had struck such terror into French hearts. Compared with World War One, losses were minimal – just over 150,000 German soldiers killed, wounded or missing in the entire campaign. The Germans could not believe it had all been so easy – a miracle seemed the only way to describe it.

How could they then imagine that they would never again know such a complete and glorious victory, and that in a few years all would end in defeat and ruin?

NOTES

1. J. Benoit-Mechin *Sixty Days That Shook the West* London: Jonathan Cape 1963.
2. ibid.
3. Gen Heinz Guderian *Panzer Leader* London: Michael Joseph 1952.
4. Alastair Home *To Lose A Battle* London: Macmillan 1969.
5. Noel Barber *The Week France Fell* London: Macmillan 1976.
6. Major L. F. Ellis *The War in France and Flanders 1939-1940* London: HMSO 1963
7. Gen Sir Edward Spears *Assignment to Catastrophe* London: The Reprint Society 1956

Index

Aa canal: 166
Abyssinia: 9
Advanced Air Striking Force (RAF): 85, 87, 150
Airborne forces (German): see Fallschirmjaeger
Air Component (RAF): 85, 87
Air Council (RAF): 85
Air forces and aircraft
 Belgium: 92, 148 et seq
 France: 74, *75*, 150
 Germany: 8, 32 et seq, *32, 58,* 60, *61, 103,* 146, 154 et seq, 158
 Great Britain: 85 et seq, *86, 87,* 150
Air to ground communications: 33
Air Raid Precautions (ARP): 15 et seq, *17,* 17n, *22, 23*
Air raids: 16, 22, 23, 24, *24,* 102, *104,* 119, 127, 146, *146*
Albert Canal plan: 131, 144, 152
Alexander, Gen Sir Harold: 171
All arms team: 27
Allied Control Commission: 3, 6
Allied strategy: 21 et seq
Allied defence plans: 131, 131 (map)
Alsace-Lorraine: 1 (map), 2
AMD White Laffly armoured car: *73*
Amiot bomber: 74, *75*
Anderson, Sir John: 15, *16,* 17 (note), 76
Anglo-Polish guarantee: 20
'Anschluss': 9, *11,* 12 (map), 106, 112, 113
Anti-Aircraft guns:
 France: *64, 69*
 Germany: 62 et seq, *62, 63,* 123
 Great Britain: 23, 85, *88,* 98
 Holland: *92*
Anti-Comintern Pact: 9
Anti-Tank guns:
 France: 69
 Germany: *137, 152, 153*
 Great Britain: *38*
Ardennes: 134 et seq
Armies:
 Belgium: 89 et seq
 France: 16, 64 et seq
 Germany: 2, 3, 41 et seq
 Great Britain: 78 et seq
 Holland: 93 et seq
 Poland: 117 (map)
Armistice: 177 et seq
Armit WO III 'Jock': 164
Armoured Cars:
 France: *73*
 Germany: *15, 28, 174*
 Holland: *95*
 Poland: *114*
 Russia: *123*
Armoured divisions:
 France: 67 et seq, 68 (chart)
 Germany: see panzer divisions
 Great Britain: 79 et seq
Arras: 162 et seq
Artillery:
 France: *72*
 Germany: *113,* 48
 Great Britain: *80, 82, 84*
 Holland: *93, 93, 94,* 148
Armstrong Whitworth 'Whitley' bomber: 87
ASDIC: 21
Assault gun: *54*
Austro-Hungarian Empire: 111

Army (Fr) 1st: 131 (map), 152, 154
 2nd: 131 (map)
 3rd: 131 (map)
 7th: 131 (map)
 9th: 131 (map)
Army Group North (Ge): 116, 117 (map)
Army Group South (Ge): 116, 117 (map)
Army Group A (Ge): 134, 135 (map), 136 (map), 154, 158, 160, 172, 179
 B: 134, 135, 136 (map), 142 (map), 158, 160, 172, 173
 C: 134, 135 (map), 136 (map), 179
Balance of power (Western Front): 140 (table)
Barratt, Air Marshal: 87
Beck, Gen Ludwig: 28
Belgian Air Force: 92, 148 et seq
 Army: 89 et seq, *89, 90, 91, 92*
 Navy: *92*
Belgium: 21, 35, 89 et seq, 128, 133, 141 et seq, 153, 168 et seq
Berghof: 41
Berlin: 8, *106,* 107, 116, 128
Besson Gen: 132
Billotte Gen: 132, 154, 160
Blanchard, Gen: 131 (map), 132
Blaskowitz, Gen Johannes: 116, 117 (map)
Blumentritt Gen: 154
Blitzkrieg: 8, 25 et seq, 29 (sketch), 111 et seq, 117, 124, 173
Bock, Gen Fodor von: 116 et seq, 123, 136 (map), 142, 158, 160, 172, 179
Bofors: 3, *88*
Bohemia and Moravia: 12
Bormann Martin: 40, 41, *134*
Boulogne: 167 et seq
Brandenbergers: 33, 141, 142
Brauchitsch, Gen Walter von: 1, 41, 116, 128, 138
Breguet light bomber: 74
Brest-Litovsk: 120, *123*
British Expeditionary Force (BEF): 22, 37, *78, 78* et seq, *128,* 129, *129,* 130, *148, 149,* 160, 163
Bristol Blenheim bomber: 87, *88*
Brooke, Lt Gen Alan: 172
Brussels: 131 et seq, 133
Busch, Gen Ernst: 136 (map)

Calais: 167
Cambrai: 163
Case Green: see Fall Grun
Case Yellow: see Fall Gelb
Case White: see Fall Weiss
Cavalry (Horsed):
 France: 70
 Germany: *10, 174, 175*
 Great Britain: 15
 Poland: *112,* 119
Cavalry Regiments, British (mechanised):
 4/7 DG: 152 et seq, 170 et seq
 5 Innis DG: 152 et seq
 12 RL: 151
 13/18 H: *150,* 169
Chamberlain, Neville: 12, *13,* 14 et seq, 21, 76, 102, 104, 113, 126, 127, 159
Chatfield, Lord: 76
China: 9
Churchill, Winston: 6, 16, 76, *98,* 102 et seq, 105, 110 (note), 115, 127, 159, 165, 170 et seq, 176, 178
Cojeul, River: 163
Cologne: *3, 4*

Cooper, Matthew: 25, 26, 54
Communications: 28, 33, 38 et seq, *39*
Compiègne: *1, 2,* 181
Conde Gen: 131 (map)
Condor Legion: 9
Corap Gen: 131, 132
Coward, Noel: 101
Curtis 'Hawk' fighter bomber: 74
Czechoslovakia: 1 (map), 9, 12, 12 (map), *13,* 106, 112, 113, 121

Daladier, Edouard: 12, 64
Danzig: 1 (map), 2, 14, 12 (map), 112, 114, 116, 119, *124*
Darlan, Admiral Jean Francois: 65, 176
DCR 1: 152, 155
DCR 3: 158
DCR 4: 161
DCR 5: 158
DLM 2: 152
DLM 3: 152, 154
Declaration of war: 107, 126, *126*
Deighton, Len: 25, 55
Denmark: 135, 139
Dentz, Gen: 175
'Deutschland' battleship: 3
Dewotine fighter: 74
Directives, Hitler's wartime: 115, 128
Dive bombing: see Junkers Ju 87
Divisional oranisation charts:
 France: Infantrie (DI) 66-67, Cuirasee Rapide (DCR) 68, Leger Mechanique (DLM) 70-71
 Germany: Infanterie 44-45, Panzer 50-51
 Great Britain: Infantry 80, Armoured 81
Doenitz, Admiral: 57
Dollmann, Gen Fredrich: 136 (map)
Dorsetshire Regiment: 130
Doumenc, Gen: 132
Duke of Wellington's Regiment: 129
Dunkirk: *24,* 166, *166,* 168 et seq, *168, 169, 170, 171, 172*
Durham Light Infantry: 163 et seq
Dutch Forces:
 Air Force:
 Army: *92,* 93 et seq, *93, 94, 94, 95, 147, 148*
 Navy: 95
Dutch East Indies: 95
Dyle Line: 131, 131 (map), 141, 151 et seq, 154, 160
'Dynamo' Operation: 171

Eban Emael: *60,* 141, 142 et seq, 148
Eden, Anthony: 76
Eire: 126
Enigma machine: 27
Escaut plan: 131, 160

Fairey Fox light bomber: 92
Fairey Battle light bomber: *75,* 87, 92, 148 et seq
Fall Gelb: 133 et seq, 136 (map), 141
Fall Grun: 113
Fall Weiss: 113, 116
Fallschirmjaeger: 33, *33,* 60 et seq, *60,* 142, 142, 144 (map); *145*
Farman light bomber: 74
'Felsnest' HQ: 41, *41, 60*
Fiat 'Falco' fighter: 92
Fiesler 'Storch' light aircraft: *58,* 60
Finland: 138 et seq, *138*
'Flak': see anti-aircraft
'Flakscheinwerfer': see searchlights

Flame throwers: 46
Flieger Divisions: 60 et seq
Fleet Air Arm: 77
Fokker, Tony: 5
Fokker aircraft: 94, 95
Fortune, Maj Gen VM: 172, 175
Fortress Holland: 142, 145 et seq, 147
Franco, Gen Francisco: 8 et seq
Franco-Belgian Treaty: 17
France:
 Air Force: 74 et seq
 Army: 16 et seq, 34, 64 et seq, 131 (map)
 Navy: 74 et seq
French Cavalry School: 179
Fritsch, Gen von: 41
Fuehrer der: see Hitler
Fuehrersonderzug (Hitler's special train): 41
Fuehrer-Begleit-Bataillon (Hitler's bodyguard): 41

Gamelin, Gen Maurice: 17, 37, 64, 126, 132, 154, 166
Gas masks: 101, *103*
Gaulle, Gen Charles de: 35, 161 et seq, 176 et seq, *177, 178*
German Air Force: see Luftwaffe, die
German Army: see Heer, das
German Navy: see Kriegsmarine
Gleiwitz: 116
Goebbels, Dr Josef: 109
George V, HM The King: 77
George VI, HM The King: 37
Georges, Gen Joseph: 64, 78, 96, 132, *132,* 158, 161, 177
Giraud, Gen: 131 (map), 132
Goering, Reich Marshal Hermann: 1, 8, *58, 59,* 142, 167
Gort, Field Marshal, Lord: 78, *78,* 96, 127, *132,* 132, 160 et seq, 163 et seq, 168, 171
Gort Line: 129
Gotha glider: 62
GHQ (Br): 79 et seq
GQG (Fr): 64 et seq
'Granite': *141,* 142 et seq
Great Britain:
 Army: 78 et seq, *80, 81, 82, 83, 84, 85, 148, 149, 150, 151, 169*
 Air Force: see RAF
 Navy: see RN
Guderian, Gen Heinz: 25 et seq, *26,* 27, 119, 121, 135, 143 (map), 155, 157, 160, 162, 166, 172, 173, 174, 179

Haakon, HM The King of Norway: 139
Halifax, Viscount: 76
Halder, Gen Franz: 55, 138, 160
Hall of Mirrors: 2
Hankey, Lord: 76
Hawker 'Hurricane' fighter: 14, 87, *87*
Heer, das: 40, 41 et seq, *42, 43, 46, 47, 48, 52, 53, 54, 151, 152, 153, 154, 156, 157, 159*
Heinkel He 111: 8, 60, *61, 103*
Hering, Gen: 175
Hess, Rudolf: 1, *134*
High Command HQs:
 France: 64 et seq
 Germany: 40 et seq, *40*
 Great Britain: 76 et seq
Hindenburg, President Paul von: 5 et seq, *5*
Hitler, Adolf: 1 et seq, *2, 4, 5, 5, 6, 8, 9, 10, 11,* 12, 14, *14, 15, 16,* 18 et seq, *19,* 20 et seq, *40, 41,* 60, 104, *106, 107,* 107 et seq, *110,* 113 et seq,

119, *124*, 125, *125*, 127, 128, *134*, *140*, 160 et seq, 168, 180 et seq, *181*
Hitler's Wartime Directives: 20, 41, 113, 115, 128, 172
Hoare, Sir Samuel: 76, 85
Hoepner, Gen Erich: 143, 152
Holland: 3, 5, 92 et seq, 141 et seq, *146*
'Hood' HMS: 76, 77
Hore-Belisha, Leslie: 76, 78
Horne, Alistair: 17 (note), 64, 138
Horses: *10*, 26, *42*, 55, 70, *112*, 124, 148, 174
Hoth, Gen Hermann: 143, 155, 162, 179
Hradzin Castle: 9
Hugenburg, Alfred: 5
Hungary: 120
Huntzinger, Gen: 131, 132

Infantry and their weapons:
 Belgium: 89 et seq, *89*, *90*
 France: 64, *65*, 66-67 (chart), 67 et seq
 Germany: *42*, 44-45 (chart), 46 et seq, *46*, *47*, *109*, *118*, *119*, 121, *133*, *134*, *135*, *139*, *151*, *152*, *153*, 157, *159*
 Great Britain: *38*, *78*, 80 (chart), *82*, *128*, *151*
 Holland: 93, *147*
Inflatable boats: *47*, *147*, *154*
Inter-Allied Control Commission: 6
Ironside, Gen Sir Edmund: 78
Italy and the Italians: 9, 21, 174, *174*

Japan: 9, *9*, 21, 23, 95
Jews: 7, *20*, *21*
Jodl, Gen Alfred: 40, *40*, 137
Junkers:
 Ju 52: 8, 60, *61*, 62, *142*, 143, 145
 Ju 87: 32, *32*, 32 (sketch), 33, 60, 124, 180
 Ju 88: 32, 60

Kaiser, The: 2
Keitel, Field Marshal Wilhelm: 1, 40, *40*, 41, 127, *134*
Kesselring, Field Marshal Albert: 116
Kleist, Gen von: 154, 155 160 et seq, 172
Kluge, Field Marshal Hans Gunther von: 116, 117 (map), 136 (map), 154, 172
Koch, Hauptman: 60, 142
Kriegsmarine, die: 40, 55 et seq, *56*
Krupp: 3, 8, *56*
Kuechler, Field Marshal Geyr von: 116, 136 (map), 147
'Kurfurst' HQ: 41

Laon: 162
League of Nations: 6, 9, 14, 24
'Lebensraum': 5, 18 et seq, 112
Lebrun, Albert: *127*, 177
Leeb, Gen Ritter von: 136 (map), 179
Leichte divisions: 46 et seq, 153 et seq, 121
Leo 45 bomber: 74
Leopold III, HM The King of Belgium: 17, 35, 89, 153, 168
Liddell-Hart, Sir Basil: 9, 26, 167
Linge, Heinz: 1
List, Field Marshal Siegmund Wilhelm von: 116, 117 (map), 136 (map), 154
Lithuania: 14, 113, 120
Lohr, Gen Alexander: 116
Lorzer, Gen: 155
'Lothringen' battleship: 3
Luftflotten: 59
Luftwaffe, die: 8, 22, 24, 32 et seq, *32*, 40, 54, *58*, 59 et seq, *59*, *61*, 62, 63, *103*, 119, 124, 155 et seq, 157 et seq
Lys, River: 168

Macksey, Kenneth: 28
Maginot André: 36
Maginot Line: 6, 17, 34-35 (sketch), 35 et seq, 36 (map), *37*, 105, 106, 116, 126, 127, 131, 133, 158, 172, 179 et seq
Malmédy: 1 (map), 2
Manstein, Gen Fritz Reich von: 135, 137, 161
Martin, Kingsley: 127
'Matilda' Mark II tank: *82*, 83, 163, *163*
Mechanisation: 37 et seq, *38*, 53
Mein Kampf: 5, 18, 107
Memel: 12 (map), 14, 113
Messerschmitt Me 109: 60
 Me 110: *58*, 60
Milch, Gen Erhard: 59
Mobilisation, Germany: 43
Molotov, Vyacheslav: 106, 115
Montcornet: 160, 162
Montgomery, Field Marshal Lord: 96 et seq, *99*
Morale:
 France: 105 et seq, 131
 Germany: 107 et seq
 Great Britain: 96 et seq
Morane Sauliner fighter: 74, *75*
Mortar 3 inch: *78*
Motorised division (Germany): 53
Mountain division (Germany): 53, *107*
Mussolini, Benito: 9, 12, 14, *14*, 114, *174*

NAAFI: 130
Nationalsozialistische Deutsche Arbeitpartei (NSDAP) Nazis: *4*, 5 et seq, *5*, 7, *11*, 107
Naval matters, general: 21, 23, 55
Naval tonnage limits: 23 et seq
Navies:
 Belgium: 92
 France: 74 et seq
 Germany: 55 et seq
 Great Britain: 76 et seq, *76*, *77*
 Holland: 95
Netherlands, the: see Holland
Newall, Marshal of the Air Force: 85
Nicholson, Brig: 167
Norway: 62, 138 et seq, *139*, 141

OKH: 40, 117, 125, 137
OKL: 40, 59 et seq
OKM: 40, 56 et seq
OKW: 40, 113, 118
Organisations:
 Allied Command Structure: 132 (table)
 British Expeditionary Force: 79, 80-81 (charts)
 France: 64 et seq, 66-67 (chart), 68 (chart), 770-71 (chart)
 Germany: 44-45 (chart), 46 et seq, 50-51 (chart), 116 (table)
 German organisation for attack on Poland: 116, 117 (map)
 German organisation for attack on France: 135 et seq, 136 (map), 143 (map)
Oslo: *139*
Ostau, Fabian von Bonin von Ostau: 108, 179, *179*
Occupation of Germany, Allied Army of: 2, *3*, *4*

Pacifism: 102
Pact of Steel: 14, 114
Panzers, types of: see German tanks

Panzer divisions, general: *15*, 31, *42*, 46 49 (tactical signs), 50-51 (chart), 120, *138*, *139*, *149*, *156*
 1st: 49, 143 (map), 155, 156, 162, 166
 2nd: 49, 143 (map), *52*, 155, 156 et seq, 174
 3rd: *13*, 49, 143 (map)
 4th: 49, 143 (map)
 5th: 31, 49, 143 (map), 153, 155, 168
 6th: 49, 121, 143 (map), 155, 160
 7th: 49, 121, 143 (map), 153, 155, 160, 162 et seq
 8th: 49, 121, 143 (map), 155
 9th: 49, 121, 143 (map)
 10th: 49, 118, 143 (map), 155-156
Panzerwaffe: 25, *25*, *28*, *30*, *31*, *42*
Paris: 58, 175, *175*
Paratroops: see Fallschirmjaeger
Pétain, Marshal: 17, 34, 177 et seq
Poison gas: 24
Poland: 14, 17, 20, 65, 111 et seq
Polish Corridor: 14
Portal, Air Chief Marshal Sir Charles: 85
Posen and West Prussia: 1 (map), 2
Posters: 11, 22, 55, *59*, *100*, *101*, *168*
Potez, light bomber: 74
Pound, Admiral Sir Dudley: 76
'Poznan' Army: 120
Prague: 9, 13, 118
Pretelat, Gen: 132
Price, Alfred: 32
Prioux, Gen: 152
Prisoners of War: *122*, *135*, *167*, *171*, *176*
Propaganda: 124 et seq, *126*, *168*

Quisling, Vidkun: 139

RAMC: 79
RASC: 37, 79
Raeder, Grand Admiral Erich: 1, 55, 56
Refugees: *24*, *104*, *153*, *158*
Reich Labour Corps: *16*
Reichstag: 6, 9, *11*, 107, 128
Reich Labour Corps: *16*
Reinberger, Major: 137
Reinhardt, Gen: 155, 160
Rémy, Pont: *172*
Reparations: 5, 17 (note)
Reynaud, Paul: 6, 64, 65, 105, 159, 175, 176
Rheinhardt, Gen Georg-Hans: 143
Rhineland: 2, 9, *10*, 12 (map), 106
Rhinemetal-Borsig factory: 7
Ribbentrop, Joachim von: 1, 106, 115
Richenau, Field Marshal Walther von: 116, 117 (map), 120, 136 (map), 142
Roehm, Ernst: 5
Romania: 14, 20
Rommel, Maj Gen Erwin: 41, 155, 162, 165, 175
Roosevelt, President Franklin: 24, 108
Rotterdam: *102*, 146, *146*
Royal Air Force: 22 et seq, 85 et seq, *85*, *87*, 127, 129, 170 et seq
'Royal Marine': 158
Royal Navy: 23, *23*, 76 et seq, 129
Royal Tank Regiment: 163 et seq
Rundstedt, Field Marshal Gerd von: 116, 135, 136, 137, 160 et seq, 166
Ruhr: 5
Russia: 19, *20*
Russian attack on Finland: 138, *138*

Saar: 1 (map), 2
Saumur: 179
'Scharnhorst' battleship: 8, *56*, 57

Schlieffen Plan: 133, 140 (note), 150
Schleswig and East Prussia: 1 (map), 2
Schmundt, Col: 41, 137, *140*
Schmidt, Gen: 143, 146
'Schnellboot': 57, *57*
'Schwarzeproduktion': 8
Schweppenburg, Gen von: *13*
Searchlights: 23, *63*, *85*
Seeckt, Gen Hans von: 26
Sensee, River: 163
Serre, River: 162
Shirer, William L: 1, 55, 108 et seq
Siegfried Line: 36, 36 (map)
Simon, Sir John: 76
Sinclair, Sir Archibald: 85
Soviet-German Pact: 106, 114 et seq
Spanish Civil War: 8, 9, 32, 59, 109
Spears, Sir Edward: 100, 131, 177 et seq
Sponeck, Maj Gen Graf von: 145 et seq
SS: 6, *6*, 54, *108*
Stahlhelm: 5
Stalin, Joseph: 20
St Valéry: 175
Student, Gen Karl: 62, 142
Stuka: see Ju 87
Submarine Protocol of 1936: 24 (note)
Sudetenland: 9, *11*, 12 (map), 12, 14
Sweden: 3, 10, 138
Supermarine 'Spitfire' fighter: 14, *86*, 87
Switzerland: 35

Tanks:
 Belgian: *90*, *91*, 92
 French: 34 et seq, 67, 70, 71, *72*, *137*, *162*
 German: 3, 4, *13*, 30, *52*, 53, *53*, *113*, 120, *120*, 121, *138*, 149
 Great Britain: 3, *81*, *82*, 83, *83*, 163
Terlinden, Lt Col Michel: 148 et seq
Thoma, Gen Ritter von: 9
Todt, Fritz: 41, 63 (note)
Toulouse: 180

U-boats: 8, 55, *56*
Ultra: 27

Versailles Treaty: 1 (map), 2, 3, 8, 9, 19, 23, 55, 108
Verdun: 160
Vollmer, Joseph: 3, 10
Vuillemin, Gen Joseph: 65
Vickers 'Wellington' bomber: 87
Vigerie, Gen d'Astier: 34

Wagner, Klaus: 18
War Cabinet (GB): 76
Warsaw: 24, 119, 120, *125*, 128
Washington Treaty of: 23
Wehrkriese: 43, 43 (map)
Wehrmacht Operations Office: 40
Weichs, Gen von: 116
Wenzel, Hauptman: 60, 143 et seq
Westland 'Lysander' army co-operation aircraft: 87
Weygand, Gen Maxime: 22 et seq, 107, 112, 166, 172, 173, 175, 176, 178
Wilhelmina, HM The Queen of Holland: 142, 147
Witzleben, Gen von: 136 (map)
Witzig, Oberleutenant: 60, 143 et seq
Wood, Sir Kingsley: 76
World War I: 2, 6, 15, 18, *18*, 23, 34, 38, 107

'Zeppelin': 41
Ziegenberg Castle: 41

183

In the Spellmount Military list:

The Territorial Battalions – A pictorial history
The Yeomanry Regiments – A pictorial history
Over the Rhine – The Last Days of War in Europe
History of the Cambridge University OTC
Yeoman Service
The Fighting Troops of the Austro-Hungarian Army
Intelligence Officer in the Peninsula
The Scottish Regiments – A pictorial history
The Royal Marines – A pictorial history
The Royal Tank Regiment – A pictorial history
The Irish Regiments – A pictorial history
British Sieges of the Peninsular War
Victoria's Victories
Heaven and Hell – German paratroop war diary
Rorke's Drift
Came the Dawn – Fifty years an Army Officer
Kitchener's Army – A pictorial history
Marlborough – As Military Commander
A Medal for Life – Capt Leefe Robinson VC
On the Word of Command – RSM's pictorial history

In the Nautical list:

Sea of Memories
Evolution of Engineering in the Royal Navy Vol I 1827-1939
In Perilous Seas

In the Aviation list:

Diary of a Bomb Aimer
Operation 'Bograt' – From France to Burma

First published in the UK in 1990 by
The Nutshell Publishing Co Ltd
12 Dene Way, Speldhurst
Tunbridge Wells, Kent TN3 0NX
ISBN 1-871876-15-X

© George Forty and John Duncan 1990

British Library Cataloguing in Publication Data
Forty, George
    The Fall of France, 1940: Disaster in the West –
    (Clash of Arms series)
    1. World War 2. Western European Campaigns
    I. Title.   II. Duncan, John 1926   III. Series
    940.5421

ISBN 1-871876-15-X

Design by Robert Hardcastle and John Ricketts
Typesetting by Vitaset, Paddock Wood, Kent
Printed in Great Britain by Courier International Ltd
Tiptree, Essex.

All rights reserved. No part of this publication may be
reproduced, stored in a retrieval system
or transmitted in any form or by any means,
electronic, mechanical, photocopying, recording or
otherwise, without prior permission in writing from
The Nutshell Publishing Co Ltd.

THE FALL OF FRANCE